At Ease in Zion

At Ease in

Social History of Southern Baptists
1865–1900

RUFUS B. SPAIN

Vanderbilt University Press: Nashville

**to
Carol, Bethanne,
John, Julie,
and David**

Preface

PROTESTANTISM greatly influenced the development of American culture in the colonial and early national periods. Foreign travelers in this country before the Civil War frequently noted the vitality and significance of religion. Ministers enjoyed universal respect and honor in the counsel halls of church and state. No form of public attraction surpassed religious revivals in drawing power. Churches dominated higher education and molded the character of public education. The religious press challenged the secular press for patronage. And public documents, novels, poems, plays, and speeches bore the unmistakable mark of religion.

During the nineteenth century, however, Protestantism declined. By 1900 secular forces far exceeded religious influences in shaping the life of the nation. Protestantism declined because it failed to remain relevant to the changing times. It had served the needs of the simple agrarian society of pre–Civil War America. Early American institutions rested on concepts which religion had helped shape. Until well into the nineteenth century, society continued to accept religion's supernatural explanation of man and the universe as revealed in the Bible. Slowly, however, but with ever-increasing speed, the modern world destroyed the simplicity of early America. The new sciences explained away the world of the supernatural. The higher criticism of the Bible cast doubt on the validity of the ultimate source of Protestant truth. On the more mundane level, technology revolutionized transportation, communication, and the way in which Americans made their living. Industrialization created social, economic, and political problems and raised moral and ethical questions for which traditional religion had no answers. In the maelstrom of these new forces Protestantism, like states'-rights politics and laissez-faire economics, seemed outmoded. American Protestantism found its world undermined.

Protestants responded to the challenge of the new era in three ways. One response was simply to ignore the modern world. Individuals embracing this view denied that the new forces of society presented any threat to their faith. They reaffirmed their orthodoxy and clung to the form and substance of the old-time religion. A second response represented the opposite extreme of the first. Those accepting this position found themselves overwhelmed by the forces of the new era. To them the new knowledge destroyed not only the religious assumptions of early America but also the gods of the Old and New Testament. Those of this group who chose to retain a religious orientation reconstructed their faith on totally different premises and found outlets for their altruistic impulses through humanitarian endeavors. The third response—and this represented the mainstream of American Protestantism—was a cautious acceptance of the new and a reluctant rejection of that which was untenable in the old. By careful and tedious pruning and grafting, adherents to this view combined much of the old and the new, hoping thereby to make Protestantism relevant to the new age. They surrendered their pre-Copernican science and compromised their cherished supernaturalism to accommodate their faith to incontrovertible scientific fact. They liberalized their theology, sought unity among their many factions, developed tolerance toward non-Protestant religions, and evolved the "social gospel" in an effort to keep religion in touch with modern man and to keep modern man in touch with God.

The new Protestantism differed most from tradition in its emphasis on ameliorating social conditions. Since the forces of the new era had blurred the vision of the heavenly city, perhaps religion could recapture some of its former vigor by focusing on the earthly city. It required no twisting of Scripture to find authority for contending that the kingdom of God was to be found on earth as well as in heaven. Consequently, Protestantism redefined its concepts of man, the world, and heaven. Whereas orthodoxy had depicted the world as Satan's domain and life on earth as a veil of tears through which man journeyed with fear and trembling toward the celestial city, the new Protestantism considered the world a worthy object of Christian redemption, an end within itself, a potential heaven which the Christian need not, and indeed should not, seek to avoid. If this constituted a tack in the course of religious history, then American Protestants had concerned themselves only too long with the otherworldly side of the gospel. The inherent danger in this new emphasis was that the pendulum would swing too far in the opposite direction. But that was a chance which Protestants had to take in an effort to regain their former prestige.

The attempt to reinvigorate Protestantism by accenting the social aspects of the gospel was only partially successful. With their less spectacular methods, the new architects of the earthly city of God failed to arouse the enthusiasm which their forerunners had inspired with their preachments of the glories of the heavenly city and the terrors of Satan's domain. Protestantism lost the dynamics of the supernatural but failed to gain another animus of equivalent vitality. By 1914 the United States entered what Winthrop S. Hudson in his *American Protestantism* (1961) calls the "post-Protestant" era.

The dramatic upheavals in American Protestantism recounted above occurred primarily in the North. Protestant churches in the South showed relatively little change during the late nineteenth and early twentieth centuries. The reason seems obvious: Southern society was affected only slightly by the forces which revolutionized the North. Southerners in general and Southern churchmen in particular were little concerned with the new sciences, Biblical criticism, industrialization, and the other innovating forces of the time. Southern churches changed less because there was less pressure for change.

If religion lost its influence in the North because of changing times, and if the South did not experience these revolutionary changes, did religion retain the place of eminence in the South which it had enjoyed throughout the country in an earlier period? Historians think so. In his book, *The Origins of the New South,* (1951, p. 448), C. Vann Woodward says:

Neither learning nor literature of the secular sort could compare with religion in power and influence over the mind and spirit of the South. The exuberant religiosity of the Southern people, the conservative orthodoxy of the dominant sects, and the overwhelming Protestantism of all but a few parts of the region were forces that persisted powerfully in the twentieth century. They were a large element in the homogeneity of the people and the readiness with which they responded to common impulses. They explained much of the survival of a distinctive regional culture, and they went far toward justifying the remark that the South was solid religiously as well as politically.

Granted then that Protestantism did exert a significant influence in Southern society long after its vitality had declined in the North, what was that influence? Was religion still a force in molding public thought and action toward certain preconceived religious and moral ends? What did Southern Protestantism say about the great problems of the post–Civil War era—the collapse of the Confederacy, Reconstruction, reunion, the Negro, sharecropping, industrialization, and the many other problems of the day?

The study presented here is an effort to answer some of these questions. It is a case study of the Southern Baptist denomination in the South during the thirty-five years after the Civil War. The term "Southern Baptist" is the official designation of the denomination composed of white Baptists who support the program of the Southern Baptist Convention. In the late nineteenth century there were eleven other groups of white Baptists in the United States, nine of which were found in the South (see Appendixes A, B, and C). For this study, only Southern Baptists have been considered and, unless otherwise noted, the terms "Baptist" or "Baptists" will refer only to this body and its adherents.

Southern Baptists have been selected for study because of their significance in the religious life of the South and of the nation. At the beginning of the period under consideration, they constituted the second-largest white denomination in the South, and before 1900 they were the largest (see Appendixes D, E, and F). Southern Baptists increased in numbers not only in the last century but they have also continued to grow in the twentieth century. By 1963 the denomination had expanded into almost every state of the Union and its membership had grown to over ten million—second only to Roman Catholics. The social attitudes of the largest denomination in a religion-oriented region should be significant in the history of the region.

The South as defined in this study consisted of the eleven ex-Confederate states and Kentucky. These states comprised the geographical area of the Old South, and more important, they exhibited the cultural image connoted by the phrase "Southern way of life." Furthermore, the vast majority of Southern Baptists resided in these twelve states. Of the 2,009,471 Southern Baptists in the United States in 1906, 1,770,303 were found in this region.

Limiting this study to the years 1865–1900 was somewhat arbitrary, although the major developments which led to the decline of Protestantism transpired during this period. The end of the Civil War was a logical starting point because it marked the end of the Old South and the beginning of a new era. Many of the problems of the South stemmed from the sectional conflict. The year 1900 as the termination date is less defensible than the beginning date. There was certainly nothing significant about turning the calendar to a new century. The logic is found in the fact that Baptist attitudes on the great social questions of the time had crystallized by then or had fallen into patterns which could be projected into the twentieth century.

The principal sources used in this study were the minutes and reports of the Southern Baptist Convention, minutes and reports of the twelve state conventions, and the denominational papers published weekly in each of the Southern states. The state papers were the most enlightening sources. They were the ready media for the expression of varying shades of opinion on any subject. Every paper featured lengthy editorials and devoted considerable space to articles and letters from readers. Although all the papers used in this study were the "official organs" of the various state conventions, they were not mere propaganda sheets controlled by denominational leaders. They were privately owned and the owners received no direct financial assistance from the denomination. The continuation of a paper depended on circulation and circulation depended on satisfied subscribers. Baptist weeklies were as amenable to the wishes of the Baptist public as they were to the desires of Baptist leadership.

Baptists were rigid congregationalists during this period; therefore, none of these sources could express *official* opinions. The difficulty of determining "the Baptist position" on a given issue is readily apparent. Fortunately, however, the very characteristic of Baptist life which precluded official pronouncements—i.e., congregationalism—also made possible an insight into Baptist thinking. The success of the denominational program rested ultimately on the voluntary support of individual members; consequently, the actions of Baptists working together in conventions and opinions expressed in reports, resolutions, and journals were designed implicitly to elicit a favorable response from the man at the bottom of the ecclesiastical pyramid. (This is not to discount the influence of individual leaders, but leaders in any democratic organization can never be very far in advance of their constituents.) Opinions gleaned from Baptist sources no doubt reflect more faithfully the thinking of the man in the pew than official decrees handed down by synods, conferences, and bishops of other denominations. What have been set forth, therefore, as "Baptist opinions" are those views which the majority of Baptists seemed to hold. Significant minority opinions have not been omitted, however. To have done so would create false impressions of unanimity, for Baptists seldom agreed completely on any issue.

The development of social Christianity among Southern churches and the interaction of religion and society are aspects of Southern social history which have not been explored adequately heretofore. The influence of Southern churches, whether reactionary, conservative, or progressive, was nevertheless important as a social force. This study of Southern Baptists, it is hoped, will reveal in some measure the social significance of the largest white denomination in the South and, consequently, will contribute to a more thorough understanding of the relationship of Southern religion to Southern society.

I want to thank the Louisiana State University Press for allowing me to reprint a portion from C. Vann Woodward's *Origins of The New South, 1877–1913,* which is Vol. IX of *A History of The South,* and the Oxford University Press, Inc., for allowing me to reprint from C. Vann Woodward's *The Strange Career of Jim Crow* (rev. ed., 1957).

I am indebted to a great many people for their assistance and encouragement in the preparation of this study. From among the many I would like to extend a special word of appreciation to the following: Dr. Norman W. Cox, former Executive Secretary of the Historical Commission of the Southern Baptist Convention, for his kind permission to use the microfilm holdings of the Commission; Miss Helen Conger, Librarian of the Dargan-Carver Library, for enabling me to have uninterrupted access to a microfilm reader; Dr. Leo T. Crismon, Librarian at the Southern Baptist Theological Seminary, Louisville, Kentucky, for permission to examine the Seminary's collection of source materials pertinent to this study; Dr. J. D. Bragg, Chairman of the Graduate Faculty Research Committee, Baylor University, and other Baylor University officials for financial assistance in the final preparation of the manuscript; and, above all, Dr. Henry Lee Swint and Dr. Herbert Weaver, sympathetic and capable advisers.

Rufus B. Spain

Baylor University
December 1966

Contents

"The South is the Baptist Zion. . . ."

Southern Baptist Convention, *Proceedings,* 1890

Introduction

IKE the South as a conscious minority, the Southern Baptist denomination did not exist until the heat of the slavery controversy destroyed Baptist unity and forged Baptists of the South into a separate fellowship. Until the 1840's most Baptists of all sections shared a common faith and supported a single program of missions and benevolences. They accepted no creed; the New Testament was their final authority in matters of faith and morals. They adhered to a modified version of Calvinism and preached the doctrine of personal salvation by faith alone. Baptists took a literal view of the virgin birth, the vicarious death, and the bodily resurrection of Christ, and they looked forward to His glorious second coming at some unknown moment in history as the consummation of God's plan for man on earth. In church government they were strict congregationalists, and they adhered faithfully to the principle of separation of Church and State.[1]

American Baptists trace their origin back through English Baptists to the amorphous communities of nonconformists who flourished on the European continent in the sixteenth century. The first Baptist church with a documented history appeared in London in 1611 or 1612. In the next decade other congregations calling themselves Baptist sprang up in various parts of England. These early Baptists did not always agree on the fine points of doctrine, but they held in common the cardinal principles which have distinguished Baptists down to the present time—reverence for the Bible as the only divine authority, religious freedom, priesthood of the believer, believer's baptism, and autonomy of the local church.[2]

1. These were the beliefs of the main body of Baptists, not necessarily those of the many splinter groups (*see* Appendix A). Two books by James Madison Pendleton presented the most popular statement of Baptist doctrine and principles during the last half of the nineteenth century: *Church Manual, Designed for the Use of Baptist Churches* (1867) and *Christian Doctrines: A Compendium of Theology* (1878). Doctrine is of little concern in this study except as it affected Baptist social attitudes and actions.

2. Robert G. Torbet, *A History of the Baptists* (rev. ed., 1963), pp. 15–83.

English immigrants introduced the Baptist faith into the New World in the 1630's. Roger Williams is usually considered the first American Baptist although he was not a Baptist when he arrived in Massachusetts Bay in 1631 and he remained a Baptist only a few months after founding the first Baptist church in America in Providence, Rhode Island, in 1639. Baptists increased in numbers very slowly in the unfriendly environment of seventeenth-century New England where the Congregational Church dominated society. In the Southern colonies, also, Baptists made little progress because of the hostile attitude of the Anglican Church. In the Middle Colonies, however, the number of Baptists grew steadily in the late seventeenth and early eighteenth centuries. The promise there of religious freedom and economic opportunity attracted Baptists from all the British Isles where they were living in constant fear of persecution and economic discrimination.[3]

During the Great Awakening in the 1740's and 1750's, Baptists increased rapidly in all sections of the country, especially in the hinterland of the Middle and Southern colonies. Baptist faith and polity were particularly attractive to settlers along the frontier. The simple, emotion-laden sermons of their poorly educated but fiery preachers found ready acceptance among the back-country folk, and the congregational structure of church government facilitated the formation of new churches. By the beginning of the Revolutionary War, Baptists constituted the third most numerous religious group in America. The rapid growth since the 1740's slowed during the Revolution and for a few years thereafter, but during the Second Awakening (the period of revival around 1800) Baptists experienced another upward surge in membership. Again their greatest gains were in the West, where their simple message of individual salvation still appealed to unsophisticated frontiersmen. In spite of the internal dissension over doctrinal differences in the second and third decades of the nineteenth century, Baptists continued to grow until the sectional controversy split their ranks in the 1840's.[4]

Baptists in Europe and in America were slow in perfecting denominational unity. Their tradition of dissent, their minor doctrinal differences, and their zealous regard for the autonomy of the local church militated against the growth of a strong ecclesiastical system. The manner in which

3. *Ibid.*, pp. 219–238.
4. *Ibid.*, pp. 239–271; J. Franklin Jameson, *The American Revolution Considered as a Social Movement* (Beacon ed., 1956), p. 85.

the faith developed in this country augmented these divisive tendencies. Baptists found little inducement toward unity either on the sparsely settled frontier or on the seaboard where the harassments of the state churches constantly reminded them of the dangers of strong ecclesiastical organization. For more than half a century after the first Baptists settled in America, they made no attempt to organize above the local church level. Pennsylvania Baptists took the first step toward unity in 1707 when they formed the Philadelphia Baptist Association, a loose affiliation of five churches for purposes of fellowship and counsel. Other Baptist churches soon followed this example, particularly during the Great Awakening. A further movement toward greater unity developed later in the century when associations and churches began forming "general associations" to promote missions and benevolences. This was the extent of denominational organization until after 1800.[5]

In 1814 Baptists from all parts of the country organized the "General Missionary Convention of the Baptist Denomination in the United States for Foreign Missions," usually called simply the General Convention, or the Triennial Convention because it met every three years. As initially conceived, the purpose of the convention was to promote home and foreign missions and other benevolent causes. By 1817 the work of the convention had been limited to foreign missions, and the promotion of home missions, publications, education, and other causes was left to separate societies without any over-all supervision by a general denominational agency. The Triennial Convention elected a Foreign Mission Board with headquarters in Boston with the responsibility of appointing missionaries and conducting the affairs of foreign missions. For thirty years the Triennial Convention and the Foreign Mission Board, usually referred to as the "Boston Board," were the most effective factors in unifying Baptist life.

The development of the anti-slavery movement threatened Baptist unity. In the 1830's elements of the denomination in New England and New York embraced abolitionism and sought to gain control of the Foreign Mission Board in order to prevent the appointment of slaveholding missionaries. Failing in this effort, the most radical of them withdrew and organized two mission societies of their own—the American Baptist Free Missionary Society and the American and Foreign Baptist Mission-

5. Torbet, *History of Baptists*, pp. 229–232 *passim.*

ary Society. Many abolitionists remained loyal to the Triennial Convention and the Boston Board, however, but they continued to agitate for control. Finally, they succeeded in usurping control of the board, and in 1844 they made public their intention to refuse appointments to slaveholders.

Baptists in the South reacted immediately and decisively to the announcement of the Boston Board. Alabama Baptists demanded a clear statement of policy: Would the board appoint slaveholders as missionaries? Before the board could reply, the Board of Managers of the Virginia Foreign Mission Society (maintained by Virginia Baptists for the purpose of raising funds for missions) published an open letter to Baptists of the South proposing a general meeting to consider a course of action in the event the Boston Board failed to give a satisfactory answer. The Boston Board answered the query of Alabama Baptists in the negative, and the general meeting suggested by Virginia Baptists convened in Augusta, Georgia, on May 8, 1845. Two hundred ninety-three delegates, representing eight Southern states and the District of Columbia, assembled at Augusta. Addressing themselves to "the Brethren in the United States . . . and to all candid men," they defended their action and blamed Baptists of the North for the existing estrangement. The Constitution of the Triennial Convention made no reference to slaveholding as a factor to be considered in the appointment of missionaries; consequently, the delegates maintained that the Foreign Mission Board had acted in violation of the constitution in its recent ruling. Continued support of the Foreign Mission Board by Southerners would be tantamount to admitting that slavery was a sin. The delegates agreed that the Boston Board had left them no choice. Before the meeting adjourned on May 12, they organized the Southern Baptist Convention. To emphasize the justice of their cause, the delegates adopted the Constitution of the Triennial Convention as their organic law with only a change in name. With few exceptions, Baptists of the slave states threw their support to the new convention.[6]

The question of slavery had divided Baptists and brought a new denomination into being. Southern Baptist historians have attempted to minimize slavery as a cause in the formation of the Southern Convention,

6. Southern Baptist Convention, *Proceedings, 1845,* pp. 12–13, 17–20; William Wright Barnes, *The Southern Baptist Convention, 1845–1953* (1954), pp. 1–30; Torbet, *History of Baptists,* pp. 219–313.

but the division of Baptists on sectional lines, like the disruption of the Union fifteen years later, would not have occurred had there been no slavery controversy.[7]

Perfecting the operation of the new denomination was less difficult than might be supposed. The adoption of a new name and the shifting of allegiance from nationwide to South-wide agencies by no means required the construction of a completely new organization. The new convention inherited the well-structured ecclesiastical system which had been developing since 1707. By 1845 four eschelons of organization, forming a pyramidal structure based on the geographical location of churches, had developed. Local churches formed the broad base of the pyramid; churches from an area the size of a county or two united to form "associations"; Baptists within the bounds of a single state organized "state conventions"; and the Southern Baptist Convention, the apex of the pyramid, co-ordinated denominational efforts for the entire South.

Associations [8] consisted primarily of delegates or messengers from local churches. Representation depended on the number of members in a given church, or the amount of contributions to the denominational program, or both. Individuals and societies (such as Sunday schools) also could be members of associations by making a stipulated monetary contribution to denominational causes through the associations. The purposes of associations were to provide means for the co-operative support of missionary and benevolent enterprises which a single church could not finance and to afford opportunities for fellowship and counsel. Churches often sent

7. Barnes, *Southern Baptist Convention*, pp. 12–32; Robert Andrew Baker, *Relations Between Northern and Southern Baptists* (1948), pp. 7–98. Baker emphasizes the dissension existing among Baptists before 1845. Baptists of the South and Southwest felt slighted by the Home Mission Society of Philadelphia, and as early as 1835 they began agitating for a Southern home mission agency. When the break over foreign missions came in 1845, Southern Baptists withdrew their support from the Home Mission Society also and organized their own Domestic Mission Board. The sectional split in the denomination was not complete in 1845 however. Southern Baptists continued to support the American Baptist Publication Society of Philadelphia until the end of the century. In 1900 Southern Baptists still were purchasing 20 percent of their Sunday school literature from this Northern agency. *See* Southern Baptist Convention, *Annual, 1900*, p. 152.

8. Associations were often designated "district associations" to distinguish them from regional or state organizations called "general associations." Baptists in Virginia and Kentucky still call their state organizations general associations rather than state conventions.

doctrinal and policy questions to associations. The judgments rendered on such questions were merely the opinions of the assembled delegates, however, not *ex cathedra* pronouncements. Nevertheless, opinions handed down by associations were highly respected by the churches, and in this respect associations exercised an important disciplinary and unifying function in the denomination. Associations were, perhaps, the nearest approach to a real ecclesiastical authority among Baptists. Associations existed, literally, only during the three or four days of the annual meeting, although work set in motion at these yearly gatherings continued throughout the year under the direction of voluntary workers.

Above associations in the organizational structure were state conventions or general associations.[9] Conventions, like district associations, were formed to provide means for enlarging the denomination's sphere of activity. Missions, education, and denominational unity were the initial emphases of conventions. The development of the convention idea was by no means uniform throughout the South. Regional "general associations," uniting the efforts of several district associations, had existed since colonial times, but state-wide organizations came into being only in the 1820's. South Carolina Baptists organized the first convention in 1821; Tennessee had no permanent convention until 1874. Even after the formation of state conventions, regional organizations continued to exist in most states. In North Carolina, for example, the Western Convention, including the fourteen counties west of the Blue Ridge, continued until 1895, although a state convention had been formed in 1834. The persistence of these regional bodies was not usually the result of factional strife but was a result rather of transportation difficulties and the reluctance of Baptists to dissolve time-honored institutions. In most instances, state conventions and regional associations exchanged "fraternal messengers," and all co-operated in supporting the program of the Southern Baptist Convention.

State conventions were composed mostly of delegates or messengers from churches, but associations, societies, and individuals also could be members on conditions similar to those already described for membership in associations. Conventions existed only during the annual meetings. Work initiated at conventions was implemented between sessions by

9. Much of this information about Baptist organization and practice has come from the sources used in this study. *See also* Torbet, *History of Baptists,* pp. 229 ff, 250; Barnes, *Southern Baptist Convention,* pp. 2–11.

permanent boards and "secretaries" elected by the conventions. Board members were usually prominent ministers of the state who served gratuitously, while secretaries and their small staffs were paid workers.

Co-ordinating the work of Baptists throughout the South was the Southern Baptist Convention. Delegates from churches, associations, state conventions, and societies comprised the membership of the convention. The basis of membership varied during the nineteenth century, but generally the number of delegates from a church or other represented body was determined by the amount of money contributed to the denominational program. Individuals also could be members of the convention by paying a stipulated sum. Like state conventions, the South-wide organization existed only during the annual sessions. Permanent secretaries and supervisory boards conducted the work of the convention between sessions.

The Southern Baptist Convention was organized for the specific purpose of combining the efforts of Baptists of the South in promoting "Foreign and Domestic Missions, and other important objects connected with the Redeemer's kingdom." [10] During its first twenty-five or thirty years, the convention restricted its efforts almost entirely to the promotion of missions. Frequently, when other matters arose for consideration, delegates objected on the ground that such proposals did not come within the purview of the constitution. Gradually, however, the "other important objects" clause of the constitution came to be interpreted broadly to include temperance, book and periodical publication, education, care of orphans, and other charitable causes. The concept of the purpose of state conventions showed similar development.

In no respect was the organization of Southern Baptists hierarchical. Each church and each individual member retained a high degree of independence within the framework of a generally accepted body of beliefs and practices. The denomination made great strides toward unity during the period, however. The enlargement of the home and foreign mission programs, the organization of a publishing house with South-wide patronage, the strengthening of its educational institutions, particularly the theological seminary in Louisville, Kentucky, and the separation from the main body of several splinter groups gave Baptists a unity of

---

10. "Preamble and Constitution of the SOUTHERN BAPTIST CONVENTION," in Southern Baptist Convention, *Proceedings, 1845*, pp. 3–5.

purpose and organization by 1900 which they had never known before. Yet, voluntary co-operation remained the key to denominational strength. Baptists were justified in insisting that they were not a "church" but merely a denomination.

Southern Baptists were homogeneous members of Southern society. By 1845, certainly by 1865, they had lost the odium associated with their forebears who constituted minor dissenter sects in England and in early America. They were found in all strata of Southern life. It is perhaps not inaccurate to say that Baptists in the late nineteenth century represented in fair proportion a cross section of Southern society. Like the mass of Southerners, the majority of Baptists resided in rural areas. No accurate statistics indicating the place of residence of Baptists during the last century are now available, but estimates made late in the nineteenth century suggest that more than 90 percent of the Baptists in some states lived in small towns or the open country.[11] As late as 1950 when reliable statistics were obtainable, 83.3 percent of the denomination's 27,788 churches with 55.4 percent of its members were still to be found in rural areas or in small towns of 2,500 population or less.[12] Of the several largest cities in the South in the 1890's, only Richmond, Virginia, was said to be a "Baptist" city.[13]

While the great majority of Baptists were unquestionably of humble birth and modest means,[14] a few individuals among them possessed considerable wealth and achieved prominence. Jabez L. M. Curry, educator and diplomat; Joseph E. Brown, industrialist and governor of Georgia; Leonidas L. Polk, editor of the *Progressive Farmer;* Basil Manly, Jr., president of the University of Alabama; James P. Eagle, governor of Arkansas; and Isaac T. Tichenor, president of Alabama Polytechnic Institute, were Baptists who rose above the masses. To this list of individ-

11. *Alabama Baptist* (Montgomery), March 1, 1888, p. 1.

12. *Southern Baptist Handbook, 1951* (1951), p. 90. These figures include the states of the South as defined in this study and Arizona, California, District of Columbia, Illinois, Kansas, Maryland, Missouri, New Mexico, Oklahoma, and Oregon.

13. Southern Baptist Convention, *Proceedings, 1894,* p. LIX.

14. That Baptists, by and large, were of the lower social and economic strata of society has been borne out by numerous statements in the course of research. Considering society as a trichotomy—lower, middle, and upper—the vast majority of Baptists were in the lower and middle classes. For evidence of the low status of Baptists in South Carolina in an earlier period, *see* Leah Townsend, *South Carolina Baptists, 1670–1805* (1935), pp. 271–305.

uals could be added the names of a number of Baptist families who ranked high in Southern society; Broadus (or Broaddus) and Jones of Virginia; Mercer and Cobb of Georgia; Fuller, Elliott, and Furman of South Carolina; and Lowery of Mississippi, to name only a few.

The opinions and reactions of Baptists toward the social questions of the time cannot be dismissed, therefore, as the captious criticism of the disinherited who had no stake in society. This fact gives relevance and meaning to this study. Did Baptists think of themselves as *Baptists* first or *Southerners* first? To what extent did Baptists shape their environment and to what extent were they shaped by their environment? Whether Baptists molded or merely reflected Southern attitudes, they were nevertheless significant.

1. Problems of Politics

H E last thirty-five years of the nineteenth century were fraught with political problems. The most portentous was that of restoring national unity after the period of sectional controversy and war. Union victory on the battlefield established the supremacy of the nation over the states, but it by no means restored a united country. For a generation after the cessation of hostilities, sectional animosity continued, nurtured by bitter memories of the war and military occupation, by the adroit devices of unscrupulous politicians, and by the vagaries of human nature. The resurgence of white supremacy in the South, tacitly approved by the North in its acceptance of the Compromise of 1877 and the Supreme Court's civil rights decision of 1883, did much to heal the breach, but sectional comity was not fully restored until near the end of the century.

Besides the difficulties resulting from the sectional conflict, the post-bellum period presented other fundamental political problems. Among the most critical was the changing role of the state in the everyday affairs of its citizens. Political laissez-faire declined between 1865 and 1900, and government at all levels intervened more and more in areas which formerly had been reserved to private initiative. The development of public education, for example, was considered by many Americans as an encroachment of the state on the domain of the church, the family, and private philanthropy. The proper relationship between church and state, the emergence of the United States as a world power, and the growth of socialism and anarchism were also problems of a political nature which provoked discussion during the last third of the century.

Southern Baptists took cognizance of these changing political conditions and expressed definite opinions about them. Their response to the events of the immediate postwar period can be understood, however, only in relation to their attitudes toward secession, the Confederacy, and the war. As the slavery controversy threatened to dissolve the Union in

1860–1861, Southern Baptists were forced to decide between the Union and their native states. In the closing weeks of 1860 they were divided on the question. Some wanted secession immediately; others wanted to wait for an overt act of aggression by the North; and others opposed secession under all circumstances. Soon after the election of Lincoln, opinion began coalescing. The Alabama Baptist State Convention, in session November 9–12, 1860, unanimously adopted a report declaring the Union a failure and pledging to support the "sovereignty and independence of the State of Alabama" in whatever course her representatives might choose to follow.[1]

Baptists in other parts of the South expressed regret at the hasty action of Alabama Baptists, which, they thought, had been unduly influenced by the recent political campaign. The editor of the *Southern Baptist* of Charleston, South Carolina, claimed to see no cause for alarm in the Republican victory or in the threatened secession of the states of the Lower South. Six or seven cotton states might withdraw from the Union, he admitted, but the separation would be peaceful. The federal government would not dare attempt a policy of coercion which could end only in failure.[2] Kentucky Baptists pursued a more cautious course. Although their state paper reflected a considerable amount of pro-Southern, and even secessionist, sentiment, their general association eventually adopted a resolution pledging loyalty to the Washington government. Kentucky Baptists failed to achieve political unanimity. Throughout the war factional strife emanating from political differences so divided the denomination that a number of churches closed their doors and all co-operative effort among the churches ceased.[3]

While the Upper South equivocated after the election of Lincoln, Baptists of the Lower South moved swiftly toward secession. Florida Baptists in convention November 24, 1860, deemed it "proper at once to express their cordial sympathy with, and hearty approbation of those who are determined to maintain the integrity of the Southern States."[4] Delegates at the Georgia Baptist Convention, April 26–29, 1861, de-

1. Alabama Baptist Convention, *Minutes, 1860*, pp. 11–12.
2. *Southern Baptist* (Charleston), November 17, 1860, p. 2; December 15, 1860, p. 2.
3. *Western Recorder* (Louisville), November 10, 1860, p. 2; December 8, 1860, p. 2; Kentucky Baptist General Association, *Minutes, 1861*, pp. 27–28; *1862*, pp. 14, 17.
4. Florida Baptist Convention, *Minutes, 1860*, pp. 7–8.

nounced the "madness of Mr. Lincoln," and vowed to let no group of Southern people exceed them in defending the Confederacy, even to the "sacrifice of treasure and of blood." [5] Members of the faculty and student body at the nascent Southern Baptist Theological Seminary in Greenville, South Carolina, debated the question of secession for several weeks, but as the states began seceding most of the students followed the lead of their native states into the Confederacy. Finally, when Virginia voted to secede, the seminary suspended classes and the remaining students left without completing their final examinations.[6]

The climax of the secessionist movement among Southern Baptists came at the meeting of the Southern Baptist Convention in Savannah, Georgia, May 10–13, 1861. Nine states had seceded from the Union by that time; the convention had to recognize or repudiate a *fait accompli*. The delegates made their sentiments unmistakable. In a long report they defended the right of secession, condemned Northern politicians and churchmen for forcing war upon the South, and pledged themselves to sustain the Confederacy with their prayers. In a final act of defiance, the delegates struck "United States" from the constitution of the convention and substituted for it "Southern States of North America." If any pro-Union sentiment existed among Southern Baptists at this convention, it is not apparent in the records.[7]

Following the action of the Southern Baptist Convention, the state conventions in all the states of the Confederacy which had not already done so proclaimed their loyalty to the Confederacy. Baptists saw God at work in the events of 1860–1861. Delegates at the South Carolina Convention in 1861 expressed the conviction that

so far as we can understand the remarkable openings and guidance of Divine Providence, we have but received, in almost every instance, the merciful blessing of our God, as approbation upon the plans our State and Southern Confederacy have deemed it best to adopt . . . [and] that in this most unrighteous and most wicked attack upon our otherwise peaceful homes, the wickedness of the wicked will return on their own heads.[8]

5. Georgia Baptist Convention, *Minutes, 1861,* pp. 5–6.
6. C. E. W. Dobbs, "Our Second Session and the Trying Days of '61," *Seminary Magazine,* III (April 1890), 123–127.
7. Southern Baptist Convention, *Proceedings, 1861,* pp. 11, 12, 57, 62–64. After the Civil War, the convention restored the original wording of its constitution. *See* Southern Baptist Convention, *Proceedings, 1866,* p. 17.
8. South Carolina Baptist Convention, *Minutes, 1861,* pp. 97–98.

Virginia Baptists found comfort in the "sweet assurance that our cause is a righteous one, and we can appeal to the God of Battles for help in this hour of darkness and peril." [9] Baptists believed that the cause of the Confederacy was in harmony with the will of God.

Until the closing months of the war, Baptists maintained their optimistic faith in the righteousness of the Confederate cause. "We solemnly reiterate our firm conviction of the rectitude of the cause of the C.S.A., and our unwavering confidence in its final success," declared Virginia Baptists in 1862.[10] Baptists of Louisiana united in a prayer of thanksgiving for the successes of Confederate arms after the first year of conflict, and concluded that Confederate victories had only served

to fasten the conviction, that the cause for which the Confederate States is struggling is just; that the existence of civil and religious liberty and the perpetuity of institutions, established by God himself, depend upon our success.[11]

The editor of the *Confederate Baptist,* a weekly established in Columbia, South Carolina, declared in 1862 in his "Salutatory" that

in regard to our civil and political *status* we may remark, that we regard the establishment of the independence of the Confererate States as a foregone conclusion, and we expect to live and die in the enjoyment of the blessings of our glorious Confederacy.[12]

As the war continued, however, and the people of the South began feeling the horrors of bloodshed and destruction, Baptists were called upon to reconcile their optimism of 1861 with military reverses. Delegates at the Virginia General Association of 1863 called Confederate defeats "tokens of God's displeasure against us for our sins," but assured their constituents that the Confederate cause was still God's cause and that success was inevitable.[13] In the same year the Southern Baptist Convention expressed similar sentiments. The events of the last two years, the delegates declared, had only

strengthened our opposition to a reunion with the United States on any terms whatever; and while deploring the dreadful evils of the war, and earnestly

9. Virginia Baptist General Association, *Minutes, 1861,* p. 16.
10. *Ibid., 1862,* p. 44.
11. Louisiana Baptist Convention, *Minutes, 1862,* p. 10.
12. *Confederate Baptist* (Charleston), October 1, 1862, p. 1.
13. Virginia Baptist General Association, *Minutes, 1863,* p. 78.

desiring peace, we have no thought of ever yielding, but will render a hearty support to the Confederate Government in all constitutional measures to secure our independence.

Although God was just in punishing the Southern people for their sins, the delegates concluded, He would ultimately bless them with success.[14]

As the war entered its final year, Baptists began reflecting the general despondency which was settling over the Confederacy. Their journals attempted to boost lagging spirits by predicting the eventual triumph of the Confederacy, but they could not avoid taking note of the setbacks to Confederate arms. The future looked dark, one editor confessed, but not every cloud that hid the sun portended immediate night. If Christians would only be true to God, "the storm-cloud which seems to be thickening over our heads shall break away, and we shall walk in the light of peace." [15] Only a month before Lee's surrender, the Virginia paper, in an editorial entitled "Away With Despondency," still expressed hope for victory but at the same time attempted to prepare its readers for inevitable defeat. In the early part of the war, the editor said, the South had been successful because the people were humble and prayerful, but success had turned their heads. The recent defeats of Southern armies were the result of the personal and collective sins of God's people. The North had the material advantage in the war, the South was cut off from outside aid, and traitors threatened the Confederacy from within; but, he continued, "if we are overcome finally, it will be because we are not worthy of freedom. . . . Our cause will be strengthened and our liberty secured as soon as we deserve it." [16] This declaration, so near the end of the war, reveals that Southern Baptists, like the devout of all ages, were caught in a dilemma of faith: How could the justice of God and the righteousness of the Southern cause be reconciled with the imminent collapse of the Confederacy?

On April 9, 1865, Lee tendered his word to Grant, and the effort of Southerners to achieve independence was over. Baptists who had gone to war four years earlier assured of God's approval now faced the problem of reconciling their confidence in victory in 1861 with the contradictory

14. Southern Baptist Convention, *Proceedings, 1863,* p. 54.
15. *Religious Herald* (Richmond), January 19, 1865, p. 1. Similar ideas are expressed in the *Christian Index* (Macon, Georgia), January 26, 1865, pp. 1, 2; February 16, 1865, p. 2; March 30, 1865, p. 2.
16. *Religious Herald* (Richmond), March 9, 1865, p. 1.

outcome of 1865. Their faith was severely tested. Defeat weighed heaviest on those whose faith had been strongest. "When the Southern Confederacy fell," wrote one editor,

thousands of hearts were crushed. . . . It is simply the *fact,* that good men, good men and true, men full of the Holy Ghost and of faith, were ardently desirous for the success of the Southern arms, and felt, when the cause failed, that Providence had sent upon them an overwhelming calamity.[17]

The North Carolina paper expressed well the sense of disillusionment:

It were useless to deny that despondency, like a thick cloud, rests on the minds of many of the people of the South. The result of the late war was unexpected to them. They believed in the justice of the cause which they espoused and believing this, looked for final success, even under the most serious reverses, till sudden, hopeless, inevitable ruin came. . . . When they turn from the past, in which so many cherished treasures, and joys, and hopes, lie buried, to the present, it only brings before them more vividly the sad realities of their condition. Confusion and uncertainty reign now, and to them the future holds out no promise of improvement, no incentive to effort.[18]

Delegates to the state conventions meeting soon after the war ignored the untenable position in which defeat had left them. They thanked God for peace and accepted their fate with resignation.[19] Baptist papers at least recognized the dilemma, although their early attempts to rationalize were little more than unreasoned assertions that God was still in His heaven and all would soon be right in the world. They continued to attribute defeat to the sins of the Southern people and to assert that the righteousness of the Southern cause, the justice of God, and the Confederate debacle could be reconciled. It hardly seems to have occurred to Southern Baptists that a forthright acknowledgment of error on their part would have solved their problem. Their effort to blame defeat on the sins of the people only hedged the question. The real dilemma was never resolved; there was no satisfactory answer as long as Baptists held to their major assumptions.

Besides the presence of unrepented sin in the lives of Southerners, Baptists offered only one other explanation for the defeat of the Confed-

17. *Christian Index* (Macon, Georgia), January 13, 1866, p. 10.
18. *Biblical Recorder* (Raleigh, North Carolina), February 22, 1866, p. 2.
19. *Minutes* of the Louisiana Baptist Convention of 1865 made no reference whatever to the end of the war.

eracy—in some mysterious way it was God's will. The editor of the Georgia paper employed a curious sort of logic in arriving at this conclusion: When the plans of Christians succeeded, he said, it could be that God was leaving them to their folly.

But when we are disappointed, it is clear that God has taken our case out of our own hands, and has substituted *his* judgment in the guidance of our affairs for our own. . . . Instead of grieving over our disappointment, therefore, we should rejoice in the evidence we have that we are in the hands of superior power. . . . If God has placed us where we are, we ought to be content with our condition.[20]

In a later issue of the same paper, the editor expressed what Baptists seemed to have accepted as the explanation of the war:

He [God] has done what he thought best. . . . He may have laid his hand heavily upon us; certainly we are deeply smitten, but in the midst of it all, we rely on his goodness, and would not, if we could, interfere with his workings of his Providence, and rejoicing ever in tribulation, we feel that it is
"Sweet to lie passive in his arms
And know no will but his." [21]

These affirmations evidently satisfied Baptists, for expressions of skepticism disappeared altogether in 1866. Attributing defeat to God's will enabled Baptists to save face and obviated the necessity of sacrificing any cherished beliefs.

Accepting the failure of the Confederacy as providential also enabled Baptists to absolve themselves of any blame in causing the war. Baptists never repudiated slavery and secession, the two alleged causes of the war. A contributor to one of the papers took sharp issue with an editorial in which the editor had suggested that the war might have been God's method of abolishing slavery. Such an idea was preposterous, the writer claimed. Slavery was sanctioned in both the Old and New Testaments:

Can it be that it was the *design* of God in the late terrible civil war to overthrow an institution which he himself ordained, established and sanctioned, and which he 'designed' should exist forever? . . . [God would not have caused all this suffering] that an inferior race might be released from a *nominal* bondage and endowed with a freedom which, to them, is but another name for licentiousness, and which must end in complete extermination, so

20. *Christian Index* (Macon, Georgia), January 13, 1866, p. 10.
21. *Ibid.,* January 20, 1866, p. 14. *See also* the issue of August 30, 1865, p. 138.

far as human foresight can judge. . . . But I cannot, I will not believe it. . . . It was Satan that ruled the hour [*i.e.,* the freeing of the slaves].[22]

A contributor to another journal saw God's hand in the emancipation of the slaves—not because slavery was wrong, but because Southern slaveowners had failed in their duty to evangelize their servants. No evil was abolished by emancipation. Southern whites, therefore, still had the same obligation to the freedmen. If they permitted the Negroes to degenerate, God would punish the white race again.[23]

As with slavery, so with secession. Baptists had no confessions of guilt. They defended the states'-rights arguments on which the doctrine of secession rested. In resorting to secession Southerners had merely followed a political philosophy which differed from that held by Northerners. The Constitution provided for the possibility of a divided loyalty between federal and state governments. Southerners had expressed first loyalty to their states; Northerners had given first allegiance to the federal government. Neither could be charged with disloyalty. At worst Southerners were guilty of treason on a technical point, not of "moral treason."[24] Because Southern Baptists considered secession a legitimate, constitutional right, they had nothing to repudiate. One editor would admit only that perhaps the South had used bad judgment in exercising its right of secession and that "the sword *is* mightier than the pen."[25]

Northern Baptists chided their Southern brethren for refusing to admit that the collapse of the Confederacy was evidence of God's disapproval of slavery and secession. To this argument one editor replied: "*Might* and *right* have *never* been wedded in this world since the fall."[26] Another paper elaborated:

It [the war] has decided questions of power, but not of morality. [The war proved that secession could not] be maintained by force of arms—and that slavery could be abolished by military [power]. . . . But the sword cannot determine moral questions. The bayonet may coerce, but it cannot convince. All questions of right—of morality—are left precisely where they were before the war. Whether secession was a legitimate or revolutionary measure?

22. *Religious Herald* (Richmond), February 22, 1866, p. 1.
23. *Christian Index* (Atlanta), February 10, 1866, p. 22.
24. *Religious Herald* (Richmond), October 19, 1865, p. 1; April 12, 1866, p. 2. These ideas were reprinted and further elaborated in the *South Carolina Baptist* (Anderson), April 20, 1866, p. 2.
25. *Christian Index* (Atlanta), March 15, 1866, p. 46. *See also Christian Index* (Macon, Georgia), November 9, 1865, p. 2.
26. *Christian Index* (Atlanta), February 10, 1866, p. 2.

whether slavery was right or wrong? whether the forcible emancipation of the slaves will prove a blessing or a curse? and whether those who engaged in the war, on either side, were innocent or guilty? are grave questions, on which the issue of the war has shed no light.[27]

Baptists persisted in these views for the remainder of the century. They refused to admit that secession and slavery were wrong in any way, constitutionally or morally, and denied any responsibility for causing the war. Because God had overridden their views through the instrumentality of war, they would accept His will, but they would change none of their views.

Having thus resolved to their satisfaction the philosophical dilemma in which the war left them, Baptists were then prepared to accept the consequences of defeat. The most obvious political results of the war were the annihilation of the Confederacy and the consequent reunion of the states. In both of these, Baptists acquiesced in *fact* if not in principle.

Baptists advocated immediate reunion, removal of all political disabilities, and the restoration of the South to its former place in the Union. There is no evidence that Baptists entertained any intentions of supporting a second effort for Southern independence. "The war is over," said the editor of the Georgia paper. "Let the evil passions which engendered it, and which it engendered, die with it." [28] In the first issue of the Virginia weekly after the war, the editor pledged to work toward peace between the sections:

Accepting the present political *status* of the country, we will advocate submission to legitimate authority and seek to heal sectional dissension, and restore a friendly intercourse between all parts of our common country; avoiding the discussion of politics, except so far as they may affect the interests of morality and religion.[29]

Later the same editor admonished Baptists to use their influence

to allay sectional strife, to promote order in society and to secure the end for which all good governments are organized—the well-being and happiness of the people.[30]

27. *Religious Herald* (Richmond), October 19, 1865, p. 2.
28. *Christian Index* (Macon, Georgia), January 13, 1866, p. 10.
29. *Religious Herald* (Richmond), October 19, 1865, p. 2.
30. *Ibid.*, November 15, 1866, p. 2.

Baptist papers castigated those die-hard Southerners who held that test oaths and oaths of allegiance were not binding since they had been administered under duress. Editors repeated St. Paul's command that Christians be submissive to civil authority as to the authority of God.[31]

Although Baptists accepted the restoration of the Union in good faith, they were not prepared to repudiate the Lost Cause and its heroes. On numerous occasions they defended Davis, Lee, Jackson, Gordon, and other Confederate leaders against the attempts of Northern journalists to defame their characters because of their participation in the war. The editor of the Virginia weekly acknowledged his readiness to accept the overthrow of the Confederacy and to work for "harmony and conciliation *in the Union;* yet," he said, "we shall ever regard it as a most sacred duty to guard the reputation and cherish the memory of those noble men who laid down their lives in the Confederate service." [32] The Alabama State Convention, meeting in November 1865, memorialized "the President of the United States in behalf of Jefferson Davis, praying that the Executive clemency be extended to him in releasing him from prison and restoring him to his full rights as a citizen." [33] On another occasion an editor admonished Southerners to exercise extreme caution in purchasing Sunday school literature and other reading materials from Northern publishers, materials which would leave the impression on the children of the South that Southerners who participated in the Confederacy "were traitors and criminals." [34]

For almost two years after the war a veritable "battle of journals" raged between religious papers of the North and South. Northern editors accused Southerners of a variety of crimes and treasonable activities—mistreatment of the Negroes before and after emancipation, insincerity in taking the oath of allegiance to the United States, plotting to re-establish the Confederacy, attempting to re-enslave the freedmen, suppression of free speech, atrocities at Andersonville and Libby prisons, and others. The most vexatious accusations, perhaps, were the attacks on Confederate leaders and the charge that Southerners, while making their bid for

31. *Christian Index* (Macon, Georgia), January 27, 1866, p. 18; *Religious Herald* (Richmond), November 22, 1866, p. 1; October 4, 1866, p. 1. The inconsistency between this advice and the Baptist advocacy of secession five years earlier is obvious.
32. *Religious Herald* (Richmond), October 19, 1865, p. 1.
33. Alabama Baptist Convention, *Minutes, 1865,* pp. 7–8.
34. *Biblical Recorder* (Raleigh, North Carolina), April 19, 1866, p. 2.

freedom, had been guilty of treason and rebellion. In answering these charges Southern Baptist editors exhibited little restraint.[35] Even the Kentucky paper, which withheld comment on political and sectional questions for more than a year following the war, broke its silence and defended the South against these attacks.[36] Baptists papers of the North (and journals of other denominations as well) seemed to demand repentance and humility of their Southern brethren as the price for restoring amicable relations. Southern Baptists adamantly refused. If reunion with the North—either religious or political—were contingent upon the South's humbling herself, said the editor of the Georgia paper, then "there can be neither union nor communion between us this side of eternity." Sectional animosity would never end as long as the North maintained its superior attitude. "More bees are caught with honey than vinegar," the editor epigrammatized.[37]

After about a year and a half of intense controversy over issues growing out of the war, Southern Baptist papers ceased almost all discussion of political affairs. During the latter years of the sixties, when Reconstruction policy was taking shape, Baptists had little to say about the affairs of state. Only an occasional article or editorial indicated their dissatisfaction with and contempt for the radical regimes.

Southern Baptists entertained little hope of Democratic victory in the election of 1868. The Georgia paper merely cautioned its readers to maintain a Christian attitude during the campaign, and other papers had nothing to say.[38] After the election was over, the Tennessee paper expressed mild disappointment at the Democratic defeat, but viewed with approval the election of a soldier to the presidency. Grant undoubtedly would bring stability to the national government and end tyranny in the South. Overconfidently, as events proved, the editor looked for the speedy enfranchisement of all Southern whites and the immediate return of white control.[39]

35. *Christian Index* (Atlanta), March 15, 1866, p. 46; August 16, 1866, p. 130; November 8, 1866, p. 178; *Religious Herald* (Richmond), March 1, 1866, p. 2; March 15, 1866, p. 2; *South Carolina Baptist* (Anderson), April 20, 1866, p. 2.

36. *Western Recorder* (Louisville), March 9, 1866, p. 3; July 28, 1866, p. 2.

37. *Christian Index* (Macon, Georgia), November 9, 1865, p. 2.

38. *Ibid.*, July 30, 1868, p. 118.

39. *The Baptist* (Memphis), November 14, 1868, p. 5.

As the carpetbaggers carried their regimes to incredible excesses in the early 1870's, Baptists spoke out in protest. A Virginia Baptist called radical rule in South Carolina a "reign of terror," [40] and a South Carolinian described conditions in his home state as thoroughly corrupt:

Villainy is the chief road to political preferment. It is the millennium of rogues and swindlers. Wealth is a sign of rascality. The honest remain poor, whilst the unprincipled and vicious are clad in purple and fine linen. . . . Will the brethren of the North interpose to break the horrible "tyranny" which, under the name of Republicanism, is destroying its very elements and establishing over the South, over their Baptist brethren—the rule of the vile, the illiterate, the vulgar and the base [?] [41]

Louisiana under military rule was, like South Carolina, "afflicted with a terrible malady in the body politic," said the South Carolina paper,[42] and Georgia Baptists extended sympathy to Louisianians who were "still under galling yoks [*sic*] of military misrule." [43]

Baptists boldly encouraged Democrats in their efforts to overthrow carpetbag rule in 1874. The editor of the Virginia Baptist weekly admitted that his paper was not a political journal, but he declared that it would be "unpardonable" if he did not comment on Democratic successes in various Southern states. The results "filled us with the most sincere delight," he said, "and inspired us with bright hopes for the future of our country." [44]

Baptists eagerly anticipated the election of 1876 with the expectation of Democratic victory. For months before the election, the journals advocated the cessation of partisan hostilities and the restoration of good will. The Virginia paper was extremely conciliatory:

We do not transcend our editorial limit, when we express the desire that our next President, whatever other qualities he may possess or lack, will not be deficient in a national spirit. The man who is most capable of rising above party and sectional influences, of obliterating the unpleasant memories of the past, of seeking to blend the nation, with its diversified interests and views, into one harmonious whole, of contemplating the future in a liberal and

40. *Religious Herald* (Richmond), May 9, 1872, p. 3.
41. *Working Christian* (Columbia, South Carolina), March 7, 1872, p. 1.
42. *Ibid.*, September 24, 1874, p. 2.
43. *Christian Index* (Atlanta), January 14, 1875, p. 5.
44. *Religious Herald* (Richmond), November 12, 1874, p. 2.

hopeful spirit, of executing the laws, with an honest purpose and firm hand, to promote the public good, and, in short, of serving the country in his high and responsible office, is our choice for the Presidency. Whether he be democrat or republican, conservative or independent, we should be pleased to see him in the Presidential chair.[45]

When first election returns indicated that Tilden had been elected, Baptists were elated. The news of Democratic victory, reported the Kentucky paper,

seemingly lifted the settled cloud of gloom which has so long rested upon the commercial and political world, and all are rejoicing together in the prospect of "the good time coming." . . . The city of Louisville wears, at this writing, a more decidedly holiday aspect than any we have witnessed for many a day.[46]

Other papers reflected the same optimistic spirit.

Optimism disappeared, however, as Tilden's apparent victory vanished in the interplay of party politics and political bargaining. By mid-February 1877, a Republican triumph seemed more and more probable. The South Carolina paper reluctantly admitted that Hayes evidently would be the next president "while the whole country admits Tilden to have been elected. . . . It is strange how partizan feeling will influence men, right or wrong." [47] Two weeks later the same editor, in obvious dejection, commented:

Our friends all know, we presume, by this time, how the Congressional Commission has fixed up matters relative to the Presidential question. We have neither the time nor heart to comment upon it. Let us trust God and fear not what man can do unto us.[48]

The people of South Carolina in 1877 were less concerned with the presidential election than with their own state elections. To all local observers, it was apparent that Wade Hampton and a Democratic slate had been elected by an overwhelming majority; yet the Republicans, with the aid of federal troops, refused to surrender the state house. Baptists in other states joined in criticizing President Grant for permitting

45. *Ibid.,* July 13, 1876, p. 2.
46. *Western Recorder* (Louisville), November 9, 1876, p. 4.
47. *Working Christian* (Columbia, South Carolina), February 15, 1877, p. 2.
48. *Ibid.,* March 1, 1877, p. 2.

the use of federal troops to support a regime composed of the "worst men of the State," whom the people had repudiated at the polls.[49] The South Carolina paper gave weekly coverage to Hampton's efforts to have his election recognized. When, after a trip to Washington, Hampton secured the removal of federal troops and the withdrawal of the puppet government, the paper devoted a large part of its April 12th issue to Hampton's triumph. In articles and editorials entitled "Governor Hampton and Reform," "A Day of Thanksgiving," "South Carolina Free at Last," and "Our Governor's Return from Washington," the paper expressed unqualified approval of Bourbon victory and the final redemption of the state.[50]

Without question, Baptists of the South were genuinely disappointed at the failure of the Democrats to capture the presidency in 1876, but the disappointment was mitigated by the removal of the remaining federal troops and the complete restoration of native white control. They were willing to accept conditions in the hope that better times were at hand.[51]

Although the events of the Reconstruction Era resulted in the reestablishment of political unity, reunion of the country in sentiment by no means followed. Baptists of both sections probably could have contributed substantially to the restoration of sectional good will by reuniting their severed denomination, but relatively few Baptists of the South gave the matter serious consideration. Some Baptists in Virginia and East Tennessee favored denominational reunion, but these were decidedly in the minority.[52]

Baptists generally preferred to maintain their own Southern organizations. For a number of years after the war, many were reluctant even to exchange "correspondence" with Northern Baptists. The *Christian Index,* the most reactionary of the state papers, categorically rejected organic reunion and agreed to a reunion "of spirit" only if "the olive branch [were] tendered by the North." [53] Baptists in Louisiana, Alabama, and Florida went so far as to refuse financial aid from the Baptist Bible and

49. *Alabama Baptist* (Marion), December 21, 1876, p. 2; *Working Christian* (Columbia, South Carolina), November 9, 1876, p. 2; December 7, 1876, p. 2.

50. *Working Christian* (Columbia, South Carolina), April 12, 1877, pp. 1, 2.

51. *Religious Herald* (Richmond), March 1, 1877, p. 1.

52. *Ibid.,* March 15, 1866, p. 2; May 22, 1879, p. 2; East Tennessee Baptist General Association, *Proceedings, 1868,* p. 8.

53. *Christian Index* (Macon, Georgia), November 9, 1865, p. 2.

Home Mission Societies of the North, unless their state conventions were given full control over expenditures.[54]

The question of closer co-operation with Northern Baptists arose at the meetings of the Southern Baptist Convention in 1867, 1868, 1869, and 1879. Nothing came from these discussions, however, except an agreement to exchange "fraternal delegates."[55] The deliberations of 1879 settled the question of organic union for the remainder of the century. Northern and Southern Baptists continued to exchange "fraternal messengers" at their annual meetings, to confer on matters of common interest, and to co-operate to a limited extent in home missions, but the restoration of denominational unity as it had existed before 1845 was not seriously discussed again. Southern Baptists came to argue that separate organizations would be desirable even if all sectional animosities could be allayed. During the years of separation, they maintained, fundamental differences, totally unrelated to the original cause of the schism and the issues of the war, had developed which rendered reunion impossible.[56]

In areas other than denominational relations, Southern Baptists also seem to have contributed as much to keeping sectionalism alive as they did to allaying ill feeling. They expressed their bitterest sectionalism immediately after the war and in the few months immediately before and after the election of 1876, but they continued to defend the South and its institutions to the end of the century. The election of 1880 was an occasion for the renewal of the sectional controversy. Democrats, especially Southerners, believed that victory had been snatched from them in 1876, and they were determined to avenge this wrong in 1880. In the early months of the election year, Baptist papers spoke objectively about politics, cautioning their readers about undue enthusiasm in the coming

54. Louisiana Baptist Convention, *Minutes, 1870,* pp. 6–7; Alabama Baptist Convention, *Minutes, 1868,* p. 10; Florida Baptist Convention, *Minutes, 1869,* pp. 13–14, 16; *1870,* pp. 9–10, 12.

55. Southern Baptist Convention, *Proceedings, 1867 passim; 1868,* pp. 20–21, 26, 27, 31, 32; *1869,* pp. 20–21.

56. Southern Baptist Convention, *Proceedings, 1879,* pp. 14, 24–26; *Religious Herald* (Richmond), May 15, 1879, p. 2; May 22, 1879, p. 2; *Christian Index* (Atlanta), August 12, 1869, p. 121; South Carolina Baptist Convention, *Minutes, 1887,* p. 23. At the convention in 1895, Isaac T. Tichenor, who had led the faction for closer co-operation with Northern Baptists in 1879, requested "as a matter of privilege" that he be permitted to insert a statement in the *Proceedings* denying that he had had any intention in 1879 of destroying the Southern Baptist Convention or any of its agencies. *See* Southern Baptist Convention, *Proceedings, 1895,* p. 41.

campaign and urging them to support the best man, regardless of party.[57] As the election drew near, however, they became less objective and, while still proclaiming their neutrality, their leanings toward Hancock became obvious.[58] After the election, the editor of the Georgia paper attributed Republican victory to corruption, bribery, and the revival of sectionalism. He regretted the fact that "the dead carcass of the 'Southern Confederacy,' that has been in its grave for fifteen or sixteen years, has been exhumed, to regale the olfactories of the 'Union saver.' " [59] The political campaign was but the focal point for a wide range of accusations and recriminations. Northern religious papers accused Southerners of the usual mistreatment of the Negroes and other derelictions of civil duty, while Southern Baptist journals employed their best polemicists in defense.[60]

Although Southern Baptists did not display their sectionalism so passionately again after 1880, they periodically expressed the defensive Southern mind until the end of the century. In 1886 and 1887 a flurry of Southern sentiment occurred with the serial publication in the *Religious Herald* of John William Jones's "Christ in the Camp, or Religion in Lee's Army." In an introductory note to the series, the author disavowed any intention of reviving the "dead issues of the war," but the accounts of God's workings among the Southern armies in Virginia, he said, quite naturally would arouse enthusiasm among ex-Confederates.[61] The many letters to the editor in response to the series indicated a strong attachment still to the memory of the Confederacy among Baptists.

President Cleveland's executive order that captured Confederate flags be returned to the South aroused a furor of protest from Union veterans. Southern Baptist papers ridiculed this Northern attitude. "One of the [Union] heroes," commented one editor,

57. *Christian Index* (Atlanta), May 27, 1880, p. 4; June 3, 1880, p. 1.

58. *Religious Herald* (Richmond), July 15, 1880, p. 1.

59. *Christian Index* (Atlanta), November 25, 1880, p. 1. *See also Baptist Courier* (Greenville, South Carolina), November 11, 1880, p. 2. The editor admitted that he was "genuinely disappointed" by the election results.

60. The controversy extended from mid-1879 until well after the election the following year. See *Christian Index* (Atlanta), June 26, 1879, p. 4; September 16, 1880, p. 5; December 23, 1880, p. 1; *Religious Herald* (Richmond), December 16, 1880, p. 2.

61. *Religious Herald* (Richmond), August 5, 1886, p. 1. The series continued intermittently into the following year. It was published later in book form as *Christ in the Camp: Or Religion in Lee's Army* (1887).

went so far as to say that the President's act would "emasculate all the manhood of the North." We hope he was mistaken in this somewhat pessimistic view, though really if the "manhood of the North" is so easily "emasculated" as this, it would seem that the sooner it is done the better.[62]

The death of Jefferson Davis on December 6, 1889, was another occasion for an outburst of Southern sentiment. Baptists throughout the South lauded their fallen hero. The Virginia paper opened its editorial on Davis's death with: "The one man enshrined in the inner sanctuary of every Southern breast is no more." [63] Another paper recounted that Davis had been ill beyond recovery for many days before his death. "However," commented the editor,

loyal Southern hearts hoped that the grand old man would be spared them yet a little longer, that they might honor him more and give attestation of their feelings to the hero of the Lost Cause. [History would place his name where it] rightly belongs—among the greatest men this country has yet produced. . . . He went to perform his duty, as did thousands of others, and the cause he espoused shall never be called the traitor's cause. Never! [64]

Without exception Baptist papers joined the lament.

Three years later when Davis's body was moved from New Orleans to Richmond for permanent interment, another mild wave of sectionalism swept the South. Along the route of the funeral train, thousands of loyal Southerners paid final tribute to the Confederacy's only president. In Greenville, South Carolina, a large crowd waited until three in the morning to view the hero's casket. "It was a memorable occasion," commented one Baptist.[65]

Another outburst of Southern sectionalism occurred in the mid-nineties. Within Baptist circles, North and South, it contributed to the failure of a plan by Northern Baptists to enlist Southern Baptists in support of the Baptist Young Peoples' Union of America. Because of old fears and suspicions Southern Baptists eventually organized their own B.Y.P.U. unaffiliated with the national group. Sectionalism was also a decided factor in preventing the closer co-operation of Southern Baptists with the

62. *Christian Index* (Atlanta), June 30, 1887, p. 1.
63. *Religious Herald* (Richmond), December 12, 1889, p. 2.
64. *Alabama Baptist* (Montgomery), December 12, 1889, p. 2.
65. *Baptist Courier* (Greenville, South Carolina), June 8, 1893, p. 2. *See also* *Religious Herald* (Richmond), June 1, 1893, p. 2; June 22, 1893, p. 1.

Northern Home Mission Society in its efforts to educate the Negroes in the South.[66]

More evidence of the persistence of sectionalism in the 1890's appeared in a review of *A History of the United States* by President Elisha Benjamin Andrews of Brown University. The reviewer, John Hart of Virginia, called Andrews an extremely prejudiced New Englander, with only "pretensions to culture." The review was principally an argument for the supremacy of Southern statesmen. Between 1789 and 1861, Hart said, the South had furnished the vast majority of presidents, supreme court justices, and other public figures.

These facts, to a candid mind, prove a remarkable ascendency of Southern public men in our Federal affairs for nigh eighty years. The most natural supposition in explanation is that these men were superior in character, culture and political sagacity. . . . One of the plain results of this long continued Southern superiority was to breed in the general Northern mind a dull jealousy passed into a deep-seated hatred, which still survives; and this hatred, born of jealousy, had far more influence in uniting the North in the purpose to crush slavery than any real sympathy with the "down-trodden" slaves.

The real cause of the Civil War, Hart continued, was the desire of Northern politicians to wrest political power from the South, and the resurgence of sectional animosity in the nineties, he concluded, resulted from the fear of Northerners that the South was regaining political supremacy.[67]

Many other articles in Baptist papers indicate the existence of strained relations between the sections in the nineties. Andrew Broaddus, one of the most highly honored Baptists of the South, severely scored Northerners for erecting a monument to John Brown:

John Brown's memory deserves to be perpetuated only as one of the foulest murderers that ever polluted the earth. . . . I venture to assert that in the history of civilized nations no other instance can be found of the erection of a monument in honor of a murderer.

66. *Religious Herald* (Richmond), January 3, 1895, p. 2; May 16, 1895, p. 2; June 6, 1895, p. 1. The controversy over the work of the Home Mission Society among the Negroes continued in almost every issue of the year.

67. *Religious Herald* (Richmond), July 18, 1895, p. 1.

The eulogies delivered in honor of Brown had raised him to the God-head, Broaddus asserted, and not even "Mariolatry" was as foul as that.[68]

This last surge of sectional strife was soon swallowed up in the groundswell of nationalism in the closing years of the century. Before noting the eventual triumph of nationalism, however, it is well to point out that Baptists by no means were totally deficient in nationalistic feelings. Although they contributed more, perhaps, to the continuation of sectionalism than to the re-establishment of sectional comity, they never-theless exhibited a degree of patriotism throughout the period. They welcomed the withdrawal of federal troops from the South in 1877 as evidence of and a contribution to the decline in sectional feelings. When Northerners contributed liberally to the relief of yellow fever victims in Memphis and New Orleans during the epidemic of 1879, Baptists hailed their action as a sign of the return of national unity: "Surely the bloody chasm has rapidly closed," said the delegates to the South-wide conven-tion.[69] Baptist editors saw in the assassination of President Garfield the hand of Providence allaying sectionalism. "The flash of an assassin's pistol," observed one editor,

revealed them [all Americans] to themselves as brethren—the report of an assassin's pistol drowned all the voices of sectional and party strife. May we not humbly believe that in this we are to see the high purpose of God, converting the most atrocious crime which the human heart can devise and the human hand can perpetrate into an instrument of glory to his name, and of blessing to our country? [70]

Not even the expressions of devotion to Jefferson Davis and the Confederacy at the time of Davis's death, declared one paper, were to be construed as

the slightest evidence of disloyalty to the American Union. The South is in the house of its fathers, there to abide and to go no more out forever. Southern citizens, of every variety of political sentiment, frankly and fully accept the result of the unhappy conflict which closed with the capitulation at Appomattox. At first, perhaps, they did so with the feelings of unspeakable sadness and hard submission; but this experience has given place, during subsequent years, to something far different from silent resignation. Our people, certainly our Christian people, believe, with all their hearts, that it

68. *Ibid.*, August 27, 1896, p. 1.
69. Southern Baptist Convention, *Proceedings, 1879*, p. 42.
70. *Baptist Courier* (Greenville, South Carolina), September 29, 1881, p. 2.

was written beyond the stars that the fabric of Southern independence should crumble into dust. There is no wish for any return to the hopes which budded and blossomed in 1861. More discerning and devout minds heartily thank God that "the peculiar institution," for whose constitutional right to remain till they were willing themselves to surrender it, Southern statesmen so ably argued and Southern valor so nobly bled and died, has been plucked up by the roots and scattered to the winds.[71]

Baptists denied that demonstrations along the route of the train carrying Davis's body to Richmond were seditious in any manner. Not a word of disloyalty was uttered along the way which the president of the United States himself might not have heard with propriety, said one paper. Although Baptists revered the past, they harbored no conflicting political allegiance. "The Confederacy is only a memory, sad, sacred, imperishable," said the South Carolina paper.[72]

Evidences of Southern sectionalism among Baptists disappeared during the patriotic upsurge accompanying the Spanish-American War. Baptists considered the war a righteous crusade for the liberation of Cuba, but "the greatest blessings," declared one editor, "will come along the line of reuniting our country in the ties of nationalism. . . . Even our colored brethren will go with the whites into battle." [73] Another journal envisioned a united America rising to meet a common foe:

Men who stood face to face as enemies in the internecine war that threatened the life of the nation thirty-five years ago now stand shoulder to shoulder in defence of their country with equal and unsuspected valor and patriotism. The last vestiges of bitter rancor and prejudice are rapidly disappearing.[74]

The Southern Baptist Convention in session in May, 1898, prayed God's blessings on the "whole country . . . and success in the war now in progress." [75] At the close of the war the editor of the Georgia paper hailed the war, not as a *cause* of reunion, but as evidence that the sections already were united:

It is taken as one of the great benefits of this war that it has served to obliterate distinctions of North and South, so far as patriotic interest in our

71. *Religious Herald* (Richmond), December 12, 1889, p. 2.
72. *Baptist Courier* (Greenville, South Carolina), June 8, 1893, p. 2; *Religious Herald* (Richmond), June 1, 1893, p. 3.
73. *Christian Index* (Atlanta), April 28, 1898, p. 6.
74. *Baptist Courier* (Greenville, South Carolina), June 9, 1898, p. 1.
75. Southern Baptist Convention, *Annual, 1898*, p. 34.

national affairs is concerned. . . . Now the president and the North see clearly what we knew all the time, that the South was loyal and sincere in its nationalism. It is this recognition that stands as the great gain from the war. . . . That recognition was worth the millions the war has cost.[76]

Within a generation after Appomattox, sectionalism of the intensity which had plunged the country into bloody conflict in 1861 was dead. Although Baptists refused to repudiate the Lost Cause and chose to retain their denominational entity along sectional lines, they nevertheless accepted and welcomed the return of political and social fraternity.

During the period from 1865 to 1900, Southern Baptists took pride in their reputation as champions of the principle of separation of church and state. They were not strict separatists to the extent that they opposed or ignored the state. On the contrary, they held a fairly distinguishable body of ideas relative to the nature and function of government. These ideas were seldom stated explicitly, neither were they held consistently throughout the period, but they were sufficiently in evidence to warrant calling them "Baptist theories" of government.

Baptists believed in the divine origin of civil government and in the obligation of citizens, especially Christians, to submit to civil authority. The sovereignty of the state was not absolute, however, for in good dissenter tradition they believed in freedom of conscience and the right of revolution. Their support of secession and the Confederacy is evidence of these beliefs. Even after the collapse of the Confederacy they continued to hold these views. "We solemnly resolve in the face of the world, and in the fear of God," declared the delegates at the Southern Baptist Convention in 1866,

that we believe civil government to be of divine appointment, and that magistrates should be prayed for, and obeyed, in all things, not contrary to the rights of conscience and the revealed will of Christ.[77]

Baptists not only believed that civil government was ordained by God, but they also held that God intervened directly in the affairs of state. Therefore, they could logically pray, as they often did, for God's blessings

76. *Christian Index* (Atlanta), August 11, 1898, p. 6.
77. Southern Baptist Convention, *Proceedings, 1866,* p. 87. Similar ideas were expressed in the *Religious Herald* (Richmond), October 4, 1866, p. 1, and many other places.

on their government and its officials. In the closing weeks of the Civil War, the editor of the Georgia paper asked his readers to pray for a miracle to save their country. Pray, he admonished, for "some special interposition on the part of Providence in our behalf. This interposition we can easily obtain by fervent prayer—and *only* by prayer." [78] The prayed-for miracle did not come, but Baptist faith was sufficient to accept the defeat as the "hand of an over-ruling power, exercising the moral government over the children of men." [79]

The elasticity of their theories enabled Baptists to support the Confederacy and then, after defeat, to return to their former place in the Union and remain loyal citizens thereafter. In spite of their defense of the Confederacy after 1865, they were not guilty of disloyalty to the United States, either in action or intent. Almost immediately after the failure of the Confederacy, they again offered sincere support to the Union which they had sought to destroy. The Constitution, said one editor, "is the gift from God, and is enshrined in the hearts of every patriot." [80]

Traditionally Baptists have held to the principle of separation of church and state. From their beginnings in Europe and America, they advocated freedom of religion in societies dominated by state churches. During the period under consideration they continued to champion the principle of separation, although in practice their actions often appeared to contradict their profession. Flagrant violations of this principle are difficult to find, but a number of instances can be cited to illustrate the difficulty which Baptists had in differentiating the legitimate sphere of action of the state from that of the church. At a time when the functions of both were expanding in society, the line of demarcation was not always clear.

During the Civil War, and to a less extent during the Spanish-American War, Baptists opposed the chaplaincy service as an encroachment of the state on the domain of the church. The Georgia Convention, for example, adopted a resolution in 1864 stating "that this Convention does not approve of the principle of appointing chaplains for the army to be paid out of the public treasury." [81] The Southern Baptist Convention was less emphatic, but it too expressed a preference for a system of army

78. *Christian Index* (Macon, Georgia), February 16, 1865, p. 2.
79. *Christian Index* (Atlanta), February 10, 1866, p. 26.
80. *Ibid.*, August 21, 1884, p. 8.
81. Georgia Baptist Convention, *Minutes, 1864*, p. 11.

evangelists and missionaries financed by the denominations and local churches.[82] During the Spanish-American War opposition to the chaplaincy was less pronounced, but Baptists still preferred church-supported missionaries rather than the chaplaincy system.[83]

Baptists were fairly consistent in their opposition to the appropriation of public funds for the support of sectarian institutions. For a number of years after the Civil War, Kentucky Baptists vehemently opposed the efforts of "the sect usually known as Campbellites" to secure state and federal appropriations and land grants for the establishment and support of their own educational institutions.[84] North Carolina Baptists, after years of protest, claimed credit for defeating a bill in the legislature which would have subsidized teacher-training programs in denominational schools. "Baptists accept no State grants for the support of their religion," said one editor of the state paper, "and they pay no taxes to support the religion of anybody else." [85] Baptists uniformly and inflexibly opposed the efforts of Catholics to secure government aid for their schools and charitable agencies.[86]

In their efforts to establish schools among the Indians in the West, however, Baptists veered from their rigid policy of refusing financial aid from the government. The Southern Baptist Convention in 1872 adopted a report on "Indian Missions" which recommended that the Domestic Mission Board accept both a land grant from the federal government and contributions of the Creek Nation for the establishment of an Indian

82. Southern Baptist Convention, *Proceedings, 1863,* pp. 12, 16, 53, 55. The Board of Domestic and Indian Missions of the convention supported seventy-eight missionaries to the Confederate armies and supplemented the salaries of eleven chaplains. *See ibid., 1886,* p. 40. Baptists furnished fewer chaplains by far than the other major denominations. *See* Herman A. Norton, "The Organization and Function of the Confederate Military Chaplaincy, 1861–1865" (Unpublished doctor's dissertation, Vanderbilt University, 1956), pp. 303–330.

83. *Christian Index* (Atlanta), May 12, 1898, p. 3; Southern Baptist Convention, *Annual, 1898,* pp. 20–21, 43. Baptists also opposed the public support of chaplains at state penitentiaries. *See Christian Index* (Atlanta), November 14, 1878, p. 45; *Religious Herald* (Richmond), November 12, 1899, p. 1; *Florida Baptist Witness* (Ocala), January 3, 1900, p. 2.

84. Kentucky Baptist General Association, *Proceedings, 1866,* pp. 18–19; *1867,* pp. 27–28; *1873,* p. 42; *1874,* p. 36; *Western Recorder* (Louisville), February 14, 1874, p. 4.

85. *Biblical Recorder* (Raleigh, North Carolina), September 22, 1880, p. 2.

86. Baptists were intensely anti-Catholic throughout the period under consideration. They opposed *everything* about the Catholic Church, not just its efforts to secure public funds for its institutions.

school. The government would allot 160 acres of land (and possibly more) and the Creek Nation promised to pay $10,000 into a building fund and $75.00 per year for each Indian child enrolled. Later conventions decided against accepting the grant of land from the federal government, but an industrial mission school was established with the aid of funds from the Creek Nation.[87] This was, in effect, accepting public funds for the support of their Indian school.

Although Baptists refused financial assistance from public funds to support denominational work (with the exception noted above), they nevertheless came to advocate and accept state aid in achieving religious and moral ends in other ways. A growing dependence on government to enforce moral precepts was a clear development in the Baptist view of what constituted legitimate governmental functions during the late nineteenth century. Baptist advocacy of prohibition by state and national legislation was the clearest example of this development, but the trend was noticeable in other respects also.[88]

During the 1870's the trend was definitely established. In 1872 the Georgia paper endorsed a bill before the legislature to strengthen divorce laws, and later in the decade it supported an anti-gambling bill. In 1875, the Virginia journal protested the chartering by the state legislature of an alleged charitable raffling company, and the following year the same paper made its first demands on the state to protect the sanctity of Sunday by enacting Sabbath observance laws.[89]

This tendency toward the reliance on government for the enforcement of morals did not go unchallenged. In an article entitled "Religion Calling for the Sword," a contributor to one paper denounced the trend as a violation of the Word of God. The Bible sanctioned only "moral suasion" in fighting evil, he said:

If civil government can specify what sins man shall not commit, then it may also specify what holy rites they shall perform. . . . The employment of

87. Southern Baptist Convention, *Proceedings*, *1872*, pp. 27–28; *1873*, p. 34; *1878*, pp. 12, 21, 35; *1880*, pp. 21, 27, 65; *1881*, p. 60.
88. *See* chapters 6, 7, and 8.
89. *Christian Index* (Atlanta), January 4, 1872, p. 1; March 2, 1876, p. 5; *Religious Herald* (Richmond), March 8, 1875, p. 2; April 13, 1876, p. 1. Sentiment in support of "blue laws" first appeared in the *Proceedings* of the Southern Baptist Convention in 1882. A similar resolution seven years later, however, met considerable opposition on the ground that it violated separation of church and state. *See* Southern Baptist Convention, *Proceedings, 1882*, p. 39; *Religious Herald* (Richmond), May 23, 1889, p. 2.

force, civil or physical, to guide [religious creed] or practice, is a full adieu to religious freedom.[90]

Other Baptists sounded similar warnings. Any religion which petitioned any branch of government to enforce morals, said a contributor in another journal, was

drifting away from the true idea of the separation of church and state. . . . It is no part of the work of a church to regulate the condnct [sic] of those outside of its pale.[91]

The trend was permanent, however, and after 1880 Baptists appealed more and more to municipal, state, and federal governments for support in their fight against evil. Tennessee Baptists called upon their legislature to establish a reformatory for juvenile delinquents; the Virginia paper urged a strong statutory rape law to "shield from outrage girls under eighteen years of age"; and in 1890 the Mississippi Convention memorialized the state constitutional convention to withhold from

immoral institutions, such as Lottery Companies, saloons, gambling hells and kindred institutions, recognition in the New Constitution, [but] rather put them under the ban of our organic law.[92]

As unstable political conditions in Cuba threatened Baptist mission work there, the Southerm Baptist Convention and several state conventions implored the federal government to protect Baptist interests and to guarantee full religious freedom to missionaries and natives alike.[93] The election of Brigham H. Roberts, a confessed polygamist, to Congress from Utah in 1898 was the occasion for an avalanche of protest from all orthodox Protestant sects. The action of the Florida Baptists is typical of the response from Baptists. At their convention in 1899 they adopted a resolution which read in part:

90. *Biblical Recorder* (Raleigh, North Carolina), March 17, 1875, p. 1.
91. *Christian Index* (Atlanta), December 8, 1892, p. 1.
92. Tennessee Baptist Convention, *Proceedings, 1880*, p. 37; *Religious Herald* (Richmond), January 26, 1888, p. 2; Mississippi Baptist Convention, *Proceedings, 1890*, p. 27.
93. Southern Baptist Convention, *Proceedings, 1895*, p. LXVI; Southern Baptist Convention, *Annual, 1898*, p. 15; Mississippi Baptist Convention, *Proceedings, 1898*, p. 14; Kentucky Baptist General Association, *Proceedings, 1898*, p. 23; Georgia Baptist Convention, *Minutes, 1898*, p. 24.

Whereas, the election of the said Roberts is a menace to every home and the honor of every woman in our land; therefore be it

Resolved, That we, the Florida Baptist Convention, representing more than 25,000 white Baptists, do ask that the members of Congress from this State use their utmost endeavors to secure the expulsion of said polygamist from the House of Representatives, and that they also work for an amendment to the Constitution forever prohibiting any polygamist from holding office under this government.[94]

By the end of the century Baptists had come to rely on the state as a valuable ally in the enforcement of moral principles. They continued to oppose financial aid from the public treasury, but the historical principle of the absolute separation of church and state had been compromised.

At the same time that Baptists were calling for the increase in governmental power to achieve certain moral ends, they were, for the most part, opposing the extension of government into other areas of national life. The Florida paper attacked labor leaders for allegedly attempting to use the power of government to further their own selfish ends. The editor declared:

Each man is to be free to work out his own fortune. Government is not a parent to help, but simply a sentinel to see that he has this freedom. . . . Now, these labor unions and combinations, which absorb the freedom of the individual, which demand that our government shall become parental, thus reducing every man to a minor, which demand that the liberties of others shall be abridged, are essentially undemocratic. The whole thing is un-American.[95]

Other writers objected to the increasing number of government employees and questioned the propriety of looking to legislation as the cure-all for the ills of society. "The State is never a charitable institution," said one editor in defining the role of the state in dispensing welfare. The state was obligated to provide education, care for the indigent, etc., but only for the good of the state, not for the benefit of the few.[96]

One of the rare expressions favorable to the expansion of government

94. Florida Baptist Convention, *Minutes, 1899*, pp. 15–16. *See also Baptist Chronicle* (Alexandria, Louisiana), January 12, 1899, p. 1.

95. *Florida Baptist Witness* (DeLand), April 1, 1886, p. 2.

96. *Biblical Recorder* (Raleigh, North Carolina), November 25, 1896, p. 1; *Western Recorder* (Louisville), June 21, 1894, p. 1.

appeared in an editorial in the Georgia paper in 1898. The editor approved a proposal to permit the city of Atlanta to assume control of the municipal electric light plant. "It is everywhere taken for granted" he said, "that it is a perfectly proper thing to do. This indicates that the principle of government control of such concerns as are of general interest is generally accepted. . . ."[97] The majority of Baptists, however, were unquestionably conservative in their attitudes toward the growth in governmental power.

One of the persistent problems facing Baptists in their relations with the state in the last third of the nineteenth century was in the area of public education. In the early years of the century Baptists had been apathetic toward or opposed to formal education—even for their ministers. But by 1865 they had come to approve the principle of an educated ministry and an educated citizenry. They supported liberal-arts schools (few deserved the name college or university) in most of the states and a theological seminary. Although they accepted the principle of universal education, they disagreed among themselves and with outsiders over details of a general education system. Controversy centered chiefly around four issues: the right of the state to enter the field of education; the validity of compulsory attendance laws; the right of the state to support higher education; and the right of the state to teach morals and religion in schools supported by public funds.

Baptists generally accepted the principle of *universal* education by 1865, but they by no means approved the idea of *public*[98] education under state control. Opposition to state schools continued for more than two decades after the Civil War. In a series of articles in the Virginia paper in 1875, a contributor, writing under the pseudonym "Civis," presented the principal arguments in opposition. His major premise was that government should touch the individual at as few points as possible. To the extent that government usurped responsibility and imposed taxation for the support of activities not absolutely necessary to its function— "to that extent," Civis said, "government is arbitrary and communistic." Since education was not a necessary function of government, taxation for education, he said,

97. *Christian Index* (Atlanta), September 15, 1898, p. 6. For further opinion on the role of government in the economy see chapter 5.

98. The term "public school" was used synonymously with "elementary school." Baptists seemed to have had only a vague concept of the role of the "high school" in public education.

is simply robbery, and harms even those for whose special benefit it was intended. Let a man know that government will educate his children, and he will cease to make efforts to educate them himself. He will, moreover, conclude, and very logically conclude, that it will feed and clothe them too. . . . Thus the public school system, and the idea upon which it is based, tend to relax individual energy by supplying its lack, and to emasculate the energies of a people. . . . I indignantly protest against the compulsory payment of a single cent for the education of the children of worthless vagabonds, who are quartered by law upon my labor for support. . . . A tax bill that takes my money to educate another man's children is a wanton and wicked aggression upon my rights, and is disastrous to all parties, and to the State at large.[99]

In a later article Civis argued that state education removed the child from the wholesome influences of home and subjected him to the immoral influences of any teacher whom the state might choose to employ. Public education crushed individualism and tended toward uniformity in violation of the laws of God and nature. Furthermore, public schools secularized education and led inevitably to "atheism or infidelity." Civis concluded,

My soul sickens in the contemplation of the terrible condition to which we are hastening with blind infatuation. Patriots, parents, Christians, let us destroy this deadly upas, ere it poison the fountains of purity and truth, and striking its roots deep down through our social fabric, sap the foundations of our strength.[100]

These articles sparked a discussion that continued for several months. By far the greater number of responses were in opposition to the views expressed by Civis. The editor finally brought the controversy to a close with a summation of the arguments on both sides and a strong statement in support of public education.[101] Sporadic opposition continued into the

99. *Religious Herald* (Richmond), April 1, 1875, p. 1.
100. *Ibid.,* April 8, 1875, p. 1. The arguments presented here are identical with those which Horace Mann, Henry Barnard, and other reformers confronted and overcame in New England fifty years earlier. Urbanized sections of the country accepted the idea of public education sooner than rural areas. The predominantly rural South resisted change longer than other major sections, but this cultural lag was by no means unique to the South. *See* Newton Edwards and Herman G. Richey, *The School in the American Social Order* (1947), pp. 322–382.
101. *Religious Herald* (Richmond), July 22, 1875, p. 1.

late 1880's, but it was obviously the work of a small minority. The majority of Baptists accepted public education as a necessary adjunct to the democratic state.

For a number of years after accepting the principle of state education, Baptists continued to oppose compulsory attendance laws. One editor said,

We are opposed to such laws. We do not think our people are prepared for compulsory laws on the subject. . . . We are willing for the State to aid and encourage, and think it should, as far as possible, aid and encourage general education, but it ought not in our opinion compel.[102]

Perilous consequences would result from compulsory education, predicted another editor:

Institute education by force—and the first step is taken toward the union of church and State—then follows the absolute ruler—not the government existing for the people, but the people for the government. A false principle is allowed to come in, and, if allowed to have sway, will produce its natural result. We believe in parents' deciding what their children shall be taught, and who shall teach them.[103]

Like the arguments against public education itself, however, opposition to compulsory attendance laws disappeared well before 1900.

Baptists came gradually to accept public education as a necessary function of the state, but they continued throughout the century to oppose the expenditure of tax funds for higher education. Objections rested on the arguments that the use of tax money for the support of colleges would constitute class legislation and would work a double hardship on parents who sent their children to church schools. Objections, even more fundamental, arose from the residual belief that college education was the peculiar province of the church and from the fear that state colleges would offer ruinous competition to denominational colleges. As early as 1875 a contributor to the Alabama paper differentiated the respective spheres of the church and state in higher education. Churches should furnish colleges for liberal-arts training, he said, while the state should provide universities for teacher training and advanced studies.[104] This idea of the division of responsibility appeared frequently

102. *Biblical Recorder* (Raleigh, North Carolina), February 7, 1877, p. 2.
103. *Baptist Courier* (Greenville, South Carolina), July 13, 1882, p. 2.
104. *Alabama Baptist* (Marion), January 5, 1875, p. 2.

thereafter. It was further developed into an all-inclusive, four-level school system with the responsibilities of the church and state specifically delineated as follows: common schools for all children through six grades at state expense; college preparatory academies, either state or privately operated; liberal-arts colleges under church control; and, finally, state universities. At the first two levels the home was to be responsible for moral training; the church assumed this responsibility at the college level; and, presumably, students at the university level were to look after their own morals.[105]

The controversy over state and denominational education raged hottest in North Carolina where Baptists united with Methodists in a losing battle against the advocates of state-supported colleges.[106] At the end of the century, Baptists were still unreconciled to the encroachments of the state on what they considered their private domain.

Another problem for Baptists concerning public education was the question of religious instruction in public schools. In this respect they encountered a contradiction of principles. They approved public education but held that education was incomplete without moral and religious training; yet they denied the state the right to teach religion.

The controversy centered largely on the reading of the Bible in public schools. For about a decade after the war, the question was hardly an issue among Baptists, or at least they took little note of it. Opinions when expressed were nearly unanimous in opposition to Bible reading in public school. Discussion increased after 1875, and from then until the nineties an ever-increasing number of Baptists came to approve Bible reading. The principal arguments advanced in support of this position were that only an education with moral and religious content was a "safe" education and that a system of education which omitted moral training would inevitably lead the country to infidelity and ruin.[107] The argument most frequently used in opposition was that any effort of the state to teach

105. *Biblical Recorder* (Raleigh, North Carolina), December 17, 1884, p. 2; *Christian Index* (Atlanta), April 7, 1898, p. 6.

106. *Biblical Recorder* (Raleigh, North Carolina), November 25, 1896, p. 2; August 3, 1898, p. 4; December 21, 1898, p. 4; North Carolina Baptist Convention, *Minutes, 1896,* p. 62; *1897,* p. 64; *1898,* p. 77; Luther L. Gobbel, *Church-State Relations in North Carolina Since 1876* (1938).

107. *Religious Herald* (Richmond), December 2, 1869, p. 2; January 13, 1876, p. 4; *Western Recorder* (Louisville), March 30, 1876, p. 4; August 18, 1887, p. 4.

religion was a violation of the principle of separation of church and state.[108] Arguments on both sides continued throughout the eighties and nineties. On the basis of the materials consulted in this study, a conclusive statement of *the* Baptist position on this issue cannot be made. The *Religious Herald* of Virginia decidedly opposed the reading of the Bible in tax-supported schools, the *Western Recorder* of Kentucky definitely approved, and the other sources presented a mixture of opinion. Taking all into consideration, however, it would appear that by the end of the century, Baptists generally had swung back to the position held immediately after the Civil War, that is, in opposition to religious instruction in public schools.

From what has been said thus far about Baptists and politics, it is evident that Baptists accepted the view that Christians should discharge their full responsibilities as citizens. Christians were citizens of two countries—the earthly and the heavenly—but this imposed no conflict of loyalties. Citizenship in the heavenly kingdom should, in fact, make a person a better citizen of his earthly state. In keeping with their belief in the separation of church and state, however, Baptists believed that Christians should exercise their political rights and privileges as *individuals* not collectively as denominations. Thus they held that churches and denominations, through their papers and religious gatherings, should remain silent on strictly political matters. Individual Christians, on the contrary, had an obligation to engage in partisan politics. Politics were corrupt, Baptists admitted, but only because Christians had failed to exert their purifying influence through active participation.[109]

In the last ten years of the century, Baptists showed an increasing awareness of their responsibility as citizens. A contributor to the Tennessee paper claimed to detect a hopeful sign in the awakening of preachers to the realization

that we need a Christian ballot in our land instead of a partisan political ballot; that political questions have a moral and ethical as well as an economic side. When the professed followers of Christ awake to the fact that every

108. *Religious Herald* (Richmond), May 2, 1878, p. 2; *Alabama Baptist* (Montgomery), October 29, 1896, p. 2.
109. *Christian Index* (Atlanta), July 30, 1868, p. 118; *Religious Herald* (Richmond), June 2, 1887, p. 1; *Tennessee Baptist* (Memphis), May 26, 1883, p. 5; *Biblical Recorder* (Raleigh, North Carolina), March 28, 1883, p. 2; *The Baptist* (Jackson, Mississippi), August 3, 1899, p. 11.

ballot not cast on the right side of any public question is morally wrong—is a sin against society, against every individual in the land—then we may lift up our heads, for our redemption from present evil conditions will draw nigh.[110]

The Mississippi Convention was equally as positive about the duty of Christians to exercise the franchize. The delegates declared,

Christian duty cannot be divorced from the citizen's duty. No man who believes God's word and professes his name has any right to neglect his duty to the State. . . . It is a transgression of Christian duty for any believer having the ballot, to wilfully fail to use it; thereby neglecting to do his part toward safe-guarding our priceless heritage of a Christian civilization and religious freedom.[111]

Although Baptists expressed the conviction that Christian laymen should participate in every phase of politics, they disagreed about the legitimate role of ministers. At one extreme were those who sanctioned the full participation of preachers in political life, even to running for public office and engaging in ward politics. At the opposite extreme were those who would limit the political activities of ministers to casting the secret ballot. After years of disagreement they had fairly well agreed by 1900 that ministers had all the political rights of citizens, although the propriety of using these rights was questionable. Preachers should vote but not seek political office; they should refrain from partisan politics; and they should preach on political questions only as those questions concerned public or private morals.[112]

In summary, between 1865 and 1900 Southern Baptists, as a denomination and as individuals, tended toward greater involvement in political affairs. With few exceptions they adhered to the principle of separation of church and state insofar as direct aid to church institutions was concerned, but they looked more and more to the state to assist in achieving certain moral and religious ends.

110. *Baptist and Reflector* (Nashville), October 3, 1895, p. 1.
111. Mississippi Baptist Convention, *Proceedings, 1899*, p. 15.
112. *Religious Herald* (Richmond), June 8, 1871, p. 2; *Christian Index* (Atlanta), July 26, 1900, p. 14; *Western Recorder* (Louisville), November 6, 1884, p. 4; *Alabama Baptist* (Montgomery), March 19, 1896, p. 1; Kentucky Baptist General Association, *Proceedings, 1890*, p. 52; John W. Million, "The Minister's Relation to Politics," *Seminary Magazine*, VI (May 1893), 441–447.

2. The Negroes: Segregation in the Churches

H E abolition of slavery was the most cataclysmic social upheaval in American history, and the consequent problem of assimilating the Negro population into the white-dominated society of the South has defied solution. Southern whites of the post–Civil War generation accepted the *fact* of emancipation, but they refused to grant the Negroes full political, social, economic, or religious equality. Forced emancipation destroyed the shackles of slavery, but it failed to alter the basic patterns of race relations which had developed in the South over the years. Essentially the same master-slave attitudes and forms of behavior continued after the war, nurtured by custom and prejudice as rigid as the laws which formerly had sustained slavery.

The Protestant churches of the South closed ranks after the Civil War in defense of the traditional relationship of the races. Except for recognizing the personal freedom of the Negroes, Southern churches exhibited no appreciable change of attitude as a result of emancipation. Since colonial times, American churchmen had been aware of the anomaly of slavery in a Christian society, but not until the slavery controversy divided the nation into antagonistic factions did the churches take decided positions on the slavery issue. The Northern wings of the major denominations drifted toward abolitionism, while the Southern branches defended slavery. Methodists divided over the issue in 1844, Baptists in 1845, and Presbyterians in 1861. Of the major Protestant denominations with sizable followings in both North and South, only the Episcopal church remained intact throughout the period of controversy and war.

Before the beginning of the highly emotional slavery controversy about 1830, masters permitted their slaves a considerable degree of freedom in their religious services—the only real freedom which most slaves ever enjoyed. After 1830, however, slaveowners became suspicious of the religious gatherings of slaves. More and more after that time, masters insisted that slaves attend services with whites. Between 1830 and 1835 most Southern states passed laws forbidding Negroes to preach, although slave "exhorters" continued to exercise their gifts before all-slave audiences with the permission of their owners and usually in the presence of whites. By 1845 practically all slave church members belonged to the same churches as their masters. Very few of them exercised all the rights and privileges which white members enjoyed, however. If the slaves were aware of what was happening to them, they must have realized that religion, which earlier had afforded them their only expression of freedom, was being used to restrict their liberty. Slaveowners cited the Bible in defense of slavery and employed "safe" slave exhorters to good effect in allaying unrest among their servants.

Emancipation disrupted the practice of biracial worship in Southern churches. Contrary to much popular belief at the time and since, Negro members were not categorically excluded from the racially mixed churches, although the whites perhaps made their withdrawal inevitable by requiring them to conform to all the restrictions which had applied before emancipation. Separation from the white-dominated churches was a natural expression of the Negroes' new freedom. The practice of segregated seating (which had developed many years before) and the presence of their former masters were constant reminders of their inferior status from which they were eager to escape. As long as they remained in the same churches with whites, they would be second-class members, but in their own churches they could participate in all phases of church life, and the most gifted Negroes could rise to positions of leadership. Restricted from full participation in political, civic, educational, and economic activities, the freedmen turned to the churches as the only area in which they could exercise complete freedom and control. The vast majority of Negroes who became church members after the war joined either Baptist or Methodist churches because of the emotional appeal of these denominations and the freedom permitted them in controlling their own affairs. The evangelical Negro churches have continued to be the institution most completely controlled by the Negroes and the one affording them the greatest opportunity for self-development.

The separation of Negro members from the white-dominated churches began before the end of the Civil War, and by 1870 the process was virtually completed. The role of religion in Southern race relations is apparent: Before the war slaveholders used the racially mixed churches to defend the institution of slavery; after emancipation Southern whites adopted the practice of segregated worship in conformity with the developing pattern of segregation in Southern society generally. In both periods the churches were *used* to support and enforce the prevailing customs of race relations.

Southern Baptists differed in no appreciable respect from other Southern Protestants in their attitudes toward their colored members. They, like other Christians in the South, failed to see the inherent contradiction between their defense of a caste system based on color and the Christian principles of the brotherhood of man, the worth of the individual, and the oneness of all mankind in the sight of God. In their attitudes toward and treatment of the Negroes, Baptists were further from the ideals of their faith than on any other issue.

Before the Civil War, Baptists expressed an awareness of their responsibilities to the slaves, but they recognized no further obligation than the preaching of the gospel. They did little, however, in an organized way toward discharging even this limited responsibility. At the first meeting of the Southern Baptist Convention in 1845, the delegates instructed the newly created Board of Domestic Missions to "take all prudent measures, for the religious instruction of our colored population,"[1] and at each session thereafter until the outbreak of the Civil War (with the exception of the 1857 meeting) the convention reiterated its concern for the slaves. But little overt action resulted. In 1849 the Board of Domestic Missions reported the appointment of two missionaries to the colored population, and in 1853 the board offered to pay half the salary of any missionary to the slaves whom any association or church would appoint. If either of these plans ever materialized, subsequent reports of the Board did not indicate it.[2]

The apathy of Southern Baptists toward the religious condition of their servants is poignantly illustrated by the disparity between what they said and did. On a number of occasions they expressed the conviction that "God sent them here to receive the word of life;"[3] yet, in defiance of what they acknowledged as the will of God, Baptists expended a minimum of organized effort in evangelizing the slaves. The resolutions and reports adopted by the Southern Baptist Convention usually shifted the responsibility for performing the actual work to state conventions, associ-

1. Southern Baptist Convention, *Proceedings, 1845*, p. 15.
2. *Ibid., 1849*, p. 64; *1853*, pp. 57–58.
3. *Ibid., 1851*, p. 13. *See also ibid., 1855*, pp. 63, 65.

ations, churches, and individual preachers and slaveowners. The number and distribution of home missionaries is perhaps indicative of the true interest of Baptists in the evangelization of the Negroes: In 1861 the Domestic and Indian Board was employing sixty-nine missionaries in the continental United States. Sixty of these were ministering to native white people. Of the remaining nine, who were working with other than native whites, six were employed outside the South (two working with the Negroes in Maryland and Washington, D.C., three with the Germans in Maryland and Missouri, and one with the Chinese in California). Of the three missionaries engaged in work with non-white or non-native peoples in the South, one was working with the Indians in Georgia and two with the Germans in Kentucky and Louisiana. The home mission agency of Southern Baptists was not employing a single missionary in the work of evangelizing the nearly four million Negroes in the South.[4]

The state conventions also recognized their responsibility to the slave population, but like the South-wide convention, they usually adopted resolutions and left the actual work to others. In the final analysis the work of winning the slaves to the Baptist faith was performed primarily by interested preachers and members of slaveholding families. That considerable numbers of slaves were won to the denomination in this manner is probable, but the boast so often made by white Baptists that the large numbers of Negro Baptists after the war attested the faithfulness of the *denomination* in evangelizing the slaves before emancipation is hardly warranted. The freedom allowed the Negroes in Baptist churches was doubtless more responsible for the large number of Negro Baptists than all the prewar missionary activities of white Baptists.

Despite the drastic changes in the relationship of the races effected by emancipation, Baptist attitudes toward the newly freed Negroes changed slowly for a year or so after the war. Baptists held that emancipation had in no way canceled their Christian responsibility to the Negroes. Besides the obligation of preaching the gospel to them—a debt which all Christians owed all men—they expressed a special sense of indebtedness to the Negroes because of their faithfulness during slavery and particularly for their loyalty during the Civil War when Southern women and children were largely at their mercy. This obligation, Baptists maintained, could best be discharged by endeavoring to elevate the Negroes spiritually and

4. *Ibid., 1861*, pp. 32–34.

morally. "The Negro still has a soul," commented the Virginia paper, "and our responsibility for his moral condition has not been abated."[5]

At the first meeting of the Southern Baptist Convention after the war, the delegates devoted considerable time discussing the best means of ministering to the freedmen. During the first year after the war, the Board of Domestic and Indian Missions employed four missionaries to work exclusively with the Negroes and others to work part-time among them.[6] This was more concerted effort than the Board had shown at any time before the war. With the exception of Georgia and Florida, all the state conventions also adopted lengthy resolutions recognizing their obligations to the former slaves. As North Carolina Baptists phrased it, the evangelization of the freedmen was "a special duty imposed by the Providence of God on Southern Christians," and because Negroes were "naturally inclined" to accept the simple truths of the Baptist faith, the responsibility rested heavily on Baptists.[7]

For all the expressions of noble intent, however, Baptists had to overcome a number of formidable obstacles before they could minister effectively to the Negroes. Their system of congregational church government presented an obvious problem. The thousands of Negro members in Baptist churches logically could expect to participate in the communion, voting, deliberations on church business, and in all the other privileges of church membership. During slavery, the whites had tolerated Negro members on a second-class basis, but after emancipation Negroes might reasonably demand equal rights with white members.

During the crucial months immediately following the war, Baptists arrived at attitudes and norms of conduct which were to determine the relations of white and Negro Baptists for generations to come. For the remainder of the year 1865 after the collapse of the Confederacy, they favored retaining Negroes in the membership of the white-controlled churches. Alabama Baptists adopted a strong statement to this effect:

The changed political status of our late slaves does not necessitate any change in their relation to our churches; and while we recognize their right to withdraw from our churches and form organizations of their own, we nevertheless believe that their highest good will be subserved by their maintain-

5. *Religious Herald* (Richmond), March 8, 1866, p. 1.
6. Southern Baptist Convention, *Proceedings, 1866,* pp. 45–48, 85–86.
7. North Carolina Baptist Convention, *Minutes, 1865,* p. 16. *See also Christian Index* (Atlanta), August 2, 1866, p. 122.

ing their present relation to those who know them, who love them, and who will labor for the promotion of their welfare.[8]

The Texas Convention admonished its constituents to

leave the subject of separate church organization, to the circumstances surrounding each church; manifesting and proving at all times, and on all occasions, our desire for their spiritual improvement and moral elevation.[9]

Opinion was decidedly in favor of maintaining a biracial membership.

The voluntary exodus of Negro members, however, soon led Baptists to realize that complete separation of the races was inevitable. "We are now satisfied," wrote the editor of the Georgia paper in February, 1866, "that their separation from the white churches is only a question of time." [10] South Carolina Baptists acknowledged at their state convention in July of the same year that "there is reason to believe that in certain localities, and under certain circumstances, they [Negroes] will prefer to be organized into separate Churches." [11] Opinion shifted rapidly in 1866 until, by the end of the year, Baptists generally favored, or at least accepted, the separation of Negro members. The North Carolina Convention meeting in November recommended to its churches that "when the numbers and abilities are sufficient, the colored members in our churches should be encouraged and assisted to organize separate and independent churches and Associations." [12] The trend was the same in other parts of the South.

Although for several months after the war Baptists expressed a willingness and even a desire to retain Negroes in their churches, they had no intention of accepting them as equals. The South Carolina Convention amended its constitution in 1866 specifically for the purpose of ensuring that every delegate to the convention would be a "white member of some Baptist Church in this State or vicinity." [13] The editor of the Virginia

8. Alabama Baptist Convention, *Minutes, 1865*, p. 10. Many Baptists favored retaining Negroes in their churches to prevent them from falling under the influence of Northern preachers and also to enable Southern whites to retain a degree of control over them.

9. Texas Baptist Convention, *Minutes, 1865*, p. 14. *See also Religious Herald* (Richmond), October 19, 1865, p. 1.

10. *Christian Index* (Atlanta), February 24, 1866, p. 35.

11. South Carolina Baptist Convention, *Minutes, 1866*, p. 240.

12. North Carolina Baptist Convention, *Minutes, 1866*, p. 19. *See also Religious Herald* (Richmond), December 20, 1866, p. 1.

13. South Carolina Baptist Convention, *Minutes, 1866*, p. 234.

paper presented it as his "settled opinion" that "freedmen should not be permitted to vote in our churches." Slaves had not been allowed a voice in church affairs before the war, he said, and emancipation had in no way qualified them to assume any new responsibilities. Furthermore, it was necessary to keep the Negroes in subordinate places to prevent the "commingling of the two discordant races." Racial differences, he added "utterly unfit them for intimate social and religious relations." [14]

When a member of the Dover Baptist Association of Virginia proposed in 1868 that Negro churches be accepted into the Association, he found no support for his measure. A fellow member expressed the hope that nothing more would be heard of "this radical change in our way of doing things in Virginia." [15] One of the warmest debates ever held at the North Carolina Convention occurred in 1867 over a committee report suggesting that churches and associations be permitted to use their own judgment in admitting Negro members. James D. Hufham, editor of the state paper, led the fight against the report. He wanted no part in any report which appeared to sanction the reception of both races, "promiscuously, with equal privileges, into our Churches, Associations and Conventions." The only way he would consent to receiving Negro members would be "on the old footing, without any voice in the discipline of the church or the management of its affairs." [16] After considerable debate the report was amended to recommend that churches encourage and assist Negro members in organizing churches of their own. [17]

Well before the end of the sixties, Baptists had come to accept the separation of their Negro members as both inevitable and desirable. This changing opinion was accompanied by—perhaps resulted from—the continued withdrawal of Negro members. Before the end of 1865, Negro Baptists from seven Negro churches in the vicinity of Richmond, Petersburg, and Manchester, Virginia, organized the Shiloh Colored Baptist Association, perhaps the first all-Negro association in the South. [18] At the same time Negro Baptists in all parts of the South were withdrawing from white churches and forming churches and associations of their

14. *Religious Herald* (Richmond), March 19, 1868, p. 2.
15. *Ibid.,* October 15, 1868, p. 2.
16. North Carolina Baptist Convention, *Minutes, May, 1867,* p. 25 (There were two conventions held in 1867, May 22–24, and October 16–19).
17. *Ibid.,* pp. 11, 17–18, 24–27.
18. *Religious Herald* (Richmond), June 6, 1867, p. 3.

own.[19] In 1866, North Carolina Negro Baptists organized the first Negro state convention, and in the following year similar conventions were perfected in Alabama and Virginia. Negro Baptists of the South made several attempts to form a nationwide organization similar to the Southern Baptist Convention, but all efforts failed until 1886 when the National Baptist Convention was formed.[20]

Statistics giving the rate of separation of Negro members from white churches are scanty and unreliable. The *Minutes* of the Georgia Convention contain the best statistics, which, while far from complete, clearly indicate the trend. In 1860 there were 27,734 Negro Baptists reported, all members of racially mixed churches. By 1866 the number had dropped to 16,055, and in 1870 only 5,745 were still listed on the rolls of white churches. In the meantime, the number of members in all-Negro churches had increased from zero in both 1860 and 1866 to 38,878 in 1870. Thereafter, the number of Negro members in white churches declined steadily while the membership of Negro churches soared rapidly. In 1895, the last year in which statistics for Negro Baptists were reported, there were thirteen Negro members still in white churches, and the membership of all-Negro churches had risen to 206,267.[21] Statistics and comments from various sources indicate that the vast majority of Negroes had withdrawn from the white churches well before 1870.

White Baptists denied all responsibility for the exodus of Negro members from their churches. On numerous occasions they made this point clear: "We prefer most decidedly," said one state paper, "that they shall take the initiative in this movement. Then we shall be innocent of

19. *Christian Index* (Macon, Georgia), January 27, 1866, p. 18; *Christian Index* (Atlanta), August 2, 1866, p. 122. It is ironic that Negroes insisted on the right to *separate* from white-dominated churches in the 1860's to prove their freedom and equality. In the 1960's they are insisting on the right to *join* hitherto all-white churches for the same reason.

20. Carter G. Woodson, *The History of the Negro Church* (2nd ed., 1945), pp. 185–201; North Carolina Baptist Convention, *Minutes, October, 1867,* pp. 19, 22; *Christian Index* (Atlanta), January 24, 1867, p. 18; April 18, 1867, p. 66.

21. Georgia Baptist Convention, *Minutes, 1861; 1867; 1871; 1895.* Pages of statistical tables were not numbered. In 1884 the Virginia General Association voted to report Negro members in footnotes in their minutes because the number was so small and to use the columns headed "White" and "Colored" on their report forms for reporting "Male" and "Female" members. *See* Virginia Baptist General Association, *Minutes, 1884,* p. 25.

any evil consequences that may arise from it." [22] Negroes *did* take the initiative, but white Baptists hastened the separation by openly declaring their intentions of limiting colored members to only those rights and privileges which they had exercised before the war.

When it became evident that the Negroes were determined to withdraw and form churches of their own, white Baptists accepted the new system of segregated churches and defended it as beneficial to both races. In 1869 Jeremiah B. Jeter, senior editor of the Virginia paper, presented the definitive rationalization for segregated worship: God did not specifically command the mingling of different races in worship, he said. Whatever was expedient, therefore, was proper. God had placed between the races "an instinctive repugnance . . . which no training and no philosophy can eradicate, and which divine grace does not." Admit Negroes into churches on an equal basis, he said, and the gates would be open for "the *mongrelization* of our noble Anglo-Saxon race. . . . Very grave consequences must flow from the admission of negroes to a full participation [in] the rights and privileges of our churches and associations. . . . In short, having taken the first step, are we not shut up to the logical necessity of admitting them into social equality, and familiar intercourse?" [23] The denomination accepted this position. In the final settlement, the bugbear of social equality more than religious principle had determined denominational policy!

With the separation of Negro members, interest of white Baptists in the Negroes' spiritual welfare correspondingly declined. This waning interest is noticeable in the deliberations and reports at the Southern Baptist Convention in the late sixties. In 1867 the Board of Domestic and Indian Missions reported that a "large number of intelligent and pious missionaries" were working among the Negroes, but the report did not designate these missionaries by name as the report of the previous year had done. The report of the Committee on the Religious Instruction of the Colored People the same year caused considerable discussion but failed to result in any concrete action.[24] In 1868 the major interest of the delegates in the Negroes centered around a proposal for evangelizing

22. *Christian Index* (Atlanta), February 24, 1866, p. 35. *See also* South Carolina Baptist Convention, *Minutes, 1866,* p. 241; *Religious Herald* (Richmond), October 3, 1867, p. 2.

23. *Religious Herald* (Richmond), August 19, 1869, p. 1.

24. Southern Baptist Convention, *Proceedings, 1867,* pp. 14, 20–22, 33, 49–51, 74–76, 79.

Africa by establishing colonies of Christianized American Negroes. The delegates debated the proposal at length but finally rejected it as financially unfeasible. Again the Board of Domestic Missions reported a "large number" of missionaries among the freedmen but did not name them.[25] In 1869 the report of the Domestic and Indian Mission Board contained only two sentences about the Negroes, while three times as much space was devoted to the Indians and five times as much to a presentation of the work among the Germans. A list of missionaries indicated only one missionary to the Negroes in the South, while twenty-two were employed in ministering to native whites and three to the Indians. Other discussion concerning the Negroes merely reiterated the duty of Baptists to them.[26]

The state conventions exhibited even more clearly the declining interest in the welfare of the Negroes. By 1870, Alabama Baptists had ceased all organized work among the freedmen, although they still considered the "colored people," along with the immigrant Chinese and the "perishing red men," worthy objects of mission endeavor.[27] Conventions in Florida, North Carolina, West Tennessee, Georgia, Louisiana, Mississippi, and South Carolina were silent on the subject by 1870, although they all earlier had acknowledged their responsibilities to the freedmen. Only in Kentucky and Virginia did Baptist work among the Negroes continue beyond 1870, but even in these states the work failed to be permanent.[28]

Another indication of the decreasing interest in the welfare of the Negroes was the changing emphasis on the kind of missionaries which Baptists believed should be employed. For several months after the war, Baptists accepted it as the responsibility of the whites to preach to the freedmen, but in 1866 they shifted emphasis to the training of Negro preachers to work among their own people. Their argument was that the Negroes needed to develop their own leaders for their own good. This could have been a correct discerning of the needs of the freedmen, or it may have been merely the shifting of responsibility.[29] Certainly it re-

25. *Ibid.*, *1868*, pp. 15, 17, 28–29, 62.
26. *Ibid.*, *1869*, pp. 17, 19–20, 24, 35–40.
27. Alabama Baptist Convention, *Minutes, 1870*, p. 16.
28. Kentucky Baptist General Association, *Proceedings, 1869*, pp. 44, 46; *1870*, pp. 13–14, 41; Virginia Baptist General Association, *Minutes, 1867*, pp. 16, 25–26.
29. *Religious Herald* (Richmond), December 20, 1866, p. 1; South Carolina Baptist Convention, *Minutes, 1867*, pp. 251, 253–254; Kentucky Baptist General Association, *Proceedings, 1866*, pp. 17–18.

flected also the hopeless groping of Baptists for an answer to a problem which, for the moment, had no solution.

The failure of Baptists to meet the spiritual needs of the Negroes had its mitigating circumstances. Forces at work made it extremely difficult for Southern whites to exert any influence over their former slaves. Of these hindrances the most formidable, perhaps, was the presence of Northern teachers, preachers, and politicians among the freedmen. Northern churches looked upon the South, especially the freedmen, as a great mission field. Missionary societies sent their agents into the South in the wake of Northern armies to evangelize and proselyte the Negroes and to establish schools for them. Among the hundreds of conscientious teachers and missionaries who went South during and after the war were many unscrupulous rakes and politicians who used the facilities of the churches to further their own or their party's interests to the detriment of the freedmen. In view of these conditions and the fact that many of these same individuals and the societies which sponsored them had supported the abolition crusade, it is not surprising that Southerners looked askance at all the work of Northerners.[30]

The delegates at the Southern Baptist Convention in 1866 expressed an unmistakable suspicion of Northern intruders:

While we are not opposed to any right-minded man aiding in this important work [of evangelizing the Negroes], it is our decided conviction, from our knowledge of the character of these people, and of the feelings of our citizens, that this work must be done mainly by ourselves.[31]

The same undercurrent of suspicion was evident in the proceedings of the state conventions as well. In 1866 the South Carolina Convention recommended the establishment of schools for freedmen to help counter the

perverting instructions of persons claiming indeed to be the special friends of the negro, but with no professed love for the Southern white man, and with little real love for the black.

The following year the executive board of the convention reported the freedmen in the state friendly and well disposed "when not deluded and

30. Henry Lee Swint, *The Northern Teacher in the South, 1862–1870* (1941), pp. 35–76, 94–142; William Warren Sweet, *The American Churches: An Interpretation* (1947), pp. 86–87; Woodson, *Negro Church*, pp. 203–204, 209.

31. Southern Baptist Convention, *Proceedings, 1866*, p. 86.

deceived by the false teachings and representations of wicked and design-ing men." [32]

The Baptist weeklies used even stronger language in expressing their contempt for Northern teachers. The editor of the Virginia paper de-nounced them as "misguided teachers, 'blind leaders of the blind,'" who were travelling through the country "instilling the most radical princi-ples" into the minds of the freedmen. On other occasions the same editor described their efforts as the "intermeddling of Yankees" bent on con-taminating the minds of the Negroes with "pernicious errors." [33] Another editor attributed the alienation of freedmen from Southern whites to the intrigues of Northern missionaries. The efforts of Southern Baptists had been thwarted, he said, "by influences from abroad estranging the colored population from the white for political ends." All the perplexities en-countered by Baptists in their attempts to reach the freedmen, he said, originated with the

industrious and wide-spread efforts of political and fanatical emissaries to alienate Baptists "of African descent" from their white brethren in the South—to induce their withdrawal from our churches—to lead them to forsake our ministry, and accept in lieu of it the ministry of ignorant persons of their own color, or of "loyal" (and often irresponsible) adventurers from a distance—to persuade them that they had never heard the "full" or even the "true" gospel from their old instructors—to create in their minds a demand for "social equality" as the condition of religious fraternity, etc., etc. [34]

An observer in Arkansas blamed Northern teachers and preachers for the low state of morals among the Negroes. Southern Negro preachers, he said,

are at the head of all their [Negroes'] stealing and wickedness generally. This, I am led to believe, originates from the pernicious influence and training of Northern men, (*abolition preachers,*) who before, and during the war, taught them, as they helped to make what Southerners had, so they had a right to appropriate whatever they wanted. Take it! Take it! was their watchword. *No wonder* that negro preachers throng our jails. [35]

32. South Carolina Baptist Convention, *Minutes, 1866,* p. 239; *1867,* p. 264. *See also* Alabama Baptist Convention, *Minutes, 1866,* p. 13; *1879,* pp. 24–27.

33. *Religious Herald* (Richmond), August 22, 1867, p. 3; March 8, 1866, p. 1; April 5, 1866, p. 2; July 30, 1868, p. 2.

34. *Christian Index* (Atlanta), June 10, 1869, p. 90.

35. *South Carolina Baptist* (Anderson), July 24, 1868, p. 2.

Without question Northern teachers and missionaries contributed to the alienation of the freedmen, but Southern whites also were to blame. By clinging to their traditional patterns of race relations and refusing to accept the complete freedom of the Negroes as proclaimed by the Thirteenth, Fourteenth, and Fifteenth Amendments to the Constitution, Southern whites were more responsible for the estrangement of the races than were outsiders. Baptists must accept a share of the blame.

Southern whites found themselves in an impasse after the war. On the one hand, the law of the land decreed the equality of the races; on the other, custom and tradition proclaimed the inferiority of the Negroes. For many Christians, the tenets of their faith which implied the essential equality of all mankind interposed a third conflicting authority. In meeting this dilemma Southerners accepted the fact of emancipation, but resisted all changes in their customary treatment of the Negroes. No presidential proclamation, nor constitutional amendments, nor a fratricidal war, nor even religious creed could effect any sweeping changes in the Southern mind.

In their relations with the freedmen, Baptists found the conventions of society stronger than the laws of God and man. Baptists appealed to the Bible, to history, to reason, to science, and to instinct to support the segregation of the races in churches and in social relations. At the end of the century when Baptists were able to view the immediate postwar period with some objectivity, they were willing to admit that religious work among the Negroes had been done always with "a proper respect for the existing and ineradicable social conditions." [36] The determination of Baptists to keep their denomination a white man's religion and to bring it into conformity with the customs of society were vital factors in shaping their attitudes and conduct toward the freedmen.

By 1870, Baptists had arrived at the attitudes and standards of conduct which were to regulate their relations with the Negroes on religious matters for the remainder of the century. As a race, Negroes were to be segregated in their own churches, but individual Negroes who were members of white churches before the war could remain as second-class members if they so desired. Baptists continued to acknowledge their Christian responsibility to the freedmen and to seek means of discharging this obligation, but the actual work of evangelization which entailed

36. Southern Baptist Convention, *Annual, 1900,* pp. CXVII–CXXVIII.

personal contact between the races was left, by and large, to the Negroes themselves or to Northerners. Baptists were careful to preserve the superior-inferior relationship in all their contacts with the Negroes. Although Negroes continued to be received at Southern Baptist gatherings as "fraternal messengers," they were required to sit in designated areas apart from whites. One journal frankly recommended that the Negro's confidence could best be won "by condescension and kindness on the part of the whites." [37] The Southern Baptist Convention *Minutes* record:

Nothing is plainer to any one who knows this race than its perfect willingness to accept a subordinate place, provided there be confidence that in that position of subordination it will receive justice and kindness.[38]

The master-servant image remained in the minds of Baptists.

For most of the thirty-year period after 1870 the attitudes of Southern Baptists toward the religious condition of the Negroes present an uneven pattern of concern and neglect. With monotonous regularity the delegates to the Southern Baptist Conventions acknowledged their responsibilities to the Negroes, advocated training Negro preachers, and pretended to see a decline in racial prejudice and a growing willingness on the part of Negroes to receive aid from Southern whites; but very little work in behalf of the Negroes followed. The report of the committee on the "Condition of the Colored People of the South" at the 1871 session is typical:

From such inquiry as they [the committee] have been able to make, they think there is an increasing disposition among this class of our population to receive kindly any efforts made by our Domestic Mission Board for their religious culture, and also to accept the aid of our brethren generally in improving their religious condition.

They evidently need every assistance that can be given to them, and especially judicious pastors and conductors of Sunday Schools. It is eminently

37. *Religious Herald* (Richmond), April 5, 1877, p. 2.
38. Southern Baptist Convention, *Proceedings, 1891,* p. XXXVI. This air of condescension may have been acceptable to the mass of ignorant Negroes, but the more enlightened ones resented it. A Negro contributor to the *Religious Herald* had this to say: "Many colored ministers complain because white ministers use them as furniture, picking them up at pleasure; calling them *brethren* in the colored brethren's meeting houses, and UNCLE in their own meeting houses, or on the street, if they are noticed. Consistency is a Jewel." *See* the issue of September 12, 1878, p. 3.

desirable that these laborers shall, as far as practicable, be furnished from among themselves; and hence it is much to be desired that schools for general education, and especially for the education of ministers, be provided for them. But your Committee do not deem it expedient for your Board at present to attempt this work.

Your Committee most earnestly recommend that the Board prosecute its Mission Work among these people with all practicable vigor and liberality.[39]

No practical plan of action resulted from this report, and little from the reports of the years that followed. By way of contrast, it is interesting to note that the Domestic and Indian Mission Board in 1871 contributed to the support of one missionary to the more than four million Negroes in the South, while it had under appointment four white and eight native missionaries to the Indians, two missionaries to the Germans, and one to the Chinese.[40]

The end of Reconstruction, Baptists hoped, would open the way for a more effective ministry to the Negroes. The report of a special "Committee on the Colored People" at the Convention in 1877 was the longest since the war. It recounted the history of the Negroes since emancipation and stressed in maudlin eloquence the obligations of Southerners to their former slaves:

When we think of the years of the past, of the homes of our childhood, of the days of our youth, of the period of our earlier manhood, they [Negroes] are associated in kindliest recollections with every scene. Memory brings forth from her silent halls no bright and joyous picture in which they do not find a place. They watched our cradle slumbers—they taught us the first steps of childhood—they hushed with tender words and with their own peculiar melodies the wayward cries of our infancy; and on their dusky bosoms sung us to our rosy rest. They watched with eager eyes our development into manhood—they rejoiced at our marriage festivities—they stood sentinel by the bed of our sick, and with hands made gentle and tender by the heart's deep love, they smoothed the pillows of dying loved ones. They robed the precious clay for its long and dreamless sleep, and with hearts overwhelmed with sincerest grief, followed them to the grave. Such memories crowd all the past of our lives, and as soon can our right hands forget their cunning and our tongues cleave to the roof of our mouths as that we can cease to feel their

39. Southern Baptist Convention, *Proceedings, 1871*, p. 23.
40. *Ibid.,* pp. 55, 58–63.

hallowed influence. . . . [Memories like these bid] us give them the bread of life.

In the judgment of your Committee the time has *now* come when the Baptists of the South ought to redouble their efforts to promote the spiritual welfare of these people. . . . Let us make the effort, honest, *earnest, manly,* and the opposing barriers will *yield* and there will be open, to its utmost bound, a field of christian activity white already unto the harvest.[41]

The enthusiasm of this report failed to stir Baptists to action, however, and the following year the convention lapsed back into its usual passivity. The nadir of Baptist concern for the Negroes came in the early eighties. The reports of the Home Mission Board for 1881 and 1882 failed even to mention the Negroes.

A reaction against the use of American Negro missionaries in Africa about this time also reflects the declining interest of white Baptists in their colored brethren. Since the war, Baptists had advocated the use of American Negroes as missionaries to Africa. They had, in fact, justified slavery as God's method of training missionaries for Africa. Almost yearly until 1880 the Foreign Mission Board pointed out the advantages of employing Negroes as missionaries to Africa—they could endure the climate better than whites, they would have no racial barrier to overcome, and they could be trained and live more cheaply than whites.[42] In the late seventies the Foreign Mission Board and the Colored Baptist State Convention of Virginia agreed to support jointly a colored missionary, Solomon Cosby, to work with white missionaries of the Southern Baptist Convention in Lagos, Africa.[43] Cosby hardly reached the mission field before the reaction against Negro missionaries set in. Included in the Foreign Mission Board report for 1881 was a letter from a white missionary in Africa expressing the opinion

that this country must be evangelized by natives, trained in this country, and under the supervision of white men. . . . I wish to divert the minds of the Board from depending upon colored laborers from the South too much.[44]

The embarrassment which Cosby's presence may have caused under these changing conditions was relieved the next year when he died of "jaun-

---

41. *Ibid.,* 1877, p. 30–31.
42. *Ibid.,* 1872, p. 37; 1877, p. 16.
43. *Ibid.,* 1879, p. 55.
44. *Ibid.,* 1881, p. 45.

dice-fever." The white missionary with whom Cosby had been working praised him highly, but in asking for a replacement said: "Send if possible, two healthy, *energetic* God-fearing *white* men." [45] From that time until late in the century only white Baptist missionaries served in Africa, although the employment of Negroes continued to be suggested from time to time.

Southern Baptists seemed content to let the Negroes work out their own salvation. Some state conventions, associations, and local churches aided Negro Baptists in organizing churches and Sunday schools and lent assistance in other ways, but the concerted efforts of Baptists were negligible. The only sustained interest centered around ministerial education. Emphasis on training Negro ministers logically followed the decision made earlier that Negro preachers could serve their own people more effectively than white preachers. [46] Until late in the century, however, Baptists devoted more lip-service than money or manpower to this work. In the early seventies, the Domestic and Indian Mission Board (name changed to Home Mission Board in 1875) reached an agreement with the Home Mission Society of Northern Baptists which permitted Southern Baptists to send Negro ministerial students to the several Home Mission Society schools scattered about the South for the paltry sum of six dollars per month per student. Under this plan Baptists contributed to the support of one student at Augusta (Georgia) Institute and another at Leland University, New Orleans, for two or three years, but in 1875 they pleaded penury as an excuse for discontinuing this work. [47]

Another method of training Negro preachers which Baptists employed with greater success was the plan known as "ministers' institutes." Baptists had used ministers' institutes since early in the nineteenth century as a means of providing a modicum of instruction for their preachers who lacked formal training. These institutes, conducted by one or sometimes several educated ministers at central locations, offered instruction in Bible and church polity for periods of from one to four weeks during the slack

45. *Ibid.*, *1882*, pp. 69–70.
46. See p. 53.
47. Southern Baptist Convention, *Proceedings, 1873*, p. 56; *1874*, pp. 46–47; *1875*, p. 31; *1878*, p. 68. The total amount contributed to these two students during the year ending June 1874 was $43.30. *See ibid.*, *1875*, p. 31. The Home Mission Board also contributed small sums to the support of a "theological instructor" at Atlanta University and Selma (Alabama) University. *See* Southern Baptist Convention, *Annual, 1898*, p. LXXIII.

farming season. Baptists had considered institutes for instructing Negro preachers on several occasions since the war, but they did nothing to implement the work until Jabez L. M. Curry presented the idea to the South-wide Convention in 1875. The plan, as perfected in the following four years, was a co-operative venture between Southern and Northern Baptists. The American Home Mission Society (North) agreed to appoint and support a full-time superintendent, and the Home Mission Board (South) was to furnish instructors at "no expense" to the Board. The Board reported in 1880 that a "large number" of institutes had been conducted during the previous year, but the co-operative plan evidently failed after one year, for reports of the Board thereafter made no reference to institute work.[48]

When the co-operative work with the Home Mission Society ceased, the Home Mission Board launched a program of ministers' institutes of its own. The plan proposed the joint support of "theological instructors" by the Board and the state conventions. The theological instructors were to organize and supervise institutes with the assistance of local pastors. In 1883 the plan went into effect in Georgia and was extended later to Alabama, Mississippi, Texas, Louisiana, and Florida. The work was immediately successful in each state, but interest soon declined. By 1895 the work had virtually ceased. The theological instructor in Alabama attributed failure to the negligence of white instructors in keeping their appointments.[49]

With the decline of institute work in the early nineties, Southern Baptists turned once again to Northern Baptists for assistance in their work with the Negroes. A definite plan began taking shape at the Southern Baptist Convention in 1894 with the appointment of a committee to confer with a similar committee of the American Baptist Home Mission Society. The proposed conference took place September 12–13, 1894, at Fortress Monroe, Virginia, and the plan of work agreed upon came to be known as the "Fortress Monroe" or "New Era" plan. This plan was in essence an expansion of the ministers' institute idea. Four agencies—the Home Mission Society, the Home Mission Board, the state conventions of white Baptists, and the state conventions of Negro Baptists—agreed to contribute to the support of state superintendents and

48. Southern Baptist Convention, *Proceedings, 1875*, p. 73; *1879*, p. 46; *1880*, p. 67.
49. *Ibid., 1883*, p. IX; *1895*, p. LXIX.

two or three district missionaries in each of the participating states. District missionaries would be responsible for organizing and conducting ministers' institutes with the aid of local ministers. The Southern Baptist Convention approved the plan at its 1895 meeting.[50]

White and Negro Baptists alike hailed the Fortress Monroe agreement as the beginning of a "new era" in the relations between white and Negro Baptists in the South (hence the name "New Era" institutes). Upon hearing of the plan, the Reverend Allen R. Griggs, a Negro missionary employed by the Texas Convention, telegraphed the Southern Baptist Convention: "God be praised for indorsement of the Fortress Monroe Conference: 'The morning light is breaking.' *Scire facias*."[51] Baptist papers and the state conventions considered the plan a great stride toward the solution of the "negro problem." The South Carolina Convention approved the plan by a "unanimous rising vote" in 1895 and credited it, a year later, with having done more to raise the moral level of Negroes and to create good feelings between the races than "all the legislation since the war."[52] The Virginia General Association asked its members to pray and work "to make this the most signal missionary movement of our century."[53] North Carolina Baptists expressed the hope that the denomination

has found the way open leading to a long neglected field which under the co-operative plan . . . is destined to accomplish great things in the training and spirital [*sic*] uplifting of the negro Baptist population of our State.[54]

Within a few months after its adoption, the New Era plan was in operation in North Carolina, Alabama, South Carolina, Virginia, Kentucky, and Georgia.

The initial wave of enthusiasm in the New Era Institutes soon subsided, however. One co-operating agency after another withdrew its support until by 1900 the work had virtually ceased.[55] The Board of

50. *Christian Index* (Atlanta), March 29, 1894, p. 4; April 5, 1894, p. 1; Southern Baptist Convention, *Proceedings, 1894*, pp. 15–16; *1895*, pp. 13–16, 42–43; *1896*, p. LXII.

51. Quoted in Southern Baptist Convention, *Proceedings, 1896*, p. 30. The Latin phrase means, "do you cause to know," or translated freely in this context, "show cause why this plan should not be executed."

52. South Carolina Baptist Convention, *Minutes, 1895*, pp. 13–14.

53. Virginia Baptist General Association, *Minutes, 1896*, p. 35.

54. North Carolina Baptist Convention, *Minutes, 1896*, p. 54.

55. Southern Baptist Convention, *Annual, 1902*, pp. 160–161.

Missions of the Alabama Convention recommended discontinuance in 1897 with only this explanation:

After a trial of two years, which is ample time to test its success, we are reluctantly driven to the conclusion that this work should be discontinued so far as it relates to our convention. . . . We are satisfied that the benefits received are not commensurate with the amount expended.[56]

Virginia Baptists continued the plan until the end of the century, but opposition mounted steadily. The editor of the state paper, quite obviously disillusioned with the results of the work after two years, quoted a "most prominent and influential Baptist worker" as saying,

We made a mistake in that new era conference held at Old Point. It is a pity that the white Baptists of the South ever permitted themselves to be pledged to raise such amounts of money annually for the support of negro mission secretaries. We can use it more wisely in other directions.[57]

Negroes and whites were responsible for the failure of the New Era work. The greater share of the blame, perhaps, rested with the whites whose long-standing prejudices rendered them incapable of working with Negroes except in a master-servant, superior-inferior relationship. On the other hand Southern Negroes in the late nineteenth century were developing a sense of racial entity which made them increasingly reluctant to accept any aid from whites—Northern or Southern—which entailed or suggested any degree of control and subordination. Southern Baptists became aware of this growing independence among Negroes in the 1880's. In 1888 the Home Mission Board reported:

While our changed relations with the colored people do not release us from the obligation to labor for their spiritual good, they do make it more difficult for white ministers to get access to this class of our population for private counsel or for preaching to them, in the great congregation, as in former times. . . . Naturally enough the negroes prefer to have their own separate local churches, and for these to be presided over by ministers of their own race. They prefer also to have their own organizations for educational, missionary and other benevolent work. It is not likely that this condition of things will be changed, nor is it desirable that it should be.

Accepting this as the settled policy of our colored brethren, and approving it, let us adopt it as our own policy, and let us encourage them to do their own

56. Alabama Baptist Convention, *Minutes, 1897,* p. 8.
57. *Religious Herald* (Richmond), September 30, 1897, p. 2.

work in their own way, giving them at the same time our sympathies and our prayers, and offering them, so far as they may indicate a willingness to accept the offer, our counsel, our men and our money to aid them in their work, and let us do all this for Jesus' sake.[58]

The desire of the Negroes to break the bonds of subservience to the whites and to go their own way was indeed real. Incidents at the Southern Baptist Conventions in 1892 and 1895 cogently illustrate this fact: Since the organization of separate Negro Baptist churches, Negro pastors in the cities where the Southern Baptist Conventions were being held had customarily invited white ministers in attendance at the conventions to preach for them. When the convention met in Atlanta in 1892 and again in Washington in 1895, Negro preachers in those areas decided to extend the usual invitation only to those white preachers who would invite Negro ministers to preach in their churches. No white ministers accepted invitations on those conditions.[59]

The Georgia paper emphatically attributed the failure of the New Era work to the independent spirit among Southern Negroes: The editor said,

In all future efforts to help the Negroes, there will have to be taken into account a new spirit which has grown up among them, and which finds expression from some of their best men. It is a spirit which leads them to feel that, in the work of their uplifting as a race, they must bear a most responsible part and, in large measure, give shape and direction to their own development.[60]

The Home Mission Board made a similar observation:

A race feeling among the Negroes in the South has been developed, and the majority of them, as we believe, seem bent on trying to run their own schools and Mission Boards, and various other enterprises.

Negroes would accept financial aid, the report continued,

but they are not willing that their white brethren, North or South, or both combined, should assume all control and give all directions as to how the help shall be spent.[61]

58. Southern Baptist Convention, *Proceedings, 1888*, p. 19. *See also* Thomas Pearce Bailey, *Race Orthodoxy in the South: and Other Aspects of the Negro Question* (1914), p. 29; Paul H. Buck, *The Road to Reunion, 1865–1900* (1938), pp. 283–297.
59. *Christian Index* (Atlanta), May 26, 1892, p. 4; *Religious Herald* (Richmond), May 16, 1895, p. 2.
60. *Christian Index* (Atlanta), August 2, 1900, p. 2.
61. Southern Baptist Convention, *Annual, 1901*, pp. 143–144.

Negroes themselves disagreed over this "new spirit." The older and more conservative ones favored retaining their subordinate position to whites and receiving aid from them on whatever terms the whites might demand. The younger and more "radical" Negroes refused to follow the moderate counsel of their elders. The result was that rival state conventions of Negro Baptists sprang up throughout the South, and white Baptists, unable to help one faction without alienating others, discontinued virtually all help. Only in Virginia, Kentucky, and North Carolina was there any appreciable co-operative work between Negroes and whites after 1900.[62]

Besides the work done by Baptists as a denomination under the auspices of the Home Mission Board, the various state conventions conducted programs of their own in behalf of the Negroes. As was true of the efforts of the Home Mission Board, however, the state conventions also failed to develop systematic and continuous programs. They adopted resolutions acknowledging their responsibility to the Negroes and discussed various schemes, but relatively few of their plans ever materialized.

Georgia and Texas Baptists experienced the greatest success. From 1878 to 1895 the Georgia Convention maintained an active institute program for training Negro preachers and deacons and also employed a number of Negro evangelists.[63] The Texas Convention co-operated with Negro Baptists of the state in supporting a Negro superintendent of missions who supervised the work of from twenty to thirty other Negro preachers. This work continued from 1886 to 1895 and ceased only when Negro Baptists split into several factions.[64]

Efforts of Baptists in other states showed even fewer tangible results. The same forces which plagued the Home Mission Board also hindered the work of the state conventions. The principal obstacle to the development of effective work, however, was perhaps the whites themselves. The Alabama State Mission Board attributed the discontinuance of its institute work after a six months trial in 1882 to a lack of funds, which the report said, only showed "that the work had but little hold upon our

62. *Ibid.*, 1903, p. 162.
63. Georgia Baptist Convention, *Minutes*, 1878, pp. 16, VII; 1895, p. 28.
64. Texas Baptist General Convention, *Proceedings*, 1886, p. 28; 1889, pp. 17–18; 1895, pp. 28–29. The amount contributed by white Baptists to this co-operative work is hard to determine. The salary of the superintendent was paid by the Negro convention, and the preachers were sustained by contributions on the field. It would appear that white Baptists contributed no money to this program through their state convention.

churches." [65] The North Carolina paper cited the "indifference" of the whites and the condescending air which they displayed in the presence of their Negro brethren as the reasons for the lack of religious intercourse between the races.[66] A committee at the South Carolina Convention in 1893 blamed the poor training of Negro preachers in that state on the "manifest apathy among the [white] brethren concerning the great need of such a work." [67]

The lack of concern among Baptists for the spiritual welfare of the Negroes at the end of the century is evident. The minutes of the state conventions of the 1890's read strikingly like those of the late 1860's. After a flurry of interest immediately after the war and in the mid-nineties, interest declined, until, by the end of both decades, the Negroes were all but ignored. The state conventions of Florida, Louisiana, and Mississippi failed to take any notice whatever of the Negroes in their deliberations in 1900, and the conventions of Alabama, Arkansas, Georgia, and South Carolina discussed their obligations to the Negroes but did nothing further. Texas Baptists appointed a committee on the "Colored People" in 1900, but the committee never reported. Only in the upper South were Baptists engaged in any religious work for the Negroes through their state-wide organizations. Baptists in Virginia, Kentucky, and North Carolina were continuing the New Era Institute work, and in Tennessee they were co-operating with the colored Baptists of the state in support of a Negro superintendent of missions and six assistants.[68]

Many individuals of the Baptist faith—Clinton C. Brown of South Carolina and Jebez L. M. Curry of Alabama, for example—worked assiduously for the betterment of the Negroes after emancipation, but their efforts were largely outside the mainstream of Baptist life.[69] Baptists as a denomination never developed a sustained program for the evangelization and religious training of the Negroes. Immediately after the war they attempted to retain the freedmen in their churches in the same relationship that had existed before the war. When the Negroes refused

65. Alabama Baptist Convention, *Minutes, 1882*, p. 7.

66. *Biblical Recorder* (Raleigh, North Carolina), May 15, 1889, p. 1.

67. South Carolina Baptist Convention, *Minutes, 1893*, p. 27.

68. Texas Baptist General Convention, *Proceedings, 1900*, p. 45; Kentucky Baptist General Association, *Proceedings, 1900*, p. 16; North Carolina Baptist Convention, *Minutes, 1900*, p. 60; Tennessee Baptist Convention, *Proceedings, 1900*, pp. 16, 56.

69. *Religious Herald* (Richmond), March 22, 1888, p. 2.

this spiritual subservience, white Baptists assisted them in organizing their own churches. By 1870 the color line in religion was clearly drawn. Thereafter, Southern Baptists insisted on segregation in church relations and, for the most part, adopted a hands-off policy toward the Negroes. They continued to express their concern through resolutions and reports, but their expressed intentions seldom materialized. All efforts at helping the Negroes were in the nature of experiments—none of which proved lasting. After the close of the century, the Home Mission Board admitted the ephemeral nature of all its efforts. In commenting on a new plan of co-operation with the National Convention (Colored), the report of the board to the convention of 1902 said,

So far as we can follow up this work it seems to be accomplishing good, but like all the work we have tried, or are trying to do to solve the spiritual problem of the Negro, it is tentative, experimental. So has it been with the Negro problem in other aspects. We can only try this thing and that, as the way seems to open before us, and trust God, not knowing assuredly whether this or that shall accomplish the purpose we have in view.[70]

Baptists offered a number of excuses for their failure to do more for the Negroes—lack of funds, indisposition of the Negroes to receive their aid, the presence of Northern teachers and politicians—all of which had some validity. But the real reasons lay in the apathy of the whites and in their latent fear that close contact with Negroes, even in religious worship, would lead to social equality.

70. Southern Baptist Convention, *Annual, 1902,* p. 161.

3. The Negroes: Segregation in Public Life

OUTHERN whites accepted emancipation in good faith, but they nevertheless expected life in the South to continue very much as before the Civil War. They advised the freedmen to remain on the farms and plantations where their labor was needed and where they were assured sustenance and lodging. But freedom to the Negroes meant freedom from gang labor and the right to leave their old homes. Consequently, Negroes flocked to towns and military camps in the wake of invading Union armies. There they subsisted on rations doled out by the army, the Freedmen's Bureau, and privated charities and awaited the distribution of land.

To relieve this congestion and to promote economic and social stability, the legislatures of the Southern states, temporarily controlled by native whites after the war, enacted the controversial Black Codes. These laws varied from state to state, but in general they reflected the true feelings of Southern whites toward the Negroes. The harshest codes would have reduced the Negroes to peonage; the most lenient would have provided a period of tutelage not at all inconsistent with the needs of a people emerging from slavery. The Black Codes were never enforced, however, because the Radical Regimes which soon replaced the native white governments expunged them from the statute books.

These efforts of Southern whites to curb the freedom of the Negroes incensed Northerners. In counter measures, a Radical Congress proposed the Fourteenth and Fifteenth Amendments, enacted civil rights legislation for the Negroes and disabling acts against Southern whites, strengthened the Freedmen's Bureau, introduced the Union League, and eventually subjected the South to military rule. Under these circumstances, carpetbaggers and scalawags assumed control in the ex-Confederate states. Southern whites struck back with the Ku Klux Klan, lynch law, political intrigue, and a public attitude of implacable hostility. For a decade the bitter sparring continued, and whites of both sections lost sight of the true welfare of the Negroes. Gradually, however, the vindictiveness and the crusading zeal of Northerners subsided, the novelty of freedom to the Negroes waned, and Southern whites had their way. By 1877 the freedmen had no choice but to accept the realities of existence in a white-dominated society which bore little resemblance to their earlier dreams of freedom.

The Compromise of 1877 and its "juristic fulfillment," the Supreme Court's civil rights decision of 1883, ended the interference of Northerners in Southern life and left Southerners free to determine once again the course of their own affairs. Southern "redeemers" eliminated the Negroes from politics or used them for their own purposes. They had little to fear from the freedmen at the time; consequently, they did little to restrict the rights of the Negroes by law. They posed as friends of the Negroes and in many respects played the benevolent role which Northern Republicans had filled for ten years after the war. The basic attitudes and behavior of Southern whites toward the Negroes remained unchanged by emancipation and Reconstruction. Race relations continued to be determined by attitudes emanating from the antebellum period. The Negroes remained the servile class; they were segregated in schools, churches, and most public places. The former caste system based on slavery became a caste system enforced by custom.

In the closing decade of the nineteenth century, Southern politics endured another period of upheaval. The discontented small-farmer element rose to challenge the conservative redeemers who had emerged victorious after Reconstruction. United by their common grievances, the yeoman farmers succeeded in capturing Democratic party leadership in most of the Southern states. Counterthrusts, however, by the combined forces of merchant-planters, bankers, and industrialists returned the conservative faction to power in most states by 1900. In this struggle for control, the Negroes again became a crucial political factor. Both conservative and the small-farmer factions appealed to and received the Negro vote at various times. Not since Reconstruction had Southern whites seen so vividly the potential of the Negro vote. Both elements of white, lower class and upper class, came to realize that a Negro majority or balance-of-power vote was more to be feared than their own rival interests. Consequently, they united to eliminate the Negroes from politics, this time by "legal" means. The Fifteenth Amendment prevented direct disfranchisement, but Southern whites achieved the same end by establishing property qualifications, literacy tests, and above all, the poll tax as prerequisites for voting.

The emergence of the lower-class whites in the nineties had further repercussions for the Negroes. The status of upper-class whites had never been threatened seriously by the Negroes, but the lower classes feared Negro competition. Once in power, therefore, the "red necks" or "wool hat boys" enacted laws to eliminate the Negro threat completely, not from politics only, but from economic and social affairs as well. The "Jim Crow" laws accomplished what Southern whites had attempted with the Black Codes a generation earlier. By 1900 the caste system was fast being enforced by law. Liberal and conservative Southerners who had exhibited little of the lower-class animus acquiesced, nevertheless, in the radical settlement of the Negro problem. The Negroes finally were put firmly in "their place."

The discriminatory laws against the Negroes in the late nineteenth century were but logical outgrowths of racial ideas which made social, political, and economic equality between the races abhorrent to Southern whites. Theories of caste and white superiority antedate the Civil War, but before emancipation elaborate racist arguments were unnecessary except as a defense against abolitionism. Emancipation, however, destroyed the constitutional and legal supports to the Southern system and necessitated the articulation of those racist ideas which Southerners had held for generations.

Between 1865 and 1900 Southern whites codified their racial theories. Seldom were their views stated systematically, but Southerners everywhere understood and gave their assent. The views of "Pitchfork" Ben Tillman may be considered representative. The Caucasian race was the "highest and noblest of the five races," Tillman said. He regarded Negroes as members of the human race but judged them "biologically inferior" and incapable of the "higher functions of civilization." Their innate deficiencies condemned them to a permanent "inferior caste." To prevent an "orgy of miscegenation" and the pollution of the white race, Tillman said, a system of legal segregation would have to be maintained.[1]

Liberals of the South deplored the extremes of Tillman's views, but most Southern whites agreed with him. They believed in the "doctrine of

1. Francis Butler Simkins, "Ben Tillman's View of the Negro," *Journal of Southern History*, III (May 1937), 161–174.

superior and inferior races" and accepted as axiomatic the assumption that "the Negro was made of inferior clay and should be suppressed in his attempts to rise politically and socially."[2] The attitudes and actions of Southern Baptists toward the Negroes must be considered in the context of this social and racial milieu.

Feelings of racial superiority constituted an integral part of Southern Baptists' social attitudes. Before the Civil War they staunchly supported the institution of slavery, even to the point of considering it divinely ordained. Evidence of their approval appears frequently in their convention minutes and denominational papers. The Southern Baptist Convention in 1851, for example, assured its preachers that anyone who made an effort to minister to the spiritual needs of the slaves would be so eagerly received

as to impress upon his mind the conviction that God sent them [slaves] here to receive the word of *life,* and that they seem, in some measure, impressed with this as a special feature in the providence of God, which has assigned them their present position.[3]

The "African . . . seems marked by Providence to be a servant," declared Kentucky Baptists in 1860, and Texas Baptists, in the midst of war, still clung to the belief that the "Bible clearly reveals to us that God has ordained the relation of master and slave, and fixed the relative duties of each."[4]

Baptists defended slavery not only as divinely instituted but also as the only satisfactory relationship between the inferior Negro race and the superior white race. A committee reported to the Texas Convention in 1860 that under the benevolent institution of American slavery, the Negroes had made greater strides toward civilization than any other "mere operatives on the face of the earth." Negroes were as dependent as children, and, left to themselves, they rapidly degenerated into "barbarity

2. *Ibid. See also* Guion Griffis Johnson, "The Ideology of White Supremacy, 1876–1910," in *Essays in Southern History,* ed. Fletcher Melvin Green, Vol. XXXI of *The James Sprunt Studies in History and Political Science,* eds. Albert Ray Newsome, *et al* (1949), pp. 124–156; Thomas Pearce Bailey, *Race Orthodoxy in the South: And Other Aspects of the Negro Question* (1914) *passim;* Edgar Gardner Murphy, *Problems of the Present South* (1909) *passim.*
3. Southern Baptist Convention, *Proceedings, 1851,* p. 13.
4. Kentucky Baptist General Association, *Proceedings, 1860,* p. 23; Texas Baptist Convention, *Minutes, 1862,* p. 6.

and misery. . . . Their energies must be directed by a superior race," the report concluded.[5]

Baptists continued to defend slavery throughout the war. They ridiculed the efforts of Lincoln to destroy slavery by executive decree. The Emancipation Proclamation by "the usurper, at Washington," declared South Carolina Baptists, was "an attempt to demoralize the people of the Confederate States, so pitifully puerile that the indignation it awakens is lost in contempt." [6]

When military victory by Union forces destroyed slavery, Baptists accepted the inevitable but did not immediately change any opinions. Delegates at the Alabama State Convention in 1866 called the freeing of the slaves the "greatest seeming calamity that could have befallen them." [7] The South Carolina Convention in the same year expressed the attitude most generally held by Baptists:

The Churches of our State, as well as of the whole South, find themselves unexpectedly in the midst of one of the greatest social changes which the history of the world presents. . . . In our land the fearful experiment of emancipation has been made on the broadest scale, and with the suddenness and violence of an earthquake. The work thus done, whether just or unjust, whether wise or foolish, is finally done. No Southern man now dreams of a reversal of this act of the Government. To us, as good citizens and Christians, the only questions left, are: *What are the duties which arise out of our changed relations?* and *How may we best perform them?* [8]

From mere acquiescence Baptists soon came to consider emancipation divinely decreed and positively good. Slavery had accomplished "its purpose" in Christianizing thousands of Africans, commented the Georgia paper; it was the "unmistakable design of Providence," therefore, that it should then be overthrown.[9] "We rejoice that slavery no longer exists in these States," said the Virginia journal in 1875, "though we had hoped that it would be gradually abolished by the influence of the gospel, and lament that emancipation was entirely a military strategem." [10]

5. Texas Baptist Convention, *Minutes, 1860,* pp. 5–6.
6. *Confederate Baptist* (Columbia, South Carolina), December 23, 1863, p. 2.
7. Alabama Baptist Convention, *Minutes, 1866,* p. 10.
8. South Carolina Baptist Convention, *Minutes, 1866,* p. 238.
9. *Christian Index* (Atlanta), June 28, 1866, p. 105.
10. *Religious Herald* (Richmond), June 11, 1874, p. 2.

Although they accepted emancipation, Baptists continued to argue that slavery was morally right and mutually beneficial to Negroes and whites. "It may well be questioned," wrote one editor, "whether any combination of capital and labor ever produced greater freedom from want and suffering, and a higher degree of contentment and cheerfulness among the laboring classes, than did Southern slavery." [11] Contrary to the arguments of Northern radicals, he asserted later, slavery had been a boon to the Negroes. Depraved and benighted when brought to this country "chiefly by the enterprising, money-loving Yankees of past generation," they had been raised to a "Christian peasantry" by the "ameliorating influence of slavery." [12] The beneficent effects of slavery were apparent, Baptists argued, when American freedmen were compared with their kinsmen who remained free in Africa. "Whatever it [slavery] might have been to other races or nations," said one editor, "to the Negroes [in America] it was, under God, a blessing." [13] Slavery and slaveholders, commented another editor, had "done more to civilize and Christianize the negro race than all other agencies of the world, literary, social, political and religious combined, and this fact should be duly acknowledged." [14] Under the enlightened guidance of Southern masters during slavery, said the delegates at the Alabama Convention in 1879, more Africans were won to Christianity

than had been accomplished by the combined agencies of Protestant Missions among the heathen for a hundred years. . . . Such an institution, we submit, as managed by the Southern people, deserves something other than pure, unmitigated hatred and vituperation. We are not apologizing for it. . . . We simply affirm that . . . it presented the mildest and most humane form in which slavery has ever existed in any country, and that the time is not distant when good men will accord to Southern slaveholders a measure of that justice which their Christian philanthropy to their servants demands.[15]

The argument most frequently used by Baptists in defense of slavery was that God had permitted Negroes to be brought to America in slavery in order that they might be Christianized and return to Africa to evangelize the Dark Continent. An excerpt from the *Proceedings* of the South-

11. *Ibid.,* October 19, 1865, p. 1.
12. *Ibid.,* August 9, 1866, p. 1.
13. *Biblical Recorder* (Raleigh, North Carolina), June 28, 1876, p. 2.
14. *Religious Herald* (Richmond), June 3, 1869, p. 2.
15. Alabama Baptist Convention, *Minutes, 1879,* p. 26.

ern Baptist Convention of 1879 will illustrate the many affirmations of
this belief:

It seems to be the design of Him who is Head over all things to His Church,
in redeeming Africa, to employ, to a large extent, American colored Christians. . . . Men had their own designs in bringing so many of the African
race to this country, to be sold into slavery, and God had His own purposes to
accomplish in permitting it to take place. What men thought may have been
evil, God meant it unto good; and it was not so much men as God who
brought them hither; it was a grand providential preparation on the part of
God for sending the Gospel back to Africa.[16]

Much of the Baptist defense of slavery was in response to attacks by
Northern religious journals. As sectional good will returned, these
charges and counter-charges declined; but Southern Baptists never aban-
doned their defense of the South's peculiar institution. The words of a
contributor to the *Christian Index* in 1868 rang true for the remainder of
the century:

Now I would certainly be opposed to the restoration of slavery in this
country; but I have undergone no change on the righteousness of slavery, nor
can I change until convinced that our Bible is not the book of God.[17]

The moral aspect of slavery and the wisdom of emancipation were
questions which could be debated or completely evaded, but one aspect of
emancipation—the presence of four million freedmen in the South—
could not be ignored. Emancipation destroyed the institution through
which race relations had been regulated for generations. Southerners were
forced to adopt a new *modus operandi*. The question was a practical one.
Even for those Southerners most kindly disposed toward them, the problem of integrating free Negroes into society presented insurmountable
difficulties.

The reactions of Southern Baptists to this situation varied. The prevailing response was to recognize the Negroes' abstract rights as freemen,
but to restrict them to the same relative position in Southern society

16. Southern Baptist Convention, *Proceedings, 1879*, p. 22. *See* pp. 59–60 for a
discussion of changing attitudes about the use of Negro missionaries in Africa.
17. *Christian Index* (Atlanta), April 9, 1868, p. 60. *See also Religious
Herald* (Richmond), September 20, 1900, p. 3. Southern Baptist Convention,
Proceedings, 1892, p. IV; South Carolina Baptist Convention, *Minutes, 1900*,
pp. 55–56.

which they had occupied before emancipation. The Negroes were free, proclaimed the editor of the Virginia paper, but they would remain "denizens of the soil, and the mutual dependence which heretofore existed, still remains." They were dependent on the whites for employment, and the whites on them for labor.[18] "It remains," said the same editor a week later, "that the whites of the South must be the guardians and benefactors of this race." [19] In a series of four articles, another Virginian argued that the Negroes should remain in the South "and occupy the position of laborer to the greater profit of his employer as well as enjoy the fruits of his own toil. . . . It is generally admitted that free labor is cheaper than slave." [20]

Baptists continued to consider the Negroes incapable of rising above the laboring class. The Mississippi Baptist Convention declared in 1887 that "they [Negroes] have been, and are yet, our servants. . . . It is a matter of self-interest for us to elevate them into a better life. They will be better servants and better citizens." [21] A contributor to the Virginia paper in 1900 revealed this same deep-seated conviction: Improvement in the Negroes had been phenomenal under slavery, and the race had reached its peak during the Civil War. "But his glory has departed," the writer maintained. Southern whites had educated the Negro, giving him political rights and made him a citizen, but they forgot that it was written,

"A servant of servants shalt thou be to thy brethren!" We should have treated him as a younger brother and led him by the hand; and he would have been useful to us, and continued to love us as of yore. We have made the mistake; let us not blame him.[22]

Although the majority of Baptists evidently believed that the Negroes were destined to live in the South in a state of semi-servitude, others envisioned different futures for them. Some Baptists believed that Negroes could not survive in a free society in competition with the whites. In an address before a group of Baptist clergymen in 1865, a prominent Virginia layman expressed the opinion that

18. *Religious Herald* (Richmond), August 9, 1866, p. 1.
19. *Ibid.,* August 16, 1866, p. 1.
20. *Ibid.,* April 12, 1866, p. 1. *See also ibid.,* April 5, 1866, p. 1; April 19, 1866, p. 1; April 26, 1866, p. 1.
21. Mississippi Baptist Convention, *Proceedings, 1887,* p. 47.
22. *Religious Herald* (Richmond), September 20, 1900, p. 3.

the cruelty [of war and emancipation] is greater upon the poor negroes than upon their owners. They are to be the sufferers, and they will melt away before the white race as did the Indians.[23]

A South Carolina Baptist reported in 1866 that few babies were being born among the freedmen in the Sea Islands. At that rate, he concluded, the Negroes would disappear sooner than the Indians and their "places will be supplied by whites, 'a consummation devoutly to be wished.' " [24] In contemplating the scarcity of labor in the South, the editor of one journal expressed grave concern for the future of the Negroes and of the South:

We cannot rely upon the freedmen. They are now far too few, and rapidly diminishing, and soon must disappear. The blacks are doomed to perish by their own vices and improvidence. No legislation can save them as freedmen. Who are to supply their place? [25]

The census reports of 1880 should have squelched the myth of the "vanishing Negro," but the idea persisted for several years. The death rate of Negroes in Richmond was nearly twice that of the whites, said one Virginia Baptist in the early eighties, which, he declared, indicated a solution to the Negro problem

on a principle that controls not only the human race but the whole animal kingdom. . . . Two races, an inferior and a superior, cannot live together except in the recognition of this relation. Human law may declare, and attempt to enforce, equality; but the eternal law of nature, which laughs to scorn human legislation, will be vindicated in the "survival of the fittest." A century hence—and in the life of a nation a century is but a point of time— the negro race, dying at the present rate, will cease to be a disturbing factor in politics and sociology.[26]

Similar arguments continued to be expressed at infrequent intervals on into the nineties.

Another idea entertained by Baptists and other Southerners as an alternative to integrating the Negroes into Southern society was the emigration of Negroes to Africa, the Caribbean islands, or the unsettled

23. *Ibid.,* October 19, 1865, pp. 1–2.
24. *Ibid.,* November 1, 1866, p. 1. *See also* Alabama Baptist Convention, *Minutes, 1866,* p. 10.
25. *The Baptist* (Memphis), November 14, 1868, p. 5.
26. *Religious Herald* (Richmond), January 19, 1882, p. 3.

areas of the United States. Since early in the eighteenth century many prominent American philanthropists had proposed the creation of a free Negro colony in Africa as a solution to Negro slavery, and early in the nineteenth century these efforts actually resulted in the establishment of Liberia. Although Liberia never accomplished the purposes of its founders, the idea of colonization quite naturally regained currency after emancipation. Always in Baptist thinking colonization was linked with evangelization. As already noted, Baptists justified slavery and emancipation on the ground that they were part of God's plan for Christianizing the Negroes. Colonization was the next logical step in God's grand scheme for taking the gospel to Africa.

Baptists looked upon colonization not only as instrumental in evangelizing the Dark Continent but also as beneficial in elevating the Negro race. In the South Negroes would ever be "hewers of wood and drawers of water," but in colonies populated by Negroes exclusively, they would be free from the domination of the superior white race, a condition "essential to their untrammeled and full development."[27] When Negroes realized their subordinate status in the South, one writer argued, they would be glad to emigrate to colonies where their full potential could be realized. Furthermore, he contended, it was not impossible that God would instill in their hearts the desire to return to "their father land. . . . Let us stand still and see the salvation of God," he exclaimed.[28]

At the Southern Baptist Convention in 1868, a delegate from Kentucky introduced a resolution requesting the convention to take steps toward organizing "bodies of converted freedmen" and aiding in settling them in Africa as a "Christian Colony." The delegates discussed the resolution at length and finally rejected it as "an experiment involving too much expense, and whose success depends on too many contingencies to justify the Convention, at the present time, in entering upon it." They referred the resolution to the Foreign Mission Board with instructions to take action as it deemed proper.[29] Nothing more appeared in the *Proceedings* on the subject.

Baptists showed less interest in colonization after 1868, but the idea was not forgotten. The passage of the Civil Rights Bill of 1875, reports of the rapidly increasing Negro population after 1880, and the acquisi-

27. *Christian Index* (Atlanta), June 28, 1866, p. 105.
28. *Religious Herald* (Richmond), April 26, 1866, p. 1.
29. Southern Baptist Convention, *Proceedings, 1868,* pp. 15, 29.

tion of tropical territory by the United States in 1898 were occasions for
renewed discussion. In response to the fear of being overwhelmed by the
increasing Negro population, Baptists presented some of their most serious arguments for colonization. If the census figures were accurate, wrote
an alarmist in the Tennessee paper in 1885,

a dark and frightful future [is] just before our beloved South. To save it from
becoming the dark portion of this continent,—to save the white population
from being soon overwhelmed and obliterated, congress should be moved to
appropriate its tens of millions, and each Southern State its millions, annually
to transport the blacks of the South back to the land of their fathers.[30]

The Florida paper proposed emigration as the only means of avoiding
race conflict and the consequent extermination of the Negroes by the
superior white race. As the continent became crowded, the editor prophe-
sied, "Shem and Japheth will jostle Ham; he never has and never will be
their equal." Another "Bishop Turner, a second Moses" must arise, he
concluded, to sound the bugle call "to the sons of Ham to go to their
native land" carrying Christian civilization with them.[31]

Opinions favorable to the mass emigration of Negroes continued to
appear occasionally in Baptist papers on into the 1890's, but by that time
most Baptists had come to oppose colonization except for those who
voluntarily chose to leave this country. A letter to the Virginia paper in
1890 expressed the opinion generally held by Baptists. The writer called
a bill before Congress which provided for federal appropriations to
finance colonization, "unmanly, impracticable and unwise." Negroes did
not want to leave the United States, he asserted, and Southern whites
could not afford to lose their labor. "While we believe in the great
Anglo-Saxon race and their right to rule in the affairs of the country," he
said, "still we do not propose to forget how well the negro served us
before the war;"[32] nor, he added by inference, "how well he serves us
now." By the end of the century more Baptists opposed than favored
colonization. With other Southerners they had reconciled themselves to
the presence of Negroes in the South and had devised a working relationship with them which guaranteed white supremacy and restricted Negroes to "their place."

30. *Tennessee Baptist* (Memphis), July 11, 1885, p. 4. There was little
missionary zeal motivating this statement!
31. *Florida Baptist Witness* (Ocala), April 17, 1889, p. 2.
32. *Religious Herald* (Richmond), February 13, 1890, p. 1.

While Southern whites theorized at leisure about the ultimate fate of the Negroes, the practical problem of how to deal with them could not be ignored or postponed. Left to their own caprice, Southern whites attempted to strip the freedmen of their political rights and reduce them to a state of peonage (as evidenced by the Black Codes), but Northern humanitarians and politicians were determined to see the Negroes exercise all their rights as free men and citizens.

For about two years after the war, Baptists had very little to say in their weekly journals about the freedmen's newly acquired political and civil rights. They seemed resigned to the most drastic changes imaginable. "All distinctions on the ground of color or race are certain to be swept away," commented one editor; the races would be equal before "the law, the witness box, the jury box, and the ballot box." [33] No result of the war was more far-reaching than the political rise of the Negroes, said another editor. "Under the new order of things," he said, the Negroes "will probably hold the balance of power in all elections for years to come." [34] Such expressions did not mean acquiescence, however. From attitudes expressed later, it is evident that Baptists had little intention of ever voluntarily permitting the Negroes all the rights of citizenship.

Before the end of 1867, Baptists were openly opposing Negro suffrage. "We cherish the hope," declared the Virginia paper,

that our Northern friends will save us from the intolerable calamity of unrestricted negro suffrage. Knowing, as we do, that the negroes are (in their present condition) utterly unqualified for the exercise of the privilege; and that, however qualified, their franchise would lead to an inevitable conflict between the white and colored races, and in many places the subjugation of the former to the latter class, we view their unconditional enfranchisement as fraught with degradation and utter ruin to the South. . . . We have strong sympathies for the negro race, would do them justice, treat them kindly and rejoice in their welfare; but our love of our own race and our views of expediency, alike impel us to deprecate the equality sought to be forced upon us, and implore our Northern friends to preserve our common, noble race from the degradation that threatens it.[35]

Thereafter expressions disapproving of Negro suffrage became more frequent.

33. *Religious Herald* (Richmond), November 1, 1866, p. 1.
34. *Biblical Recorder* (Raleigh, North Carolina), April 24, 1867, p. 2.
35. *Religious Herald* (Richmond), November 14, 1867, p. 2.

An episode at the Southern Baptist Convention in 1870 illustrates the
aversion which Baptists had toward granting political rights to Negroes.
In 1869 the convention adopted a report of a joint committee composed
of Northern and Southern Baptists which recommended that Baptists of
both sections join "heart and hand" in promoting missionary and educational work among the Negroes. This joint endeavor, the committee
hoped, would result in "raising up millions of freedmen to the exercise of
all the rights and duties of citizenship." The wording of the report created
a furor among Baptists throughout the South. At the convention in 1870,
George E. Brewer of Rockford, Alabama, introduced a resolution, previously adopted by his association, which asserted "that we dissent from,
and disown" that part of the report adopted the previous year which
called for the elevating of Negroes to full citizenship. Such views could
not be approved, Brewer's resolution stated, "without violating the plain
teachings of God's Word." A number of delegates assured Brewer that
the previous convention had entertained no intention of approving any
plans which would raise the freedmen to equality with the whites. Discussion continued for some time and the delegates finally tabled the resolution. Efforts later to take the resolution from the table failed, but the
convention decided to publish the discussion in its *Proceedings* to allay
any misunderstanding which others like Brewer might have had.[36] Discussion continued in the journals after the convention adjourned. Brewer
called the invitation of Northern Baptists to unite in elevating the
freedmen to higher levels of "citizenship and Christian brotherhood" an
invitation "to complete our own degradation by making our former
servants, wrested from us by force, not only the political equals of
ourselves, but the superiors of those who formerly were our legislators
and executive officers." [37] Brewer's views were extreme, but even those
who opposed his resolution agreed with him in his distrust of Northern
efforts to raise the Negroes to the full status of citizens. The whole
incident illustrates clearly the reluctance of Baptists to grant the freedmen all the rights and privileges which citizenship implied.

As Reconstruction continued and the abuses of radical rule became
more flagrant, Baptists showed less and less restraint in opposing the

36. Southern Baptist Convention, *Proceedings, 1870*, pp. 13–14, 18. *See also*
The Baptist (Memphis), May 14, 1870, p. 4; *Religious Herald* (Richmond),
May 19, 1870, p. 2.
37. *Christian Index* (Atlanta), August 4, 1870, p. 117.

participation of Negroes in politics. In a lead editorial in 1874, the editor of the Virginia paper attributed all the political and racial problems of the South to the entrance of Negroes into politics:

There is no use in denying that in most of the States there is antagonism between the white and colored races. However the political parties may be denominated, the simple question that divides them is whether the whites or the negroes shall exercise the supreme authority. Every other question is dust in the balance, compared with this. That the whites have cause to be anxious on this point, is evinced by the fate of the unfortunate States of South Carolina, Louisiana, Arkansas, in short, every State in which the negroes have ruled. We would infinitely prefer any form of government, military, aristocratic, royal or imperial, to that of the ignorant, lawless and rapacious negroes, led by a few white men, who affiliate with them to gain office and fill their empty pockets.[38]

Baptists continued their denunciation of Negro suffrage until after the crucial campaign and election of 1876. "The right of suffrage is so solemn a trust that it ought never to be universal," asserted one editor. No republic could survive if it conferred the franchise on all classes regardless of their qualifications. The Negro vote had become a "commercial commodity" to be sold to the highest bidder. What else but corruption "could have been anticipated when slaves were suddenly freed —freed, not through philanthropy, but as a desperate military strategy— and invested with such power?" he asked.[39] In an effort to ridicule the idea of extending Negroes the ballot, the papers cited instances of Negro stupidity and ignorance. One editor declared personal knowledge of the fact that many freedmen, in the expectation of receiving something to eat, were herded to the polls like cattle.[40] Another editor recounted a conversation he had overheard between two Negroes on their way to vote: One freedman declared his intention to vote the Republican ticket because, he said, the Democrats were the enemies of Christ. When his companion asked what he meant, he replied that Christ had described Himself as the "friend of 'Publicans and sinners'"; therefore, the Democrats must be His enemies.[41]

With the end of Reconstruction, Baptists exhibited a decided change in

38. *Religious Herald* (Richmond), September 3, 1874, p. 2.
39. *Ibid.*, June 1, 1876, p. 2.
40. *Ibid.*
41. *Alabama Baptist* (Marion), December 21, 1876, p. 2.

attitude. For a short time they seemed to favor the participation of Negroes in politics. "Heaven send the day," said the Virginia paper, "when there shall be new political parties, with new names, and each party shall include both white people and black people." The Negroes' right to vote "is secured to them by constitutional enactments, State and Federal, and is not likely to be materially abridged." [42] Later the same paper recognized the right of Negroes to elect members of their own race to office "if they have brethren capable of framing wise and salutary laws." [43] The Southern Baptist Convention in 1878 acknowledged the right of the freedmen to vote, and accepted a share of the responsibility of preparing them for this duty.[44] The significance of this change in attitude should be considered in the context of the political conditions of the times. Southern whites were again in control of politics. They could use the Negro vote to their own advantage or restrict the Negro vote if they desired. Furthermore, the sincerity of Baptists in their apparent willingness to grant full political rights to the Negroes becomes highly suspect in light of the attitudes which they had expressed before the end of Reconstruction and were to express again before the end of the century.

For a period of about ten years after 1879, Baptists again showed little concern for the political rights of the Negroes. During this time Southern politicians were manipulating the Negro vote as the radical Republicans had done or eliminating the Negroes from politics altogether. In this process Baptists evidently concurred. The few articles and editorials in the Baptist press on the subject expressed or implied approval. The Virginia paper defended the South Carolina "eight box election law" as merely putting *"ignorance at a discount."* [45] But, the editor explained later, the number of Negro voters in South Carolina had declined only because Negroes "don't want to vote." [46] Another editor defended the

42. *Religious Herald* (Richmond), November 23, 1876, p. 2; March 8, 1877, p. 2.
43. *Ibid.,* March 29, 1877, p. 2.
44. Southern Baptist Convention, *Proceedings, 1878,* pp. 24–26.
45. *Religious Herald* (Richmond), January 25, 1883, p. 1. The Eight Box Law of 1882 required separate ballots and boxes for each office to be filled. Ballots deposited in the wrong boxes were disqualified. *See* Francis Butler Simkins, *The South Old and New: A History, 1820–1947* (1956), pp. 227–228.
46. *Religious Herald* (Richmond), December 18, 1884, p. 1.

Negroes' right to vote but judged them unprepared for the ballot. "The negro as he is today," he said, "is fit for little but to count his hours of toil, go through with his drudgery, eat and sleep." [47] The absence of all protest against the abridgement of the Negroes' political rights can be taken only as tacit approval or culpable lack of interest.

After a decade of relative silence, the Negro problem again became a topic of major concern among Baptists. During the remaining ten or twelve years of the century, all the Southern states systematically and "legally" eliminated the Negroes from politics by constitutional or statutory restraints. Baptists concurred in these proscriptive measures. The Mississippi paper reported favorably a speech by Senator James Z. George in which the Senator advocated eliminating Negroes from politics "by legal means" and thereby securing to the people of Mississippi and their posterity the "blessings of white supremacy." Unrestricted Negro suffrage, he continued, would lead to a "domination of ignorance" which Southern whites would not tolerate. In commenting on George's speech the editor agreed that the Anglo-Saxon race, true to its glorious tradition, would have to find a *legal* means of restricting the voting privileges of Negroes rather than continue the extra-legal devices employed since Reconstruction. [48]

Alabama Baptists defended the elimination of the Negroes from politics as the first step toward political and social tranquillity. The editor of the state paper asked:

What are the whites to do? Must they sit still and let the negroes take possession of the government? Are they required either by patriotism or religion to allow an inferior race to dominate them? . . . The solid South is largely a local condition. It is not so much a solidity against the North as against the negroes. . . . The race issue is growing sharper every day. The color line is growing into a chasm which it is to be feared will yet be a bloody chasm. The white people of the South mean to rule, and they will rule. [49]

Opposition to Negro voting among Baptists became even more pronounced in the nineties. James B. Gambrell, president of Georgia Baptists' Mercer University wrote:

47. *Western Recorder* (Louisville), May 4, 1882, p. 4.
48. *Southern Baptist Record* (Meridian, Mississippi), October 31, 1889, p. 2.
49. *Alabama Baptist* (Montgomery), November 28, 1889, p. 1.

As I see it, if all history furnishes an account of one political blunder, which must have prominence for magnitude, the enfranchisement of the negroes was that one. The whole history of it is a record of partizan hate and blindness, of misrule, corruption, stealing, bloodshed and strife. The negroes were not prepared for it, and are not now. It has wrought evil, and only evil, to both races. . . . Negro suffrage was a blunder and a crime.[50]

A contributor to the Georgia paper called enfranchisement the "colossal mistake of the century. . . . American institutions staggered at the blow," and only the disfranchisement of the Negroes could relieve the country of the danger. He congratulated Mississippians and other Southerners who had already denied Negroes the ballot. "We only regret Georgia had not taken the lead," he concluded.[51]

Baptists approved the disfranchising techniques which a number of Southern states incorporated into their new constitutions during the nineties. The North Carolina paper repeatedly agreed with gubernatorial candidate Charles B. Aycock's position on Negro suffrage: "He bluntly denies that the negro is fitted to vote," commented the editor. "One cannot read what he says without confessing that he seems to be speaking in clear sentences what the whole country has known."[52] Baptist papers in Virginia and Alabama also sanctioned disfranchisement through constitutional provisions.[53] At the close of the century, Baptists were unmistakably in agreement with the movement throughout the South to eliminate the Negroes from politics. At the same time, however, they were loud in proclaiming their advocacy of Negro rights. "The only way then to deal with the black man whom we find in America," said Professor Basil Manly of the Southern Baptist Theological Seminary, "is to GIVE HIM HIS RIGHTS, cordially, frankly, fully."[54] But in Baptist thinking, Negro "rights" did not include the right to vote and participate in politics.

The meaning of freedom differed widely in the minds of the Negroes after the Civil War, but universally they interpreted freedom to mean

50. *Christian Index* (Atlanta), April 5, 1894, p. 1.

51. *Ibid.,* May 25, 1899, p. 3. *See also Baptist Standard* (Dallas), August 18, 1898, p. 1.

52. *Biblical Recorder* (Raleigh, North Carolina), May 2, 1900, p. 1.

53. *Religious Herald* (Richmond), September 20, 1900, p. 3; *Alabama Baptist* (Montgomery), May 17, 1900, p. 4.

54. Basil Manly, "Our Brother in Black," *Seminary Magazine,* II (May 1889), 137.

the right and opportunity to receive an education. State laws before 1865 had prohibited educating the slaves, and although these laws were not rigidly enforced, the overwhelming majority of Negroes were still without the rudiments of formal education at the time of emancipation. To provide schools for the thousands of newly freed Negroes in an area where no public schools—white or Negro—had existed previously was an impossible task for the prostrate South. The resources of the federal government, Northern churches, and private philanthropy were therefore added to the appropriations of the Southern state governments in an effort to finance this gigantic undertaking. Providing physical facilities was but one of many obstacles to the development of an effective educational system for the freedmen: Who would teach the Negroes? Would Negro and white children attend the same schools? Could the Negroes be educated at all? If so, what kind of education was best suited for a people emerging from slavery? Conflicting opinions about these and other questions rendered the task of educating the freedmen extremely difficult.

Within a few months after the end of the war, Baptists arrived at answers to most of the questions concerning Negro education. They approved the principle of educating the Negroes although they disagreed for many years over the degree of educability of Negroes and the most appropriate curriculum for them. They insisted that Southern whites teach the freedmen until Southern Negro teachers could be trained. And they demanded without equivocation that the races be educated in separate systems.

Baptists unanimously agreed that Negroes should be educated, at least to the extent of enabling them to read the Bible. "It never was a necessary part of the institution of slavery to keep the slaves in ignorance," declared Professor John A. Broadus of the Southern Baptist Seminary in 1866, and after emancipation there could be no excuse for holding them longer in darkness.[55] "We shall endeavor to promote their *mental improvement*," said the Virginia paper in its first issue after the war. "Let them be taught, in Sunday schools and day schools."[56] The Southern Baptist Convention of 1866 went on record in favor of educating the freedmen "that they should become able to read for themselves

55. *Religious Herald* (Richmond), May 10, 1866, p. 1.
56. *Ibid.,* October 19, 1865, p. 2.

the blessed Word of salvation."[57] "Let the New Testament be made a text book" for the freedmen, declared the South Carolina Convention in the same year.[58] And on numerous other occasions immediately after the war Baptists expressed their approval of Negro education.

Besides supporting the principle of Negro education, Baptists expressed some definite views on the practical aspects of the problem. They were adamant in their determination that Southern whites should teach the freedmen. Northern help would be welcomed, said the Georgia paper in 1866,

> but we want no pseudo-philanthropic adventurers to come among us to associate exclusively with blacks, to make them believe that they are to look abroad for friends and education, and to stir up antagonism between the races. . . . It is our interest to do it; it is the interest of the blacks that we should do it.[59]

Delegates to the North Carolina Convention in 1866 declared that it was the "dispensation of his Providence" that freedmen should be taught by Southerners, their former owners and instructors and those best qualified to teach them.[60] John A. Broadus encouraged Southern white teachers to consider devoting their lives to teaching the Negroes:

> The teachers who come from [the North] must be mainly such as are not greatly in demand at home. . . . These, with all the prejudice and fanaticism of ignorance, would exert an evil influence by alienating the colored people from the Southern whites to whom, under God, they must mainly look, not only for employment and protection, but for education and religion.[61]

If Southerners did not choose to make a profession of teaching the Negroes, then, Broadus urged, they should teach them in their spare time, gratuitously if necessary. Whatever the arrangement, Southern whites had to do the job. The urgency of the appeal for Southern white teachers arose not out of a sense of obligation to the Negroes, but rather from fear of the consequences which might ensue if the Negroes came under the influence of Northern teachers. In spite of the eloquent appeal,

57. Southern Baptist Convention, *Proceedings, 1866*, p. 32.
58. South Carolina Baptist Convention, *Minutes, 1866*, p. 240.
59. *Christian Index* (Atlanta), April 26, 1866, p. 71.
60. North Carolina Baptist Convention, *Minutes, 1866*, p. 20.
61. *Religious Herald* (Richmond), May 10, 1866, p. 1.

however, few Southern whites offered their services as teachers, and the task of educating the freedmen fell to Northerners.

The many Northern teachers in the South during Reconstruction were a constant source of irritation to Baptists. A contributor to the Georgia paper epitomized the attitude of most Baptists. He denounced Northern teachers as

abolition emissaries, in the shape of a *"school marm,"* sent out professedly to teach the negroes, but, in truth to engender strife and disaffection, to encourage the negro in insolent assumption, and to fan the flames to open hostility between the races.[62]

Baptists could find nothing worthy of commendation in the work of the Northern teachers.

After Reconstruction the question of who should teach the Negroes— indeed, the whole problem of Negro education—ceased to be important. The great host of Northern "meddlers" lost their zeal and went home, and the Negroes' intense desire for education subsided. Southern whites, again in control, were content to entrust the major task of educating the Negroes to Northern churches and charities or to leave them ignorant, a condition commensurate with their "place" in Southern society. Southern Baptists did nothing to provide white teachers for Negro schools.

Another phase of Negro education on which Baptists agreed was that the races be segregated in separate school systems. "Everybody knows," said a Virginia Baptist in 1866, "that it will not do for the negro children to go to school with the whites. . . . So there must be separate schools." [63] Georgia had no mixed schools for Negro and white children, admitted the editor of the state Baptist paper in 1866 and, he said, we "trust that we never shall have." [64] Segregation of the races in public schools was never a controversial issue among Baptists at any time between 1865 and 1900. They considered it a necessity. When they discussed the question, it was only to add new arguments to their inflexible position. In criticizing the efforts of the American Baptist Home Mission Society to integrate the races in its schools, the editor of the

62. *Christian Index* (Atlanta), June 17, 1869, p. 93.
63. *Religious Herald* (Richmond), May 10, 1866, p. 1.
64. *Christian Index* (Atlanta), May 24, 1866, p. 86.

Virginia paper declared that mixing the races would only degrade the "tastes, manners, habits and morals of the [white] pupils." He continued:

To this influence the Southern whites are not willing to subject their children. . . . The inevitable tendency of it would be to corrupt and degrade the white society of the South; and we do not believe that the intelligent, refined and respectable classes of the North, in circumstances like ours, would subject their children to such a contaminating influence. . . . Any attempt to force mixed schools on the South, by legal enactments, would be a flagrant injustice, and an utter failure. It would be to tax the whites heavily to support schools, from which their own children, by a social law, more binding than any legal enactment, would be excluded. . . . We cannot endure any measures which tend to Africanize and mongrelize [our race]. God has made us different from the negro race, physically, intellectually and socially, and with due love to all his creatures, and due reverence for all his laws, we shall recognize that difference, and accept all the consequences that legitimately flow from it. Until it can be shown, by a fair interpretation of the Scriptures, that he requires us to have mixed schools, we shall follow the strong instincts of our nature in patronizing schools of our own complexion of our own blood.[65]

The same editor strengthened his argument in a tirade against the Civil Rights Bill of 1875 which originally included integrating the races in public schools. Education was a *state* function, he said, but if the federal government insisted on legislating in the field, it should consider local "prejudices" and sentiments.

We do not concede, however, [he continued] that the aversion of the people of the South to mixed schools is a prejudice. We maintain, on the contrary, that it is an instinct, divinely implanted, for the wise and beneficent purpose of keeping separate races which are, by nature, widely different in color, social qualities and moral tendencies. God has made the differences, and human government should not ignore it. . . . [The effect of the bill] will be not only to obliterate all social distinction between the races, but to blend them into a common mass. This calamity must not be endured, if, by any possible means, it can be averted. We know the people of the South too well to doubt for a moment that they will do and endure anything rather than submit to this social degradation. We do not believe that one white person in a hundred, including natives and immigrants, will consent that his children shall attend a mixed school.

65. *Religious Herald* (Richmond), June 22, 1871, p. 2.

Should the bill become a law, then the whites of the South will owe it to themselves, to their children, to their race, to future generations, and to God, who has made the distinction between the Anglo-Saxon and the negro, to adopt the best methods to counteract its pernicious influence. Whatever can be done by State legislation to prevent or to diminish the evil should be, and, no doubt, will be, promptly done. If necessary, let the public schools be abolished. If they are required by constitutional enactments, the constitutions should be amended. If, however, State legislation can bring no relief, then let the whites be taxed to support schools for the education of the colored children, while private arrangements are made for the instruction of white children. If the poverty of the whites should prevent them from educating their children, let them grow up in ignorance rather than be taught in mixed schools. . . . Greatly as we would dread barbarism, we prefer it infinitely to *mongrelization*. From a state of barbarism our noble Anglo-Saxon race would rise to civilization, refinement and power; but from the effeminacy, degradation and misery of a mixture of uncongenial races there is no redemption. . . . And believing, as we do most firmly, that mixed schools and the unrestricted social intercourse of the white and colored races tend to that result, we deprecate them as a greater calamity than barbarism, famine, pestilence, or even national destruction.[66]

Baptists contributed only one more substantial argument against integrated schools during the remainder of the century. This was that integrated schools would be unfair to the Negroes. In competition with the superior white children, Negro children would be denied opportunities for full development. Separate schools, therefore, were essential to the progress of the Negroes themselves.[67]

The editor of the Virginia paper in 1877 summed up the attitude of Baptists toward integrated schools for many years to follow. "Whether mixed schools are wise or desirable, is a question which need not be discussed;" he said, "their establishment is *simply impossible*."[68] From this position Baptists never wavered.

That Negroes should be educated, that Southern whites should control their education, and that the races should be educated in separate systems were presuppositions which Baptists accepted. They expressed considerable disagreement, however, over the objectives of Negro education and,

66. *Ibid.,* January 8, 1874, p. 2. The similarity between these arguments and those of Southern segregationists since 1954 are striking.
67. *Ibid.,* May 10, 1894, p. 1.
68. *Ibid.,* March 15, 1877, p. 2.

consequently, over the kind of schools which could best achieve those ends. The consensus of Baptists immediately after the war was that freedmen should be taught to read the Bible, but how much education Negroes could assimilate beyond the elementary level was a matter of debate. Differences arose from divergent opinions about the mental capacity of the Negroes. A contributor to one paper, whom the editor described as a Virginian of "intelligence, piety, social standing, and purity of character," presented the extreme view of those who held that Negroes were incapable of mastering advanced knowledge. He contended,

that the negro race, in mental endowment, is inferior to all other races; and that so great is this inferiority, that the negro can neither build up of himself civilized society, nor, if left to himself, sustain and perpetuate a civilization once imparted to him by other races. . . . That, stamped by creative power, with an inferior mental capacity, human agency cannot elevate the negro to equality with the white race.[69]

In contradiction to this view another Virginian asserted a few months later that it was "all a mistake that the colored people cannot excel in acquiring knowledge," and he cited the achievements of a number of Negro ministers as proof.[70] As the years passed Baptists tended more and more to admit that Negroes had the capacity for acquiring knowledge, but they continued to consider them inferior to the whites. In 1866 Professor John A. Broadus expressed what was to become the general opinion of Baptists by the end of the century:

They are a greatly inferior race to the whites, but their intellectual and moral endowments are not radically different; and there are individual negroes, as everybody knows, who are greatly superior, in intelligence and character, to some white men.[71]

From the belief that Negroes were inferior to the whites in native intelligence, it was but a logical step to the view that Negroes should be educated differently. Baptists came to advocate as a "proper" education for the Negroes that type of training which would equip them for filling their "place" in Southern life. The condition of the Negroes was unfavorable to "the development of a literary stimulant," said one journal in 1877, and "their menial service and their agricultural and mechanical

69. *Ibid.,* February 19, 1874, p. 1.
70. *Ibid.,* May 21, 1874, p. 3.
71. *Ibid.,* May 10, 1866, p. 1.

labors do not require high mental culture." [72] After 1880 Baptists frequently expressed the opinion that Negroes should be educated only as laborers. Negroes did not need training in science, philosophy, literature, and languages, said the Kentucky paper in 1882, but they needed instruction in that which would "give them a knowledge of life and of citizenship and their responsibilities, a knowledge of their own value, of the possibilities that their being enwraps. . . . to be instructed in the principles of art and handicraft." [73] In the same year the Georgia paper advised "those who have charge of the education of our black people" to "teach them that the object of education is to make them efficient in their necessary position in life, and not to lift them *above* it." [74] The North Carolina journal sanctioned industrial and mechanical training for the Negroes. Negroes could find ready employment in the South as blacksmiths, barbers, shoemakers, and other craftsmen, the editor said, but education for the professions was wasted effort since Negroes could not compete with whites in those fields. [75] "A training that gives a [Negro] man a handicraft," said the Georgia paper, "enables him to earn an honest living, and makes him a useful citizen," but a liberal arts course "turns him out a thriftless, educated idler." [76]

Baptists unanimously approved Booker T. Washington's plan for manual training and self-improvement for Negroes. The Kentucky journal in 1900 printed this:

For our part, we believe that the course of education outlined by President Booker T. Washington, is in far closer accord with the ultimate facts of the race inheritance of the negroes than the well-meaning but futile attempts to elevate the negroes as a mass by giving them the education that would be suitable to the white children of a New England town. [77]

Another paper commended Washington's Tuskegee Institute:

Probably no other institution stands for more useful effort, or more promotes the healthiest relations between the races than this one. [78]

72. *Ibid.,* March 15, 1877, p. 2.
73. *Western Recorder* (Louisville), May 4, 1882, p. 4.
74. *Christian Index* (Atlanta), November 2, 1882, p. 8.
75. *Biblical Recorder* (Raleigh, North Carolina), May 13, 1885, p. 2.
76. *Christian Index* (Atlanta), June 11, 1891, p. 8.
77. *Western Recorder* (Louisville), November 8, 1900, p. 1.
78. *Christian Index* (Atlanta), January 4, 1900, p. 6.

And the Virginia paper asserted that at Tuskegee the Negro race was being educated to realize that the relations between the races will only improve so far as the negro improves his education. He must produce something which the white man wants, before he will be recognized.[79]

At the close of the century, Baptists had come to favor only that kind of education for Negroes which would enable them to read the Bible and to earn a living as unskilled or semi-skilled laborers. A few Negroes could profit from higher education, admitted one editor, but college education only ruined the masses

so far as manual labor is concerned. The men scorn to become servants or field hands, and the women will suffer for the necessaries of life before they will cook or wash, or work in the fields. Are we not stating facts? A little learning is a very dangerous thing to the negro, and but few of them have the capacity, the brain power to get more than a "little." [80]

Negroes should be taught, said another Baptist, "but not taught books; for statistics of our penal institutions show that the book-learned Negro is our bad negro." [81]

These views expressed in 1900 were identical with those held by Baptists since the war. In 1874, for example, a contributor to the Virginia paper asserted that to attempt to train Negroes to a high degree of technical skill was

zeal without knowledge . . . and any system designed to withdraw from the fields and workshop our colored population, in the school-rooms, in which to fit them for the highest duties in our advanced social life, is radically wrong, and will surely bring only misfortune and misery. In the higher spheres of duty, he may not compete with his white brother; in menial labors he may. Fit him for this, and all is done which can be well done.[82]

And later the same paper declared:

The Negro should be made to understand that his sphere is that of a laborer, under the guidance of the white man. Much of what is called educating the Negro is simply unfitting him for the only sphere in which he will ever be a useful and happy member of society. . . . It is cruel to attempt to train an ox

79. *Religious Herald* (Richmond), April 9, 1896, p. 1.
80. *Alabama Baptist* (Montgomery), May 17, 1900, p. 4.
81. *Religious Herald* (Richmond), September 20, 1900, p. 3.
82. *Ibid.,* February 19, 1874, p. 1.

to trot at 2:40. You may *kill* your ox by striving to force him out of the sphere to which he naturally belongs.[83]

The South Carolina paper in 1900 presented one of the rare arguments for educating Negroes the same as whites. The editor said:

The only safe education for the Negro is the same as the only safe education for the Caucasian, namely, a harmonious, liberal education, adapting the person to his environment at all points. . . . But he must, at the same time, be educated in all directions in which, as a human being, he is capable of receiving education, since under our form of government we cannot have a class of helots, or "hewers of wood and drawers of water." . . . No, we should say, let the Negro be educated, so far as possible, exactly as the white race is educated.[84]

This view was clearly at variance with the majority opinion of Baptists.

The attitudes of Baptists toward Negro education suggest their pre-conceptions about the place of Negroes in the Southern economy. Deprived of all but the rudiments of learning, Negroes could be expected to perform only manual labor. Baptists concurred in the opinion prevailing in the South that Negroes should do the same kinds of work which they had performed as slaves. They considered Negroes the natural laborers for the South and looked to the exploitation of their labor to restore Southern prosperity through agriculture. In a resolution at their state convention in 1866, Mississippi Baptists pledged that they would,

by example and precept, inculcate a sentiment of kindness and justice towards this dependent class, and we will use our influence in securing to them just compensation for their labor, and protection and security against fraud or injustice.[85]

Baptists gave no hint in this report that they expected Negroes to engage in any occupation except that of farm laborers in the employ of the whites. Why cannot the black man remain in the South "and occupy the position of laborer to the greater profit of his employer as well as enjoy the fruits of his own toil?" asked a contributor to the Virginia paper.[86] A Baptist in the Mississippi Delta expressed the opinion in 1869 that the

83. *Ibid.,* March 8, 1883, p. 2.
84. *Baptist Courier* (Greenville, South Carolina), February 8, 1900, p. 4.
85. Mississippi Baptist Convention, *Proceedings, 1866,* p. 23.
86. *Religious Herald* (Richmond), April 12, 1866, p. 1.

Negroes' efforts to establish themselves as "an independent element" in the Southern economy had failed:

The negro, left to himself, is a helpless creature, doomed to penury and want. The *Anglo-Saxon*—the *manor born sons and daughters of the South,* must develop [the South's] vast resources. . . . The colored man accepting the situation, instinctively turns to the white man for protection, as he tills these broad acres to enrich again his former master.[87]

The difficulties encountered by Southern whites in their attempts to keep the Negroes in a state of peonage convinced many of them that free Negroes were unreliable as laborers and that a new source of labor had to be found. Europe was a possible source, but China was more promising. For a few years after the war, Baptists encouraged the importation of Chinese coolies to replace Negroes. They expected Chinese labor to be more dependable and less costly than Negro labor, and they anticipated no political troubles from the Orientals—"if the carpetbaggers and scalawags will not seek to corrupt the celestials, as they have the negro." [88] A few Chinese came to the South but not in sufficient numbers to affect materially the labor supply. By the early seventies, Southerners had become disillusioned with the prospects of imported labor, and again they turned to the Negroes as the only possible laborers for the South. The question was not *where* farm laborers were coming from, but *how* to employ most effectively the Negroes already in the South. One Baptist paper counseled:

The policy of managing freedmen is, to act firmly, and truly, and honestly with them, and require them to do the same; and as good stimulus to do this, never pay them more than half wages til the end of the time for which they contracted to work.[89]

. . . .

Conciliation, firmness and justice, are the elements by which we are to control the negro . . . and when this is done, there is no nation of people so well suited to our purposes as the African.[90]

Farm labor continued to be a problem for the rest of the century, but Baptists considered no people except Negroes suitable for the task.

87. *Western Recorder* (Louisville), May 29, 1869, p. 1.
88. *Religious Herald* (Richmond), August 12, 1869, p. 1.
89. *Ibid.,* January 19, 1871, p. 4.
90. *Ibid.,* September 12, 1872, p. 4.

While freely offering their advice about how to treat Negroes in order to get the most work from them, Baptists had surprisingly little to say about specific farm-labor systems. From the few editorials and articles in their papers (mostly reprints from farm journals), Baptists seemed to favor money-rent and wage-labor systems rather than sharecropping.[91]

Baptists considered the great mass of Negroes suited only for unskilled agricultural labor, but they believed that a small minority were capable of engaging in occupations requiring higher skills. Consequently, Baptists held that Negroes with ability should be permitted to enter certain skilled and semi-skilled trades. In reply to Northern criticism of the Southerners' treatment of the Negroes, Baptists took great delight in pointing out that Negro craftsmen—carpenters, masons, barbers, and draymen—had greater freedom in practicing their trades in the South than in the North.[92] And because of this greater economic freedom and the kind treatment of Negroes generally by Southern whites, Baptists argued, Negroes in the South were happier than Negroes in the North. Northerners cited the "Exodus of 1879" as evidence of the Negroes' dissatisfaction in the South. But Baptists denied this and attributed the exodus instead to the generally depressed condition of agriculture in the South and to the enticements of "shrewd and unprincipled sharpers" who lured Southern Negroes into undeveloped areas of Kansas for personal gain.[93] The migration of Negroes from the South was only temporary, said the Georgia paper, and "the end of it all will be that the negroes will find that their old home is the best place for them, and that their old masters are their best friends."[94] Negroes who had migrated to Kansas, said another paper, would soon learn that the South, by comparison, was the "poor negro's paradise."[95]

By the closing decade of the century, Negroes had found their place in the Southern economy. Baptists, with other Southerners, expected them to

91. *See* pp. 128–130 for further discussion of Baptist views on the farm labor problem.

92. *Christian Index* (Atlanta), August 1, 1889, p. 1; September 5, 1889, p. 1; November 14, 1889, p. 1.

93. *Biblical Recorder* (Raleigh, North Carolina), May 7, 1879, p. 2. *See also Religious Herald* (Richmond), June 12, 1879, p. 1; *Alabama Baptist* (Selma), May 15, 1879, p. 2; John G. Van Deusen, "The Exodus of 1879," *Journal of Negro History*, XXI (April 1936), 111–129.

94. *Christian Index* (Atlanta), December 4, 1879, p. 4.

95. *Western Recorder* (Louisville), April 17, 1879, p. 4.

4. The Negroes: Segregation in Social Relations

 A N T E B E L L U M concepts of race relations continued unchanged in the South after the Civil War. The combined forces of war, legislative action, constitutional amendment, and judicial decision were ineffectual in altering the social customs of Southern whites. Baptists, too, remained distinctly Southern in their social views. In defiance of powerful pressures for racial equality, they persistently proclaimed their determination to prevent social intercourse between the races.

The biracial membership of Baptist churches after the war presented an immediate and complicated social problem for Baptists. If Negro members remained in the churches, a certain amount of social mingling was inevitable. Yet, if they were permitted or forced to withdraw, white Baptists would lose a valuable controlling influence over the Negroes and would subject themselves to charges of unchristian conduct. The Dover Baptist Association of Virginia grappled with this problem at its annual meeting in 1869 and eventually approved the severance of religious ties between white and Negro Baptists as essential to the preservation of social distinctions. A special committee appointed to study the problem reported that Christian brotherhood

is an equality of religious benefits, not of social position or of moral responsibility. Christianity does not propose to abolish the natural, civil or social distinctions among men.

Furthermore, the report continued:

Believing that the admission of colored persons into our churches and associations is not divinely required of us—that it is not necessary to their religious instruction and welfare—and that it would lead to social evils that all should deprecate and guard against, your committee earnestly recommend that your constitution shall not be so changed as to admit colored delegates to seats in the body. We make this recommendation more heartily because a different course would involve a change of policy far-reaching, and, in our opinion, very disastrous in its consequences.[1]

The delegates at the Southern Baptist Convention in 1869 discussed the same question and also decided against mixing the races.[2] A delegate who refrained from speaking at the convention while everyone had *"negro on the brain,"* aired his views at length in the Georgia paper later:

My own convictions are that we should, frankly and firmly, discountenance the first movement towards equality between the white man and the negro, as well in *religious* as in political assemblies. If my religion forbids the denial of their equality at our Conventions and Associations, I cannot understand how it will justify that denial in our own churches and at our firesides. Authority, supreme in itself, and dangerous to contravene, has established a distinction, and all that we do should indicate the plain, undisguised fact, that our solemn, conscientious determination is to maintain and preserve that distinction. To act otherwise can result in no good to the negro, and must prove a serious and widespread evil to the white man.

. . . .

[W]hen the distinction which the Great Ruler of the Universe has made, ceases to be observed—when, by common consent, the white man and the negro meet on equal terms, in all the relations of life—then will our religious and civil liberty—the noble institutions which commanded the respect and admiration of the world—be among the things that have passed away, and the oft-repeated declaration in regard to Republics be verified in our downfall and disgrace.[3]

Baptists throughout the South agreed that segregation was the solution to the problem of race relations within the denomination. Everywhere they found the divisive forces of social custom and racial prejudice stronger than the bonds of Christian brotherhood.

By 1870 Baptists had settled the question of race relations within the denomination, but the problem of racial mingling in society at large remained a live issue for the remainder of Reconstruction—not that Southern whites were indecisive, but the presence of federal troops in the various states prevented whites from settling the problem to their satis-

1. *Religious Herald* (Richmond), August 19, 1869, p. 1.
2. *Christian Index* (Atlanta), May 13, 1869, p. 74. The *Minutes* of the Southern Baptist Convention did not record the discussion.
3. *Christian Index* (Atlanta), June 17, 1869, p. 93.

faction. As the radical regimes fell in state after state, Southern whites resumed control and imposed their system of total segregation. Baptists agreed completely with the emerging patterns of racial discrimination. They often were reluctant during Reconstruction to reveal their true feelings about the political and civil rights of the Negroes, but they were uninhibited in expressing their opposition to social equality between the races. Can the "black man be received into perfect social equality with the white man?" asked a contributor to the Virginia paper. "No," he replied to his own question. Natural differences compelled the separation of the races and kindness to the inferior race also demanded it, for by separating the races the inferior "is saved from constant mortification, and is better satisfied with the condition in which the providence of God has placed him." God has established "insuperable barriers" between the races, he continued, to keep each "in his proper place."

Then let not man confound, by bringing into too close alliance, what God hath separated. . . . Every white man, of refined tastes, stands agast [*sic*] at the thought of taking to his bosom, as his companion for life, the coal black damsel of African descent. The instincts of nature . . . creates [*sic*] the repellency. . . . The instincts of both white and black say that full social equality is impossible.[4]

A few weeks later the editor of the same paper commented, "Beyond all question, a good colored man is to be preferred to a bad white one," and he admitted knowing some Negroes of refinement whose company he could enjoy and "with whom we could heartily commune at the Lord's table." But, he confessed, he was unable to accept any Negro into full social relationships without doing violence "to the feelings of our nature. This aversion may be a weakness—a prejudice—an evil—but we have it in common with our race. We would not, if we could, destroy this instinct."[5] Still later in the year the same editor again expressed his opposition to social intercourse: "As for equality, either social or political, between the races, that cannot be, must not be—and if it ever exists, it will be the fault of the whites. . . . Let no man try to bring together what God has sent so far asunder."[6]

Although Baptists insisted on the complete separation of the races,

4. *Religious Herald* (Richmond), April 19, 1866, p. 1.
5. *Ibid.,* June 28, 1866, p. 2.
6. *Ibid.,* September 20, 1866, p. 1.

they maintained that segregation did not necessitate the suppression of the Negroes. They proclaimed their belief in the right of Negroes to develop to the extent of their capacity, but they insisted that such development be parallel to, not commingled with, the culture of the whites. "What God requires is kindness, not social intercourse," said the Virginia editor. "We do not object to social equality," he continued, "but to social intercourse. Let them be millionaires, nobles, rulers, anything; but still our repugnance to social intimacy with them would not be overcome. We could not consent for a colored senator, or even emperor, to escort our daughter to church." [7] Barring an "extraordinary revolution," the Negroes seemed destined to become the *"peasantry* of the South,"* commented the same editor, but even if Negroes were able to develop a civilization equal to the whites "they still must have *their society entirely among themselves."* [8]

In a series of articles entitled "fragments of Southern Civilization," a Virginia Baptist listed as one of the distinctive features of Southern life the coexistence of the races in separate spheres. The future of the Negroes was unknown, he said, but

one point is certain: their social relations with the whites will not be materially changed. The races are separated by a gulf which no human ingenuity can bridge. . . . The negro may be cultivated, refined, become rich, live in splendor and luxury; but to become the associate and the equal of the Caucasian, he never will. In his normal state, he does not desire this intimacy. He is moved, by a deep-rooted instinct, to prefer and cleave to his own race. The white man, when not influenced by a false humanitarianism, or governed by a blind fanaticism, loathes the union. Before he would consent to the marriage of his daughter with the most intelligent, virtuous and respectable negro on the earth, he would gladly follow her to her grave. There is no need, however, to discuss this point. If there is anything on which the white Southerner is resolved, it is to maintain, at all hazards, and through all changes, the purity and the social elevation of his race; and to this course he is impelled alike by natural instincts, by a sound policy, and by the unmistakable indications of the will of the Supreme Ruler. [9]

The sincerity of Baptists in assenting to the principle of separate-but-equal existence of the races is questionable in view of their approval of

7. *Ibid.,* December 25, 1873, p. 2.
8. *Ibid.,* October 4, 1866, p. 1.
9. *Ibid.,* November 26, 1874, p. 2.

proscriptive measures against the Negroes later in the century. Further-more, Baptists evidently felt no trepidation in conceding the right of unrestricted development to the Negroes, because, in their opinion, Ne-groes were incapable of achieving the cultural level of whites. In all probability they acknowledged the right of the Negroes to develop freely in their own society for argumentative reasons. Such expressions made excellent counter-propaganda against Northern charges of racial discrimi-nation.

Baptists knew, however, that complete separation of the races was impossible, and they insisted that social distinctions be maintained rigidly when contact between the races was necessary. In advising white farmers on how to treat a Negro laborer, the North Carolina paper admonished: Treat him kindly, but

in your kind treatment, never so lose sight of your own self-respect as to socialize with him; if you do, you at once subvert your influence and destroy your mutual interest. You [may] concede to him all the immunities and privileges which he enjoys under Providence and his government, and may go so far as to even encourage his education in all the systems and branches which you may yourself enjoy—but avoid the suicidal policy of making him believe he is as good as you are—he will drop you at once, and naturally and justly should—your veneering being so thin, you breed his contempt.[10]

Baptists unleashed the full fury of their contempt for social equality against the Civil Rights Bill of 1875. The bill was a misnomer, declared the editor of the Virginia paper:

The Civil Rights Bill, so called, is really a *Social Coercion Bill*. A whole race is opposed to social intercourse and intimacy with another and a very different race; and the Bill proposes, in opposition to the instincts, rights and protestations of the race, by heavy penalties, to enforce this intercourse. . . . It is not right; and it is an abuse of language to call it right.[11]

For months thereafter the editor continued the tirade:

In our deliberate judgment, an attempt to force distinct races into intimate social intercourse would be as flagrant an infringement of right, as heartless an injustice, and as gross an assault on the laws of nature as any government has ever perpetrated.[12]

10. *Biblical Recorder* (Raleigh, North Carolina), June 25, 1873, p. 4.
11. *Religious Herald* (Richmond), October 8, 1874, p. 2.
12. *Ibid.*, January 14, 1875, p. 1.

Furthermore, he contended, Congress was exceeding its legitimate authority in attempting to enter

into every department of social life, and, for the sake of the freedmen, to
convert the United States Government into a vast, oppressive inquisition,
armed with powers which do not belong even to the States. . . . The attempt
to invade the public schools, the hotels, the places of recreation within the
States, under their auspices, and to exercise a censorship over all the minute
details of their economy, this is a usurpation—a despotism never to be
tolerated by a free people.[13]

When the bill, "emasculated of the clause requiring the coeducation of
the races," became law, the editor noted its passage with contempt:

It secures to the colored people equal rights in public conveyances, hotels and
places of public amusement, but fails to give them rights in churches and
cemeteries. The Bill, we think, is of little practical importance; and some of
the soundest Republican lawyers pronounce it unconstitutional. . . . It is
altogether a measure of little meaning, little worth. This law merely secures to
all persons, without distinction of race, birth, or previous condition, willing to
pay for them, the right to equal accommodations in railroad cars, hotels and
theatres. We see nothing in this act which was not secured to the colored
population by the fourteenth amendment to the Constitution.[14]

The protest of Baptists against the Civil Rights Bill was their last
outburst against social equality during Reconstruction. After 1875 the
amount of space in Baptist journals devoted to the question declined
sharply, and for the next thirteen or fourteen years, social equality ceased
to be an issue. In 1879 the Virginia paper reported:

There is scarcely any social intercourse between the whites and negroes of the
South. Whether this separation is right or wrong, we need not inquire. It
exists, and is controlled by laws as immutable as those of the Medes and
Persians. Instinct, custom, interest, and, as we think, the highest welfare of
the races, combine to perpetuate it.[15]

When the papers did take note of race relations, the same arguments
which had been presented so frequently during the first decade after the
war were repeated with little variation. The Georgia paper took issue
with George Washington Cable's article, "The Freedmen's Case in

13. *Ibid.,* January 7, 1875, p. 2.
14. *Ibid.,* March 11, 1875, p. 3.
15. *Ibid.,* June 19, 1879, p. 2.

Equity," published in *Century* in 1885, in which Cable called the Negroes a "greatly outraged people," and proposed "that the only remedy for their wrongs is for the two races to intermingle as freely as [if] they were all of one color." The editor denied that such discrimination as Cable described existed in the South, but if it did, Cable's remedy would be worse than the alleged trouble. When races mixed, he said, "it is usually only the dregs of each race that come together," and their offspring usually amounted to nothing.[16]

The same editor later admitted that Negroes were denied admittance as "first class guests at hotels, . . . theatres, and other places of amusement, . . . waiting rooms of the railroads, [and] . . . in the trains." But, he maintained, the charges of discrimination were not as serious as they might appear, for Negroes did not desire to associate with whites in first-class accommodations. The solution to these apparent discriminations was simple: "Whenever it will *pay* to set up first-class hotels [theatres, trains, etc.] for Negroes, the supply will be found equal to the demand." As for other problems growing out of the coexistence of the races in the South, they would be solved, the editor concluded, "by Providence, and not by men." [17]

Following the period of relative quiescence, Baptists renewed their discussion of the Negro problem in the late eighties. The attitudes and arguments expressed in the remaining years of the century varied to no appreciable extent from these presented earlier except that Baptists were generally more argumentative and defensive and bolder in proclaiming the necessity for and the justice of the complete segregation of the races.

The renewed interest in the Negroes in the late eighties was occasioned in part by the recognition among Southerners that the Negroes had become a "problem." Before the Civil War when law and custom carefully regulated race relations, the Negroes were not considered a social problem. After emancipation, the whites expected their former slaves to continue to occupy essentially the same relative positions. Had this condition prevailed, no Negro problem would have developed, but the Negroes refused to accept docilely their "place" in Southern society. The refusal of the Negroes to accept the status which the whites had designated for them and the determination of the whites to maintain white

16. *Christian Index* (Atlanta), January 8, 1885, p. 8. Cable's article appeared in *Century Magazine*, XXIX (January 1885), 409–418.
17. *Christian Index* (Atlanta), February 10, 1887, p. 8.

supremacy constituted the essence of the "Negro problem" in the late nineteenth century.

Baptists began recognizing the Negroes as a problem as early as 1879. In commenting on the "Exodus" of that year, the Kentucky paper pleaded: "O for the advent of a little common sense to take the place of sentiment and mock philanthropy in the treatment of this everlasting 'negro problem'!" [18] Thereafter Baptists used the term with increasing frequency in their papers, and in 1886 it appeared for the first time in the *Proceedings* of the Southern Baptist Convention. [19]

Baptists expressed varying opinions about what the Negro problem was and how it could be solved. Some opposed any and all discussion of the question in public meetings and the press while others thought it should be discussed freely. By 1890, however, they had come to a general understanding as to what the problem was (although it was never clearly defined) and they also had come to agree that it should be discussed in order to be solved. The problem, for Baptists, involved a contradiction of social views and Christian principles. Having accepted the Southern position on the race question, Baptists were confronted with the problem of equating these views with Christian principles. They seem not to have questioned the rightness of their social views. It was their Christian ethics which had to be bent to conform to their social views.

Baptists never arrived at a specific solution to the Negro problem, although they all agreed that the solution would be found through an application of the gospel. Since they refused to acknowledge the possibility of error in their social attitudes, the inference was that if Negroes were made Christians, they would therefore be satisfied in their assigned status in life.

Baptists failed to realize the seriousness of the Negro problem until very late in the century. John J. D. Renfroe, a prominent Alabama minister, declared in 1886 that the Southern Baptist Convention had solved the Negro problem in that year by appropriating $1,000 for work among the Negroes through the Home Mission Board. [20] A North Carolinian declared that white ministers by showing "kind, fraternal feelings toward colored churches and pastors" and by preaching for the Negroes "when they can spare the time," could "do much toward solving the great

18. *Western Recorder* (Louisville), April 17, 1879, p. 4.
19. Southern Baptist Convention, *Proceedings, 1886*, pp. 15, 17.
20. *Religious Herald* (Richmond), May 27, 1886, p. 1.

question of the day, and at the same time discharge our duty toward them as a people." [21] A contributor to the Florida paper in 1889 still looked to colonization as the final solution to the problem, but he admonished Florida Baptists to continue their efforts in educating and evangelizing "their weaker brother," and "leave the final solution of this seemingly knotty problem to an All-Wise Providence." [22] "The gospel of Jesus Christ solves all problems," declared Texas Baptists in 1890; "with it let the race question find speedy and permanent adjudication." [23] In arguments based primarily on census returns and observation, the editor of the Tennessee paper claimed to see an end to the race question:

Thus, I have demonstrated, by facts and figures convincingly and conclusively, that the race question is solving itself in natural ways; that nature is repeating in the South the lessons she has taught in all other countries and ages, where inferior races have been brought in contact with the superior—that the civilization of the latter means to the former a rapid declination.

Tennessee and Arkansas, he concluded, would soon cease "to have any particular interest in the negro problem." [24] In similar vein another paper argued that racial tension would become less and less a problem and that "the solution may reasonably be left to the operation of physiological and economic laws." [25] Another editor saw the solution in "southern institutions" which he defined as those measures already employed in the South to ensure the complete segregation of the races. [26] A prominent Virginia Baptist declared in 1894,

The only 'negro problem,' is to find out how to stop conceited, impertinent and ignorant intermeddlers, who know nothing about the negroes, but who think they 'know it all,' from eternally orating about 'the negro problem.' If the negroes and the Southern whites are let alone, they will get on as well together as the characters of the two races will permit. [27]

The most absurd understatement of the Negro problem and the ease with which it could be solved occurred at the Southern Baptist Conven-

21. *Biblical Recorder* (Raleigh, North Carolina), May 15, 1889, p. 1.
22. *Florida Baptist Witness* (Ocala), April 17, 1889, p. 2.
23. Texas Baptist General Convention, *Proceedings, 1890,* pp. 18–19.
24. *Baptist and Reflector* (Nashville), March 19, 1891, p. 7.
25. *Alabama Baptist* (Montgomery), July 30, 1891, p. 2.
26. *Baptist Courier* (Greenville, South Carolina), November 10, 1892, p. 2.
27. *Religious Herald* (Richmond), December 6, 1894, p. 1.

tion in 1891. In that year the convention adopted the "report of the Home Mission Board" which read in part:

The race problem, as it is called, has been deemed by statesmen the most perplexing of all questions affecting our society and our political institutions. We venture the assertion that it can and will be found of easy solution.

Nothing is plainer to any one who knows this race than its perfect willingness to accept a subordinate place, provided there be confidence that in that position of subordination it will receive justice and kindness. That is the condition it prefers above all others, and this is the condition in which it attains the highest development of every attribute of manhood. Whenever it shall understandingly and cheerfully accept this condition, the race problem is settled forever.

The only thing needed now on his part is the assurance that he may confidently rely upon the justice and kindness which such a condition always demands and should always receive.

This assurance the Christian men and women of this Southern land ought to give. . . . It is perfectly in the power of the Baptist people of the South to do all and give all that is needed to accomplish this end.

With the great mass of the professed Christians among them members of Baptist churches, with three fourths of this entire population under Baptist influence, we have but to take hold of their religious interests with an earnestness becoming Christian men, and they will respond to such expressions of kindness with an alacrity and a sincerity that will surprise every beholder. If the Baptists of the South will but open their eyes to see their opportunity and open their hearts to the stimulating influences of Christian obligation to these people, they will themselves be amazed and gratified at the ease and rapidity with which the end will be attained. We do not hesitate to affirm our confident belief that an expenditure under the best conditions by our Home Mission and State Boards of fifty thousand dollars a year for the next ten years will settle this race question forever.

What greater good could come to our country, or what grander triumph to Christianity than so easy and perfect a solution of a question which has been and is now the despair of the statesmanship of the world? [28]

Successive conventions evidently failed to concur in the sentiments of this report, because the "fifty thousand dollars a year for the next ten years" which was supposed to "settle this race question forever" was not appropriated.

Notwithstanding the display of optimism and the many suggested solutions, the race problem was no nearer solution in 1900 than it was at

28. Southern Baptist Convention, *Proceedings, 1891*, p. XXXVI.

any time earlier in the century. Baptists had made some progress, however, for at least they had come to face the problem realistically. The pessimistic report of the "Committee on Work Among the Negroes" adopted at the Southern Baptist Convention in 1900 was in marked contrast to the sanguine report of the Home Mission Board of 1891: "With all possible emphasis," the report read, "your committee declares its conviction that the negro problem in the South is the gravest that confronts us as a people." [29] The Alabama weekly reflected the same pessimism:

The race question is practically the one and only question of any importance before the people of the South. Nearly all other questions are either involved in or related to this. Solve this, and a thousand others will be solved.[30]

At the beginning of the new century, the South still had its Negro problem. None of the remedies which Baptists had entertained had brought the problem nearer solution. The Negroes had refused to emigrate, they had continued to multiply in defiance of "physiological and economic laws," and not even the gospel had produced any obviously salutary effects.

The renewed discussion of the Negro problem in the late eighties and early nineties and the efforts of Southerners to circumscribe the rights of the Negroes by "legal" measures evoked new attacks by the Northern press, both religious and secular. Southern Baptists again defended the South's handling of the race question, but their defense was not apologetic as it had been during the "babble of the journals" in Reconstruction days. Employing ridicule and countercharges of discrimination, Baptists launched out boldly in defense of Southern "institutions." The Georgia paper, for example, castigated the Cincinnati *Journal* for its Pharisaism in criticizing racial discrimination in the South, while at the same time, the editor asserted, the people of Cincinnati were practicing racial segregation as rigidly as Southerners:

All this clatter about race-prejudice is sheer hypocrisy; it comes from men who are just as full of the so-called race-prejudice as anybody else; or, we may say, as everybody else; for the feeling is universal. It is not a prejudice, however; it is an instinct.[31]

29. Southern Baptist Convention, *Annual, 1900*, p. 36.
30. *Alabama Baptist* (Montgomery), June 22, 1899, p. 3.
31. *Christian Index* (Atlanta), August 22, 1889, p. 1.

A week later the same editor called the New York *Independent* the "most negrolatrous paper in the United States." He went on to defend the South's treatment of the Negroes both before and after emancipation. American Negroes, he said, under the "influence of the Southern whites, cavaliers by descent and Christians by the grace of God," had attained the highest civilization known among any Negroes on earth. Northern criticism of the South was unchristian and unjust.[32] All the arguments between the sections served only to fix more firmly upon the South the patterns of race relations which had developed since emancipation.

Baptists defended segregation in the closing years of the century as divinely ordained. "The color line," said one paper, "remains just where the Almighty put it, and there it will remain."[33] A Georgia pastor denied that he was "drawing the 'color' line" in supporting segregation. "I am only showing that it exists," he said, "and that the Creator in His wisdom decreed it."[34]

Baptists also held that both races preferred segregation. Negroes as well as whites demanded it and racial harmony required it. The Georgia paper asserted:

The line of demarcation is observed as rigidly by Negroes as by whites. So it is, so it has been, and so it will be, and it is right. . . . Living together and in parallel lines, there is perfect peace between the races, but if forced into as close association as some of the Northern people seem to desire, there will be dreadful collisions, and eventually extermination of the weaker race. We are for peace.[35]

Whites who worked for integration did themselves and Negroes a disservice, declared the Virginia paper. Negroes "feel an inexpressible contempt for the whites that would force themselves upon" them.[36]

In contradiction to this view, the editor of the Georgia paper accused the Negro preachers in Atlanta of seeking integration of the races in 1892 when they proposed a mutual exchange of pulpits with white preachers:

The whole movement is a step, and quite a bold step, in the direction of social equality. . . . We have had the kindest feelings toward the negro

32. *Ibid.*, August 29, 1889, p. 1.
33. *Ibid.*, July 4, 1889, p. 1.
34. *Baptist Courier* (Greenville, South Carolina), November 21, 1889, p. 1.
35. *Christian Index* (Atlanta), September 5, 1889, p. 1.
36. *Religious Herald* (Richmond), May 14, 1891, p. 1.

race. . . . But if separation from the whites, entirely, is what they demand, or else indiscriminate commingling of the races, we say, most emphatically, let the separation come, and let it be complete. . . . When he [the Negro] begins to demand social equality he steps into a territory he can never occupy. The sooner this lesson is learned and practiced the sooner he will have settled security in the enjoyment of his civil rights. . . . Race prejudice is as deep seated in the minds of the white people of the north as of the south. It is an ineradicable antipathy, planted by nature in the very constitution of both races. It can not be removed until all the white people are made negroes, or all the negroes made white people. Neither bayonets or bullets, neither human laws nor the laws of God as revealed in the Bible can change the natural instincts of either race. The only hope of peace, psosperity [*sic*], and progress for either the black or white man is for each to make himself contented and useful and faithful in the sphere where God has placed him. . . . Let each know his place, stay in it, and do his duty there, and we shall have no trouble, otherwise, there will be conflict, bloodshed, extinction.[37]

In all their media of expression Baptists manifested the same determination as other Southern whites to keep the Negroes separated from and subordinated to themselves. The delegates to the Southern Baptist Convention repeatedly proclaimed the inferiority of Negroes. They admitted that their mission program to Negroes was predicated on the assumption that Negroes would accept a subordinate position.[38] The Mississippi Convention adopted a report in 1894 which acknowledged that

for their good as well as ours we must stand in ranks unbroken on the line that separates us as distinct races and give no place for social equality. Then we shall have their respect. . . . We must take care of him, for in his place he is the best man in the South and for the South, now or ever will be, in our judgment.[39]

In 1900 Baptists still maintained that whatever work was done among the Negroes would be done with "proper respect for the existing and ineradicable social conditions" of the races.[40]

Baptists preferred to maintain segregation and white supremacy by legal, or at least nonviolent means, but they were not averse to sanction-

37. *Christian Index* (Atlanta), May 26, 1892, p. 4.
38. Southern Baptist Convention, *Proceedings, 1891,* p. XXXVI; *Christian Index* (Atlanta), May 26, 1892, p. 4.
39. Mississippi Baptist Convention, *Proceedings, 1894,* p. 26.
40. Southern Baptist Convention, *Annual, 1900,* p. CXXVII.

ing or giving tacit approval to the use of extra-legal methods and even violence in achieving desired ends. They remained ominously silent toward the Ku Klux Klan and similar organizations after the war. In one of the rare references to the Klan during the sixties, the editor of the Georgia paper declared in a reply to a question from the Boston *Christian Era* that he was not a member of the Klan and that he had opposed it and would continue to do so.[41] A careful reading of the paper, however, failed to reveal a single word of reproof against the Klan before or after this time.

The Virginia weekly in 1871 defended the actions of the Ku Klux Klan and similar organizations under certain circumstances. Although the editor asserted his respect for the principle of law and order, he said:

We think it possible that cases may occur, in which, from the defects of laws, or the failure to execute them, honest men may unite to defend their rights, by means outside the laws.

Dishonesty in government, bribery and perjury in the courts, unlawful use of Negro troops, and other corrupt practices during Black Reconstruction, created circumstances which warranted the use of extra-legal methods, he maintained.[42] In the same issue a resident of South Carolina obliquely sanctioned the Klan. He denied that the Klan or any klan-like organization disturbed anyone, black or white, Democratic or Republican, "whose character is good and whose conduct has been orderly." The Klan, he continued, had never been known to inflict injury upon "any but bad men." In defense of the Klan against specific accusations, he continued:

The store that was burned by them was a thieves' den; the demagogue that was driven off was a felon or an incendiary; the negroes that were hung, without judge or jury, were assassins. . . . A disguised vigilance committee, they have inflicted the rude justice which the powers of the State refused or proved unable to do. The white robes they wore were the ermine of Judge Lynch. . . . We do not approve such organizations, but if ever any vigilance committee could plead an extenuation for its illegal performances, this can find many an excuse in the present condition of affairs at the South. In its application to a variety of crimes and criminals, the law of the land is a dead letter. In such a case, men do become "a law unto themselves." [43]

41. *Christian Index* (Atlanta), July 8, 1869, p. 106.
42. *Religious Herald* (Richmond), May 18, 1871, p. 1.
43. *Ibid.*

Other papers offered excuses for or defended the tactics of night riders. At no time during Reconstruction did Southern Baptists condemn unequivocally the extra-legal methods employed by Southern whites to bring the Negroes under control.

At the end of Reconstruction, however, Baptists rather abruptly changed their attitudes toward the personal and property rights of Negroes, and for the succeeding twelve or fifteen years they catagorically denounced acts of racial violence. "We set our face like a flint against mob law under any and all circumstances," wrote one editor.[44] The response of the Virginia paper to the lynching of a Negro woman in Rockingham County, Virginia, for allegedly burning a barn was typical of many outbursts of Baptist papers against crimes inflicted on the Negroes:

The hanging of the colored woman by the Rockingham mob was murder—murder by the laws of the State, by the voice of Christendom, and by law of God—murder in the first degree, for it was committed by the instigation of the devil, and with malice aforethought—and murder, we may add, with scarcely the semblance of an apology. . . . We sincerely lament the unfortunate event. . . . The whole county, indeed the whole State, must share in the reproach and ill effects of this outrage.[45]

In the late eighties and early nineties, Baptists, especially in the Lower South, again underwent a marked change of attitude toward lynching and mob rule. As in Reconstruction days, they did not condone acts of violence against the Negroes, but they offered grounds for justification. Lynchings continued, Baptists claimed, because of lax law enforcement, inept juries, unscrupulous lawyers, and, above all, the persistence of the Negroes in committing the "crimes which lie at the bottom of these lynchings." [46] The Georgia paper declared in 1892:

There is swift justice awaiting the brutes who are guilty of the fearful crime for which negroes are usually lynched in the South. We do not defend the lynching, but he who commiserates the brute is far more despicable than the lynchers.[47]

44. *Christian Index* (Atlanta), March 7, 1889, p. 1.
45. *Religious Herald* (Richmond), March 21, 1878, p. 2.
46. *Christian Index* (Atlanta), June 9, 1892, p. 1.
47. *Ibid.,* June 16, 1892, p. 1.

The great majority of lynchings in the United States occurred in the South, the Georgia paper admitted. This was true not because Southern whites lacked Christian character as Northerners charged, but because "they have a high sense of honor and highest regard for female character, so they lynch the black rapist." The remedy for lynching was to eliminate the cause, not denounce lynchers. "When the cause passes away or the courts mete out prompt punishment these things will change perhaps, and not before." The best way to eradicate lynching was to "elevate and Christianize the negro, to give him a moral uplift, above the commission of arson, assassination, rape, this, we think is the most excellent way for them to help to put down lynching." Negro men would have to be persuaded to stop committing the most "henious crime." [48]

Later in the decade of the nineties, opinion again shifted. Baptists ceased arguing that lynching for rape was the result of the uncertainty of lawful punishment, for evidently the argument was fallacious. As the Virginia paper repeatedly pointed out, no Negro who committed rape against a white woman ever escaped punishment in the courts. The law might operate more slowly than the public desired, but the punishment of a Negro guilty of the "nameless crime" was inevitable. [49] At the end of the century, Baptists achieved near unanimity in condemning crimes against Negroes. Most of the state papers spoke out boldly, and a number of state conventions also offered their protests. Of the twelve Baptist weeklies in the South, only the Georgia paper continued to justify lynching, but only for the act of rape. The editor said,

By common consent, lynching for rape has been made an offense to be condoned. But only when, by common consent, all other forms of mob violence are utterly repudiated, can we justify ourselves among civilized people.[50]

A short time later a prominent Georgia minister echoed the same views toward lynching: "We must abate the crime which provokes it," he said. "The ravisher must cease to assault our wives and daughters." [51] Except for these few instances and perhaps their failure to protest more vigor-

48. *Ibid.,* July 28, 1892, p. 4; November 2, 1893, p. 4.
49. *Religious Herald* (Richmond), September 14, 1893, p. 1.
50. *Christian Index* (Atlanta), March 23, 1899, p. 6.
51. *Ibid.,* May 11, 1899, p. 2.

ously against lynching and other injustices inflicted against the Negroes, Baptists were making a creditable record in defending the Negroes' rights to life, personal safety, and property at the close of the century.

By the close of the turbulent decade of the 1890's, Southern whites had solved the Negro problem to their satisfaction. The Negroes' status in society had now been defined by law as well as custom. Baptists were in full sympathy with the settlement. They welcomed the new state constitutions and franchise laws which successfully eliminated Negroes from politics, they firmly resisted all social contact between the races, they subscribed to the view that Negroes were destined to provide the labor force for the South, and they resolutely refused to admit Negroes into their churches.[52]

An examination of the attitudes and beliefs of Baptists about Negroes and whites indicates that Baptists subscribed to a fairly definite body of racist ideas. These ideas were neither logically developed nor systematically stated, nor were they held exclusively by Baptists. They constituted an integral part of the cultural heritage of Southern whites which Baptists understood and defended.

Underlying the racial views of Baptists were four basic concepts:
1. that mankind was a unity, created by God of "one blood,"
2. that God had divided mankind into races,
3. that races differed biologically, the principal distinguishing characteristic being that of color, and
4. that the white race was superior to the colored race and that Anglo-Saxons were superior to all other branches of the white race.

52. Rather surprisingly, perhaps, Baptists had little to say about the "Jim Crow" laws being enacted in the closing years of the century. The term "Jim Crow" appeared only once in the materials covered in this study. A contributor to the Virginia paper commented in 1900, "When the negro can be made to feel that his is an inferior race and must be satisfied to remain as such, then, and only then will his real improvement begin. As a means to this end, we hail the 'Jim Crow' car bill, and ask that further legislation will provide separate waiting-rooms at all railway stations."—*See Religious Herald* (Richmond), September 20, 1900, p. 3. Also, Baptists gave very little attention to the far-reaching Supreme Court decision, *Plessy v. Ferguson*. In the only reference to the decision noted in the course of research, the editor of the Tennessee paper simply observed that the decision would have effects throughout the South. *See Baptist and Reflector* (Nashville), May 21, 1896, p. 1. Although Baptist commented very little on specific segregation laws, many other statements reveal their approval of these proscriptive measures.

From these basic ideas Baptists deduced a number of corollaries:

a. that God intended the differentiations of mankind to be permanent,
b. that a "law of race," evidenced by instinct and natural antipathy between the races, forbade amalgamation,
c. that science could verify racial differences and rate them qualitatively,
d. that miscegenation polluted the superior race,
e. that hybrid races (and individuals) were inferior to both parent races and that hybrids tended to revert to a parent type,
f. that *complete* separation of the races was necessary to prevent amalgamation, except under circumstances in which both whites and Negroes recognized and accepted their respective superior and inferior statuses,
g. that no amount of training and education could lift the Negro race to the level of the white race; removed completely from the influence of whites, Negroes would lapse back into barbarity,
h. that Anglo-Saxons were chosen by God to rule America and the world or at least spread their superior civilization throughout the world,
i. that the superiority of the white race was confirmed by history, observation, and the Bible,
j. that some Negroes were superior to some whites, but (contrary to point e) superior Negroes always had a mixture of white blood, and
k. that the slightest trace of Negro blood made a person "colored." [53]

To trace the development of each basic and secondary idea separately would involve unnecessary tedium. The "Baptist" concept of race will be discussed, therefore, as a whole, noting periods of stress and change.

Baptist ideas of race were *not* the product of the post–Civil War period. Erroneous conclusions about the origin of racism in the South have been drawn from the revival of racial tensions and the passage of the Jim Crow laws in the late nineteenth century. The paucity of well-articulated racist doctrines and the absence of segregation legislation before about 1890 have been confused with an absence of racism. Even so prominent a historian as C. Vann Woodward was guilty of leaving

53. These ideas accord generally with the popular views of race still prevalent in the South in the twentieth century. *See* Gunnar Myrdal, *An American Dilemma: The Negro Problem and Modern Democracy* (1944), I, chap. IV. The word "blood" is here used as it was commonly used in the nineteenth century to denote the carrier of genetic characteristics.

a false impression about the rise of racism in the first edition of his book, *The Strange Career of Jim Crow* (New York, 1955). This impression was corrected in a subsequent edition, in the Foreword of which Woodward said:

The new edition of this book provides a welcome opportunity to treat of some of those things and to clarify points that the original edition left unclear.

In the first place, although the segregation system is relatively new, it is grounded upon theories and attitudes that are not at all new. It is a mistake to assume that the ideas of innate Negro inferiority and white supremacy originated along with the Jim Crow system, for they are much older. . . . In so far as segregation is based upon these assumptions [Anglo-Saxon superiority and African inferiority], therefore, it is based upon the old proslavery argument and has remote roots in the slavery period.[54]

The only thing new about racism in the late nineteenth century was the claim that racism had a basis in science. The attempt to justify racism scientifically stemmed from the efforts of Blumenbach and others who sought to classify man as Linnaeus and Buffon had classified the plant and lower animal kingdoms. The attempt was unsuccessful, but classifications —many of them—appeared anyway, neatly arranging the races of man in orders of ascending and descending value qualities. Racists could *use* this "scientific" evidence to strengthen their arguments, but such evidence added little to racism because racism was a conglomeration of feelings, attitudes, emotions, and suppositions and not a demonstrable fact. The times demanded a new statement of old ideas and science furnished the vehicle, but the essence of the thing being expressed was the same.[55]

Baptist ideas of race, therefore, extend far back into the past and provide a continuing basis for determining the relationship between the races in the South which even the Civil War and Reconstruction could not materially alter. To antebellum Southerners, Negroes were not simply unfortunate persons caught in the system of slavery; they were inferior beings, incapable of rising to the level of white men under any

54. *The Strange Career of Jim Crow* (rev. ed., 1957), pp. xi–xii.
55. Pre–Civil War concepts of race are treated in the following: Oscar Handlin, *Race and Nationality in American Life* (1957), pp. 3–73; M. F. Ashley Montagu, *Man's Most Dangerous Myth: The Fallacy of Race* (3rd ed., rev. and enl., 1952), pp. 1–32; and Stanley M. Elkins, *Slavery: A Problem in American Institutional and Intellectual Life* (1959), pp. 61–62.

circumstances. Southern whites accorded free Negroes no higher standing in society than slaves simply because they were free. Free Negroes were subject to the same prejudices and discriminations as Negroes still in bondage. It is not the purpose of this study to trace the complete history of racist theories among Southern Baptists, but a few citations from prewar records are useful in indicating the existence of definite racist views long before emancipation. The Texas Baptist Convention in 1860, for example, designated the Negroes as "mere operatives" who, "without guidance of another race, relapse back into their original barbarity and misery." [56] The Kentucky General Association in the same year spoke of the Negro as

marked by Providence to be a servant. We know that this fact is disputed by many, still among the white race in the Southern States there is no difference of opinion upon this subject; all are united in opinion in reference to the political, intellectual and social inequality between the colored and the white races. And the people of our Commonwealth generally feel that the present condition of the colored race in this country accords both with the Word and the providence of God.[57]

The Louisiana Convention called the Negroes a "class of humanity" among whom the gospel seemed to spread faster than among "their superiors." [58] The essentials of racism are evident in these expressions.

The Civil War and emancipation intensified race feelings and led to the further elaboration of racist doctrines. During the first two or three years after the war, Baptists expressed most of the racist views which they were to hold for the remainder of the century. Basic to their concept of race was the idea that mankind was a single species, created by God in a single, miraculous act. Their authority for this belief was the story of creation as related in the first three chapters of Genesis and St. Paul's statement that God "hath made of one blood all nations of men for to dwell on all the face of the earth, and hath determined the times before appointed, and the bounds of their habitation." [59] In accepting the unity of the races Baptists differed from many people in both North and South. No less an authority than Louis Agassiz advanced the theory that

56. Texas Baptist Convention, *Minutes, 1860*, p. 5.
57. Kentucky Baptist General Association, *Proceedings, 1860*, p. 23.
58. Louisiana Baptist Convention, *Minutes, 1862*, p. 13.
59. Genesis 1:26–28; 2:7, 18–25; 3:20; Acts 17:26.

Negroes and whites were the results of separate acts of creation. The Virginia paper accepted Agassiz's "scientific proof" of the differences between the races, but denied that such distinctions had resulted from different creative acts.[60] Baptists generally condemned the popular forty-eight page pamphlet entitled *The Negro* by Ariel,[61] which denied the descent of Negroes from Adam and Eve. The arguments contradicted the Bible, they said, and its author deserved to be classed with "Gibbon, Paine, and other atheists." [62]

While holding that all human beings had descended from God's one creative act through a single pair of parents, Baptists nevertheless believed that mankind had been divided into races differing fundamentally from one another. They did not agree on how the differentiation had come about, but they attributed it to God's creative will. Some Baptists surmised that the races may have originated at Babel where God, according to the Genesis account, had confused the tongues of men. "I know not but that color and language went together," said a contributor to one paper.[63] Others believed that God had created man "under laws which developed the differences which science has demonstrated." Still others held that God, "for wise and beneficent purposes, by direct interposition" has impressed racial differences upon certain peoples.[64] This last view was the one most widely held by Baptists. They offered no detailed explanation of the origin of the all races, but the black race, they believed, was descended from Ham, whom Noah had cursed with perpetual servitude. As a sign of the curse, God placed on Ham and his descendants a "mark," which Baptists interpreted as black skin.[65]

By whatever method the races may have been distinguished, Baptists considered it the work and will of God and, therefore, intended to be permanent. To ensure the separation of the races, God had imposed biological differences on each race, differences which everyone could observe and which science could demonstrate. The most obvious biologi-

60. *Religious Herald* (Richmond), June 13, 1867, p. 1.
61. Ariel [Buckner H. Payne], *The Negro: What is his Ethnological Status? Is he the Progeny of Ham? Is he a Descendant of Adam and Eve? . . . What is his Relation to the White Race?* (1867).
62. *Biblical Recorder* (Raleigh, North Carolina), February 5, 1868, p. 1.
63. *Religious Herald* (Richmond), April 19, 1866, p. 1.
64. *Ibid.,* June 13, 1867, p. 1.
65. *Ibid.,* August 16, 1866, p. 1. The story of Ham is related in detail, pp. 120–121.

cal characteristic was skin coloring, described by one writer as the "handiwork of God" benignly given to keep the races apart.[66] Besides skin color, races differed in temperament, intelligence, and potentiality; and to preserve these differences, God had implanted in each race a natural aversion to all other races. The editor of the Virginia paper said,

These differences utterly unfit [the different races] for intimate social and religious relations. These differences God has ordained, and we should not endeavor to efface them.[67]

Baptists' insistence on keeping the races separated was a logical consequence of their belief in the superiority of the white race, especially Anglo-Saxon whites. Contrary to the opinions of some of his fellow-Southerners, the editor of the Virginia paper saw no danger in educating the freedmen:

Let them be taught in Sunday schools and day schools. . . . We need cherish no jealousy of their improvement. The Anglo-Saxons can have no cause to fear competition, in any department of enterprise, with any race of men; and certainly not with the African race.[68]

In an address before the Alabama Legislature, Issac T. Tichenor also pleaded for schools and kind treatment for the freedmen. The "white people of the South, with our superior culture, intelligence and christianity," he said, should develop a "benign attitude" toward the "weak and dependent" ex-slaves who "now have the misfortune to be free." [69] Negroes were "a greatly inferior race to the whites," said Professor John A. Broadus, and the Virginia paper described them as the race "farthest removed, perhaps, in their physical, mental and moral characteristics from us." [70]

The Reverend James C. Hiden, a leading Baptist minister in Virginia, grew belligerent at the suggestion that a "natural equality" existed between the races. "Natural equality, indeed!" he exclaimed,

when science has demonstrated—not conjectured—that there is not a bone, nor a muscle, nor a drop of blood, nor indeed any single organ of the negro which is the same in material and in structure with the corresponding organ

66. *Religious Herald* (Richmond), August 23, 1866, p. 1.
67. *Ibid.,* May 19, 1868, p. 2.
68. *Ibid.,* October 19, 1865, p. 2.
69. *Christian Index* (Atlanta), February 17, 1866, p. 29.
70. *Religious Herald* (Richmond), May 10, 1866, p. 1.

of the white man; and that there are as many, as real and as wide differences between the negro and the white man, as between the Arabian race-horse and the common ass. . . . [God] has shown himself to be no leveler. . . . This wild and chimerical notion of universal human equality is essentially opposed to the divine model.[71]

While disagreeing with Agassiz over the origin of race, the Virginia paper, nevertheless, accepted his description of the differences between whites and Negroes. There were greater structural differences between a white man and a Negro man than between a Negro man and a chimpanzee, the editor said. Quoting a letter from Agassiz, he continued:

"In his bones, muscles, nerves and fibres, the chimpanzee has not much further to progress to become a negro than a negro has to become a white man. This fact science inexorably demonstrates. . . . The negro is no more the white man's brother than the owl is the sister of the eagle, or the ass is the brother of the horse." [72]

The belief that the white race was superior to the Negro race was the most widely held tenet of Baptists' racial creed.

Believing then that the white race was superior to the Negro, Baptists logically opposed the contamination of the superior race by intermarriage. Two quotations from the many that could be cited will illustrate this view:

Let us hold in just abhorrence the miscegenationist, who, warring against the law of the Creator, would degrade our noble saxon race—the race of Newton, Milton and Washington—to a race of degenerate mongrels.[73]

· · · · · · · · · · · · · · · · · · ·

We, belonging to the more improved class, should do what we can to promote the physical, intellectual and religious welfare of the negroes; but we owe it to our race, our history, and our posterity, and to civilization, to maintain the purity of our blood, and to perpetuate the distinctions which have their foundation in nature. We shrink, with absolute abhorrence, from all approach to the commingling of the two discordant races.[74]

The foregoing views expressed in the two- or three-year period immediately following the Civil War remained essentially the "Baptist" view

71. *Ibid.,* May 13, 1875, p. 1.
72. *Ibid.,* June 13, 1867, p. 1. Quotation from the *Medical and Surgical Reporter* (Philadelphia), May 25, 1867.
73. *Religious Herald* (Richmond), June 28, 1866, p. 2.
74. *Ibid.,* March 19, 1868, p. 2.

of race until the end of the century. Baptists' relations with Negroes always were predicated on the assumption that Negroes were inferior to whites and that this relationship was unchangeable. Theories of race were as much a part of Southern Baptist thinking as the Virgin Birth or the Second Coming.

If the number of articles appearing in their journals is a criterion, the early 1870's was the period in which Baptists were most keenly interested in the race problem. Hardly any phase of the issue—theoretical or practical—escaped their attention. In a series of seven articles in the Tennessee paper in 1872, a contributor presented what he called the definitive exposition of the origin of race. Citing the biblical story of Noah and his sons Japheth, Shem, and Ham as his authority, he said,

I object to and condemn equality of the races, because I conscientiously believe, with all the power of my soul, that the law of races as given by Noah most positively and pointedly forbids it.[75]

In succeeding articles he developed his thesis in detail: After the flood, by which God destroyed all mankind except Noah and his family, Noah blessed Japheth and Shem but cursed Ham and condemned him to the permanent status of servant. The mark of the curse was dark skin. On these propositions, the writer said, "hinge the whole argument." Japheth became the progenitor of the white race, Ham fled to Africa and fathered the black race, while Shem drifted eastward and founded the Asiatic races. Color, the writer asserted,

is a primordial characteristic, impressed on the three great races of mankind in the immediate family of Noah. . . . The color of the Japhetic race points them out as a superior race. What is so attractive amongst all the races as the beautifully fair and ruddy complexion of that race?[76]

The descendants of Japheth—the Greeks, Romans, and north Europeans —conquered the Asiatics and enslaved the Africans, he continued, and "the whites, the pure Caucassian [sic] blood, have ruled ever since." In

75. *The Baptist* (Memphis), September 7, 1872, p. 1. The passage cited as authority was Genesis 9:25–27: "And he [Noah] Said, Cursed be Canaan; a servant of servants shall he be unto his brethren. And he said, Blessed be the Lord God of Shem; and Canaan shall be his servant. God shall enlarge Japheth, and he shall dwell in the tents of Shem; and Canaan shall be his servant." Two points are often confused in retelling the Biblical account: "Ham's curse" was actually pronounced by Noah (not God) on Canaan (not Ham).

76. *The Baptist* (Memphis), October 26, 1872, p. 1.

view of the sacred account of Noah's prophecy and its fulfillment in history, "how dare any assert that all men are equal, and claim an equal share of privileges and immunities?" he asked. Baptists generally accepted this explanation of the origin of races.[77]

During the period of intense discussion in the early 1870's when Baptists were reaffirming their racial views, they reiterated no tenet of their creed more frequently nor defended any more eloquently than their belief in the necessity of maintaining racial purity. Intermarriage would elevate the Negro race, one writer admitted, but at the tragic cost of degrading the superior white race:

Amalgamation gives a hybrid race, inferior in physique and moralé [*sic*] to the white, superior to the black. . . . If we could not reach the conclusion, that the hybrid is physically and morally inferior to the white, by reasoning from the natural endowment of races, it needs but poor Mexico to demonstrate it by experiment. Weak in body and dull in intellect, such a population can add nothing to the glory, and little to power, of a country. . . . Break down the influence of caste, and this process of absorption will be greatly accelerated. . . . To level downwards is a crime against the nobler race; it mars the variety and beauty of the natural creation; introduces confusion in the handiwork of the Creator; obstructs the progress and injures the well-being of society. Thus to alloy the purest intellect . . . is high crime against the God who made us. To shield us from such a calamity, is a work worthy of the highest effort of the noblest statesman.[78]

A long editorial in the Virginia paper described racial mixing as the greatest tragedy which could befall mankind. The English-speaking people (whom the editor equated with the "white race") were superior to all

77. *Ibid.*, September 7, 1872, p. 2. Attributing the origin of the Negroes to the curse of Noah was not original with Southern Baptists. The idea was prevalent at least as early as 1700. See Charles H. Wesley, "The Concept of the Inferiority of the Negro in American Thought," *Journal of Negro History*, XXV (October 1940), 542. Research failed to reveal any Southern Baptists who accepted Darwinian evolution as the explanation of the races, although a few references suggest that some Baptists may have accepted theistic evolution. "We feel almost compelled," proclaimed a Virginia Baptist in 1874, "to suppose a more extensive succession of ages [than the 6,000 years commonly attributed to man's residence on earth] during which external causes have produced and fixed, by transmission, so many peculiarities" on the different races. He emphatically denied the atheistic implications of Darwinian evolution, however.—See *Religious Herald* (Richmond), September 24, 1874, p. 2.

78. *Religious Herald* (Richmond), February 19, 1874, p. 1.

other peoples in all fields or would soon be, he contended. To mix the
superior white race with other races would imperil their superiority:

The maintenance of its [Anglo-Saxon race] purity and the perpetuation of
its influence are a solemn, sacred duty. To place any portion of it under the
control of an inferior race, and to adopt laws for the purpose of forcing it
into social relations and intercourse with such a race, obliterating the distinctions which nature has made, and tending to its mongrelization, is a war upon
civilization, and outrage against humanity, and disloyalty to the Supreme
Ruler. But when it is proposed to subordinate the highest to the lowest race
of mankind, or to force them, by rigid laws, into social intercourse and unity,
no language can express the folly, injustice and mischiefs of the measure. Just
think of it. A race that leads the world in art, commerce, religion, and every
noble enterprise—the only people capable of self-government—to be placed
under the heel of a race, or to be coerced into social amalgamation with it,
that, in thousands of years, has never written a book, or built a ship, or
opened a road, or subordinated a beast to its use, or made any progress in
civilization, except in a state of slavery, or as the result of it, is too bad. There
is no portion of the Anglo-Saxon race, not blinded by fanaticism, degraded by
oppression, or misled by a shallow humanitarianism, that would for a moment
submit to it, except at the point of the bayonet, and under the relentless grasp
of tyranny. . . . There are instincts of race that cannot be repressed by legal
enactments. There are rights of nature, pertaining to the Anglo-Saxon race, as
well as to other races of men, that cannot be invaded, without the stern
uprising of all that is true, and noble, and heroic in humanity, to resist the
outrage.
    In conclusion, we say: Let all races and classes of men have their rights;
nay, more, let them be treated kindly and generously; but, if it can be done
without violence, let the independence and the supremacy of the Anglo-Saxon
race be maintained; and, at all hazards and every sacrifice, let its purity and its
social instincts and respectability be preserved.[79]

Following the period of extreme racist expressions in the early and
mid-seventies, Baptists had relatively little to say about race for the next
ten or twelve years. During this time they refused to recognize the
Negroes as anything more than freed slaves and continued to affirm their
faith in white supremacy. One audacious young preacher from Alabama
went so far as to proclaim the whole Bible as nothing more than the
history of the white race:

79. *Ibid.,* September 17, 1874, p. 2.

The *ethnological difficulties* are greatly diminished, if not done away, by accepting what more and more becomes apparent, that the Bible history is, in the main, an account of the fortunes and achievements of the white race through which the Savior, the printing press, the steam engine, the telegraph, and all else worth anything to the world, were ordained to come.[80]

In an attempt to explain to Northern critics why Southern whites refused to accept Negroes as equal, John A. Broadus described the majority of Negroes in the South as depraved savages. There were three distinct "races" among Southern Negroes, Broadus maintained. The smallest and most intelligent group was composed of "brown negroes" who had come from central Africa. The second group were the "black negroes" with "good features." They had thin noses and lips and high foreheads and exhibited but slightly less intelligence than the brown Negroes. The third and largest element of the Negro population was the "black negroes" who had been brought from Guinea and the Congo. These were distinguished by the

flat nose, thick lips, low forehead, and ill-shaped skull. If any of these show high intelligence, the cases must be very rare. And unfortunately the overwhelming majority of American negroes are of this class. . . . They are a sadly low grade of savages.[81]

In 1883 one of the associate editors of the Georgia paper presented what he called the "orthodox" position on the race question. He proclaimed good will toward all races, "yet," he said, "we have our preferences. . . . The ties of blood we can not ignore, and race is only another name for blood." He professed great love for all mankind, but greater love for the English-speaking people, still more for the American English-speaking people, and the greatest love for "those known as the 'Southern people' of that race. . . ." He continued:

Our affection for peoples shades off according as they are more remote from us, either in race, or in nationality, or in geographical position. . . . We do not believe that "all men are created equal," as the Declaration of Independence declares them to be; nor that they will ever become equal in this world, and perhaps not in the world to come. . . . We believe that some of these various races are inferior to others in physical organization, in intellectual ability, and in capacity for development, political, social, moral, or religious,

---

80. *Alabama Baptist* (Selma), November 17, 1881, p. 2.
81. *Religious Herald* (Richmond), April 20, 1882, p. 2.

and that they will so remain until the end of time. . . . We think that our own race is incomparably superior to any other, and that our distant cousins of the Aryan family in India are next best. The people of Terra del Fuego are perhaps the worst. . . . As to the Negro, we do not know where to place him; perhaps not at the bottom of the list, but certainly not near the top. We believe that fusion of two or more of these races would be an injury to all, and a still greater injury to posterity. We think that the race-line is providential, and that Providence intended that it should be perpetuated unless a new dispensation should blot it out. . . . [Any mingling of races is evil for] it must have its origin in sin. We think that any legislation, preaching, teaching, or action, which tends to promote great intermingling, unnecessarily, is unwise and wrong. We have no dealings with other races than our own except to do them good, or for purposes of business, and we prefer to have as little business with them as possible. . . . Instinct is unconquerable; and it *ought* to be. . . . This is our "Confession of Faith." We think that we are orthodox. If we are not so, we should be glad for someone to point out the heresy.[82]

Evidently this editor's views were orthodox, for no one pointed out any "heresy."

After the ten or twelve years of relative silence, discussion of the Negro problem increased perceptibly in the last decade of the century. During this time Baptists identified themselves fully with Southern "conservatives" who were determined to maintain the "blessings of white supremacy" at all costs. At their conventions and in their papers they repeatedly expressed their contempt for the inferior Negro race. So outspoken were they that one of their own preachers cautioned them against stating the obvious too often: "Grant that the race is inferior," he said, "we remind them of it often enough without putting it in every declaration about our religious relations to them." [83]

Baptists added little that was new to their views of race in the closing years of the century, except to elaborate more fully their belief in Anglo-Saxonism. They saw in the conflicts in Cuba, the Philippines, and South Africa the beginnings of white domination in those areas. "The English-speaking people are rapidly becoming the dominant race of the globe," declared the Report of the Home Mission Board in 1896: "Their ancestry, whose history begins with the morning twilight of the world, built

82. *Christian Index* (Atlanta), March 22, 1883, p. 4.
83. *Baptist Courier* (Greenville, South Carolina), January 28, 1897, p. 1.

their growing power on their love of home, their love of land and their unconquerable desire for personal independence. Home and country and liberty became the watchword of their progress, and from the dawn of history to the present hour have reverberated down the centuries." A segment of this race founded the Indian Empire, the report continued; other elements swarmed over the plains of Persia, other groups founded the civilizations of Greece and Rome, still other tribes of whites settled England, Scotland, and Ireland. The nearly one hundred twenty million people who "speak their language" were those "whose industry and skill and enterprise and courage and intelligence and moral power is unexampled among the nations past or present." [84]

The triumph of the Anglo-Saxon race, Baptists believed, was not by chance, nor by the workings of natural laws only, but by the expressed will of God, whose ultimate purpose in favoring the race was to use it in spreading the word of salvation to all the world. The delegates at the Southern Baptist Convention in 1890 expressed the belief "that the religious destiny of the world is lodged in the hands of the English-speaking people. To the Anglo-Saxon race God seems to have committed the enterprise of the world's salvation." [85] Although God had chosen the whole Anglo-Saxon race to work out His purpose in the world, Baptists felt that He had given the greatest responsibility to Americans and especially to Southerners. The Georgia paper declared,

There is a vast community in this Southern land of ladies and gentlemen, of blue blood, and high breeding, many of them refined by grace, and all of them fair representatives of the very best part of the Anglo-Saxon, or rather of the Anglo-Norman race. Blood will tell, and the cavalier still lives; and a Christian cavalier is a cavalier indeed, and a Christian indeed.[86]

The South, with its purity of race, its abounding wealth, and its orthodox religion, was the home base from which the gospel was to be spread around the world. The Southern Baptist Convention declared in 1896,

No portion of this [Anglo-Saxon] race has been dowered with more magnificent advantages than that one which inhabits this Southern land. . . . Who can doubt that he means to give it the post of honor as the light-bearer of the world? . . . We hail every increase of material power [in the South],

84. Southern Baptist Convention, *Proceedings, 1896*, p. LXVII.
85. Southern Baptist Convention, *Proceedings, 1890*, p. VIII.
86. *Christian Index* (Atlanta), June 20, 1889, p. 1.

every field of springing grain, every opening mine, every rising manufactory, every extending railroad, every new channel of commerce, every steamer that plows the deep as God's agent working to accomplish his will, of filling the earth with his glory.[87]

An article entitled "The White Man's Burden" in the *Christian Index* of Georgia in 1899 expressed the epitome of Anglo-Saxonism:

Blessed with the marked favor of God, endowed with the cream of earth's intellect, given power and dominion on land and sea, and acknowledged the world's peers in diplomatic skill, they stand before God to-day as the chosen people of his Providence, and as the leaven to leaven the lump of his purposes. . . . Every victory for American arms means in the Philippines, as it did in Cuba and in the conquering of the savage Indians, an advancement of the plans of God in the calling out of his sheep which shall hear his voice and follow him. . . . Oh, let the stars and stripes, intertwined with the flag of old England, wave o'er the continents and islands of earth, and through the instrumentality of the Anglo-Saxon race, the kingdoms of this world shall become the kingdoms of our Lord and his Christ! May the Eagle's scream and the Lion's roar echo and reverberate over earth's mountains and valleys, sending terror to the heart of tyranny and freedom to the shackled slave.[88]

Baptists fully supported the prevailing racist views of Southern whites throughout the late nineteenth century. Arguing from the Bible, history, science, instinct, and observation, they proclaimed the eternal supremacy of the white race. Any solution to the Negro problem, they maintained, would have to come within the range of action approved by Southern society. "Let him [the Negro] stay absolutely in his own sphere, and let us manfully, religiously and patriotically maintain our dignity, supremacy and social status in our own sphere," cautioned the *Alabama Baptist*.[89] The Baptist view of race was the Southern view!

87. Southern Baptist Convention, *Proceedings, 1896,* pp. LXVII–LXVIII.
88. *Christian Index* (Atlanta), August 3, 1899, p. 3.
89. *Alabama Baptist* (Montgomery), April 26, 1900, p. 4.

5. Economic Problems

ETWEEN 1865 and 1900 the basis of the American economy shifted from agriculture to industry. The census reports of 1890 indicated for the first time that the value of industrial goods had come to exceed the value of agricultural products. American industry had come of age. Industrialization proceeded most rapidly in the North and Northeast, but with the development of textiles, steel, lumbering, and other industries, the South too was experiencing significant change by the turn of the century.

Agriculture remained the chief economic activity of the South, however, and the problem of its revival after the devastation of war remained the South's primary economic problem. Southern agriculture suffered from the disruption of its labor system, the destruction of land improvements and capital investments, the scarcity of credit facilities, competition of foreign cotton, a wasteful but expanding tenant system, and the debilitating hold of the one-crop system. The economic recovery of the South depended on the solution to these problems—and few were solved before the end of the century.

Industrialization and the peculiar problems of the South created economic and social problems and raised moral and ethical questions for which tradition furnished no answers. Proposed solutions ranged from complete socialism to an unyielding defense of the status quo. American churches were slow in recognizing the significance of the changes going on about them; consequently, they had little to offer toward solving the problems of the new age. For the most part, religion constituted a mainstay in the conservative defense.

Baptists as a denomination had few suggestions for solving the South's farm problems. With a membership drawn predominantly from rural areas, the denomination might logically have concerned itself with the farmers' plight, but such was hardly the case. Journals and convention deliberations indicated little interest in ameliorating the economic condition of farmers. All the state papers carried special farm columns from time to time, but these columns contained mostly quoted material from farm journals and practical suggestions for curing hay, seeding tobacco, spreading manure, repairing machinery, and the like. Seldom did the papers grapple directly with specific problems. Baptist papers were not unaware of the farm problem, however. Editors devoted considerable space to lamenting the farmers' plight, but suggestions offered to meet specific problems evinced little zeal or originality. Most suggestions merely emphasized the virtues of hard work. Suggested remedies were not often pursued in subsequent issues.

On the crucial problem of farm labor, Baptists expressed the belief and the hope immediately after the war that immigrants would replace the freedmen, whom Southerners considered unreliable and undesirable as farm labors in their new status. Chinese coolies were considered a possible source of cheap labor for the South.[1] Very few Chinese immigrants settled in the South, however, and Baptists then advocated diverting the stream of European immigration southward—a suggestion voiced at intervals for the remainder of the century. This source of labor also failed to materialize, and by the early 1870's Southerners were compelled to admit that farm labor would have to come from the South itself. By this time the Negroes were returning to the farms and plantations after their first fling of freedom. Contrary to earlier speculation, they had neither migrated in large numbers, nor had they become a "vanishing race." The freedmen, whose emancipation had created the labor problem, would also be the solution to the problem. The real problem was how to employ them most effectively.[2]

1. *Religious Herald* (Richmond), August 12, 1869, p. 1; *Christian Index* (Atlanta), April 25, 1867, p. 72; Southern Baptist Convention, *Proceedings, 1871*, pp. 24, 55. One Baptist, after a trip to an area of California where a large number of Oriental immigrants had settled, declared that Chinese laborers would never solve the South's labor problem. After only a few years in California, he said, they were already making more money than Negroes in the South. Orientals would not be content to remain laborers but would rise to the independent farmer class. Furthermore, he added, Chinese would make undesirable farm laborers because of their non-Christian religious and moral beliefs.—*See Western Recorder* (Louisville), June 26, 1879, p. 1.

2. *Biblical Recorder* (Raleigh, North Carolina), June 9, 1869, p. 4; *Western Recorder* (Louisville), December 18, 1869, p. 1; *Religious Herald* (Richmond), August 3, 1871, p. 4; *Christian Index* (Atlanta), May 6, 1880, p. 5. The problem of farm labor was restricted primarily to the large plantations where

As a means of easing the labor problem, Baptists frequently suggested that farmers with large acreage sell part of their land and cultivate the remainder with few or no hired workers. Not only would this solve the labor problem but it also would provide cash for immediate use. Furthermore, crop yields would improve as a result of more intense cultivation.[3] Dividing the plantations was not the solution, however, for large landowners were reluctant to part with their land. For those who wished to continue the plantation system, the labor problem remained most difficult.

Baptists were generous, and often contradictory, with their advice to the planter class. Baptists accepted emancipation as an accomplished fact, and they agreed that the freedmen should be treated with firmness, honesty, and impartiality, but beyond this there was little agreement. The majority favored a wage-labor system rather than sharecropping, but they differed on specific plans. The editor of the Virginia paper advised large farmers to contract their laborers for wages and to maintain stores of supplies for resale to them "at a profit sufficient to pay all risk and interest on the money." And, he continued, "Never pay them more than half wages till the end of the time for which they contract to work."[4] In contrast, another Virginia Baptist admonished:

In dealing with the colored population we have found that the only way we can manage them is to pay them promptly for what they do. They are utterly incapable as a class of looking to the future, and the prospect of immediate reward is the only thing that will stimulate them to exertion.[5]

A contributor in another journal found after years of experience that the best system was to hire Negroes for an entire year, pay them a portion of their wages each month, but withhold most of their pay until the end of the year. This would give them an incentive to work month by month and also to remain until the end of the year.[6]

Although a wage system was preferable, few Southern farmers had

---

slaves had done most of the work before emancipation. The majority of Southern farmers continued to work their small farms in much the same manner as before the Civil War.

3. *Religious Herald* (Richmond), September 7, 1871, p. 4; *Christian Index* (Atlanta), March 28, 1867, p. 56.
4. *Religious Herald* (Richmond), January 19, 1871, p. 4.
5. *Ibid.,* March 6, 1873, p. 4.
6. *Biblical Recorder* (Raleigh, North Carolina), January 9, 1884, p. 4.

sufficient cash to pay wages. Sharecropping, therefore, was the only recourse. For a few years after the war, Baptists considered sharecropping wasteful and ruinous to landowners but *potentially* advantageous to tenants. If a tenant were energetic and frugal, he might rise to the landowning class. But after observing the system in operation a few years, they conceded that sharecropping was harmful to tenants also because it destroyed ambition and encouraged slothfulness. Although they recognized the disadvantages of sharecropping, they accepted it as inevitable.[7]

Significant as an indication of conservative Baptist thinking on economic matters was the scarcity of radical suggestions for solving the labor problem, such as the destruction of the plantation system and the division of land among the landless classes. The following excerpt from the Georgia paper is a rare exception to the general attitude:

We know that the landed aristocracy look with much disapprobation upon the efforts the middle and lower classes are making to procure homes of their own; that they are endeavoring to prevent the division of their large estates, and trying, by fine promises, to hoodwink the laboring classes into a kind of feudal tenancy system, by which their estates may remain entire, cheap labor supplied to them, their influence felt, and themselves allowed to revel in sumptuous idleness. But, my brother laborers, pay no heed to the false flatteries, cunning expostulations, or imperative threats of these landsharks. It is the *duty of every man* to work for his living. . . . Yes, let us, brother farmers, abandon these drones to their own *aches* and acres; go to work upon land of our own . . . and pretty soon we shall see the aristocracy coming to us for bread, or better, perhaps, see them with laudable zeal taking hold with their own hands to cull from the soil a living. Let us welcome and aid those that are so doing.[8]

That more expressions of this kind did not appear reflects, perhaps, the upper-class control of Baptist papers (or at least a striving by those who controlled the papers for upper-class status) or, perhaps more important, the absence of class consciousness and antagonism among Southern whites. As a whole, Baptists found little fault with the class structure and recommended changes in the plantation system only as a practical necessity.

    7. *Religious Herald* (Richmond), June 13, 1872, p. 4; *Christian Index* (Atlanta), July 24, 1879, p. 2; July 23, 1887, p. 13.
    8. *Christian Index* (Atlanta), June 17, 1869, p. 96.

Another difficulty confronting Southern farmers after the Civil War was the lack of capital and credit facilities. This was even a greater hindrance to agricultural recovery than the labor problem because it affected small and large farmers alike. The war destroyed the South's financial structure and left farmers the unhappy choice of attempting to farm without cash and credit or of seeking credit from Northern sources at ruinous rates of interest. Since credit was a necessity, Southern farmers had no choice but to borrow money wherever it could be found. Excessive interest payments drained the South of its precious profits and helped fix on it the one-crop system.[9]

Baptists were aware of the money problem, but their suggested remedies usually were shallow and unimaginative and totally within the framework of conservative economic thinking. They urged farmers to live frugally, to work hard, to buy on credit as little as possible, to diversify their farms and depend less on outside purchases, and, most frequently, to sell part of their land and use the proceeds as operating capital. Baptists had very little to say about free silver or any of the soft-money ideas of the time. A Mississippian advanced the only radical scheme noted in the course of research. He proposed that Congress print an unlimited supply of paper money and lend it to the states. The states then would make it available to farmers in renewable loans at 6 percent interest, payable January first of each year.[10] Evidently Baptists saw little merit in this plan, for they did not mention it again.

The tenant and credit systems devised in the South after the war to meet the labor and money problems resulted in the one-crop system. Because cotton was always marketable, landowners and moneylenders insisted that farmers over whom they had control cultivate cotton to the near exclusion of foodstuffs and produce of questionable market value. These three elements—cotton, credit, and cropping—remained the nemesis of Southern agriculture for the remainder of the century.

Baptists expressed near unanimity in condemning the one-crop system and in extolling the virtues of diversified farming. They advised farmers to raise more corn, to devote part of their land to cattle and sheep grazing, to plant cover crops which could be cut for forage or turned

9. Charles H. Otken, *The Ills of the South* (1894) *passim;* E. Merton Coulter, *South During Reconstruction* (1947), pp. 190–195; C. Vann Woodward, *Origins of the New South,* (1951), pp. 180–184.

10. *Southern Baptist Record* (Meridian, Mississippi), February 12, 1891, p. 1.

under for fertilizer, to raise fibers for clothing and return to home manufacturing of wearing apparel, to grow grapes and even to initiate wine manufacturing, to experiment in tea and silk culture, to introduce commercial poultry farming, and in other ways to break away from their total dependence on cotton. Most Baptists agreed with the editor who said: "The trouble with the average cotton planter is that he believes too much in cotton and too little in breadstuffs. He ought to raise his own produce and have his cotton money extra." [11] The advice was good, but few farmers were able or willing to declare independence from King Cotton.

The efforts of farmers to improve their lot by organizing received the approbation of Baptists generally. During Reconstruction Baptist papers ardently supported farmers who united to oppose Northern opportunists. Southern farmers "must band together," said a South Carolinian, "or be immolated by the cormorants, land sharks, and skinflints infesting every village, town and city, throughout our land." Farmers' clubs could go far toward solving the labor problem by regulating Negro labor, he continued, and more important, they could break the power of middlemen, railroads, corporations, bankers, market manipulators, packing houses, and millers who exploited the disunited farmers. Simply by publishing accurate production figures, for example, farm organizations could prevent market manipulation by "speculators and traders, who put their goods at a high price, and the poor man's cotton at a low one." [12] Farmers were at the mercy of "wealthy gentlemen of elegant enterprise, seated in a private parlor or around a board of direction," argued another Baptist, because farmers were

cut up into isolated fragments. . . . All other interests are armed and constantly on a war footing. Among the powerful nations of Europe, when one arms, all must arm. So it is in all communities. When every interest is cared for, when every interest is prepared for defense, all are cared for. Then there is equity, justice, peace and prosperity for all.[13]

Although united action promised beneficial results, Southern farmers were apathetic toward organizing. Baptists did little to encourage organization. For a few years after the war, they recommended argicultural fairs

11. *Religious Herald* (Richmond), May 28, 1885, p. 1.
12. *South Carolina Baptist* (Anderson), October 2, 1868, p. 4.
13. *Religious Herald* (Richmond), May 20, 1869, p. 4.

as rallying points around which farmers could organize, but when fairs came under the control of large planters who used them for their own purposes, often to the detriment of small farmers, Baptists withdrew their support. Furthermore, Baptists were reluctant to endorse agricultural fairs when horse racing and sideshows became the chief attractions.[14]

The *idea* of co-operative action for the betterment of agriculture remained attractive to Baptists, but they could not agree on the objectives to be sought nor the methods to be employed. Generally they approved farmers' clubs for the dissemination of information and the co-operative expression of protest against specific evils, but they only partially supported, or more often opposed, those organizations which meddled in politics and religion. For example, the Baptist press both praised and condemned the Patrons of Husbandry (or Grange). The Virginia paper commended the Grange in 1873 for its successes in the West and expressed the hope that farmers in all sections would lend their support. Thereafter, however, the paper gave little attention to the Grange and even criticized its secret ritual and hierarchical organization.[15] In contrast, the Georgia paper fervently supported the Grange. For several years in the 1870's it even carried a special column headed "The Patrons of Husbandry" in which it reported the activities of the Georgia Grange in detail.[16] Baptists as a whole did not support the Grange, however.

Toward the Farmers Alliance Movement, the most powerful farm organization for political action in the nineteenth century, Baptist opinion ranged from lukewarm support to open hostility. The Georgia paper wrote approvingly of the Alliance Movement in 1888: "This is an indication of the gigantic efforts being made by the farmers to improve their condition. . . . The agriculturists of the country have aroused from their lethargy, and are determined to rank with those enterprising and progressive spirits that are moving onward and upward in other industries of the country." But, the editor continued, the farmer's success depended "principally on his own individual effort, thrift and

14. *Ibid.,* April 29, 1869, p. 4; October 13, 1870, p. 4; *Christian Index* (Atlanta), April 1, 1869, p. 51.

15. *Religious Herald* (Richmond), October 16, 1873, p. 4; December 4, 1873, p. 4; July 2, 1874, p. 1; March 1, 1883, p. 3.

16. *Christian Index* (Atlanta), November 13, 1873, p. 6. The support given the Grange by the *Christian Index* raises the suspicion that some connection existed between the two, but none was discovered in the course of this study.

economy." [17] An editorial in the Alabama paper criticizing the Alliance evoked a letter in defense of the Alliance. The Alliance, the reader said, would hurt no one except "anarchists, communists, socialists and monopolists. . . . 19/20th of our churches are supplied by preachers who are mostly farmers [and] the membership of our churches are [*sic*] mostly farmers." Baptists therefore should support the Alliance. It would make them better farmers and better churchmembers. [18] The most serious indictment of the Alliance came from a successful Virginia planter, Major A. H. Drewry. The Alliance, he said,

can do me no good. I need no office. I have no ax to grind. . . . I do not believe in being run by a miserable set of old hacks who will fleece the farmers just as the carpetbagger did the negroes at the close of the war. They are doing it now, and their zeal for the poor farmer is a hollow pretense. [19]

Not even so prominent a Baptist and Allianceman as Leonidas L. Polk could evoke much enthusiasm from Baptists for the Alliance movement, even in his native North Carolina. [20] The reasons for the failure of Baptists to support the Alliance are not readily apparent. The reasons most often advanced were the distrust of Alliance leadership and the implication of the movement in politics. Whether Baptists feared the Alliance as a possible threat to white supremacy in only conjectural. It is true, nevertheless, that Baptist papers remained ominously silent on the Alliance movement when it entered politics as the Populist Party in the crucial election of 1892 and 1896. [21]

Baptist attitudes toward farm organizations ranged, therefore, from enthusiastic support of the *idea* to complete disapproval of specific efforts. Baptists most friendly to the idea considered united action the means by which "the farmer class is to cut the gordian knot that has bound him so long and so completely to the chariot of his oppressor," [22] while at the

17. *Christian Index* (Atlanta), June 7, 1888, p. 13.

18. *Alabama Baptist* (Montgomery), March 1, 1888, p. 1. The editorial referred to appeared in the issue of February 9, 1888, p. 2.

19. *Religious Herald* (Richmond), October 1, 1891, p. 2.

20. Polk was founder and editor of the *Progressive Farmer*, president of the Southern Alliance, and president of the North Carolina State Baptist Convention.

21. C. Vann Woodward attributes the defeat of the Alliance Movement in the South to the fear among Southerners of splitting the white vote. *See* his *Origins of the New South*, pp. 244, 254–263. This study of Baptists neither confirms nor denies this view.

22. *Biblical Recorder* (Raleigh, North Carolina), March 4, 1885, p. 4.

opposite extreme were those who viewed any co-operative action with suspicion.

The demand by certain malcontent farm groups for federal and state aid to agriculture as a means of bettering farm conditions received scant support in Baptist circles. Baptist papers usually expressed approval of laws to protect farmers from market manipulators and businessmen in general, but they generally opposed as unnecessary expenditure of tax funds, any direct aid to farmers in the form of state-supported agricultural colleges, state commissioners of agriculture, a federal department of agriculture, and statistical reports by state and federal agencies.[23] Baptists considered the farm problem outside the province of governmental action.

What was the Baptist solution to the farm problem? As individuals Baptists proposed a variety of remedies, but as a denomination they did little more than espouse the Puritan ethic. They agreed that economic prosperity bore a relationship to spiritual well-being. As one Florida Baptist put it, the farmers' troubles could be traced to the same source whence issued all the ills of mankind—"the World, the Flesh and the Devil." Against this enemy, he concluded, only the gospel could prevail.[24] Similarly viewing the farmers' plight as basically spiritual, a Tennessee Baptist advised farmers who were caught in the predicament of high interest payments, low income, high prices, and market manipulations to remember that "all things work together for good to those who love the Lord." Furthermore, he advised farmers not to lose their religious zeal, "do not stop taking your religious paper," and "lay not up for yourselves treasures on earth. . . ." If Baptist farmers, smarting under their grievances, found little of practical value in these suggestions, they must have been less than comforted by the writer's parting benediction: "May God bless you and prosper you."[25] As impractical as these suggestions may appear, they are more representative of Baptist thinking on the farm problem than the remedies proposed by Grangers, Alliancemen, and Populists.

While the South was struggling to revive its agricultural economy after the Civil War, the North was experiencing the revolutionary effects

23. Expressions favorable to state and federal aid to agriculture appeared mostly in the ten-year period after the Civil War.
24. *Florida Baptist Witness* (Ocala), December 25, 1890, p. 2.
25. *Baptist and Reflector* (Nashville), July 10, 1890, p. 8.

of industrialization. By the turn of the century, industrialization had reshaped every phase of society in the North. Enterprising industrialists and financiers had amassed fortunes and power which staggered the imagination. Wealth had become the criterion of status, and, protest as they might, the old aristocracy was forced to yield to the irresistible onsurge of the *nouveau riche.* Paradoxically, the same machines which produce the *parvenu* also created a new proletarian class which shared only scantily in the new wealth of the machine age. Constantly increasing from the influx of workers from rural American and from the flood of the new immigration, the labor class concentrated around the factory sites and created unprecedented problems of urban existence.

The new age of big business brought with it its own standards of morality and conduct. The new businessman who operated behind the façades of the impersonal corporation could not be bound by the moral code which had regulated the activities of business men in a simpler era. The new age obviously challenged the traditional Protestant business ethics. According to the Protestant ethic, the greatest returns should go to the man who worked the hardest, but the new age rewarded the cunning manipulator and unscrupulous monopolist. Could the accumulation of wealth by such dubious means be equated with the traditional Protestant morality? Could rugged individualism which benefited the few and exploited the many be justified in the light of Christian principles? Could wealth be considered a mark of God's favor as formerly believed? Was poverty, the lot of the sluggard to Poor Richard, necessarily the result of a man's slothfulness in a system which restricted individual opportunity? The new era of rugged individualism had its defenders in William Graham Sumner and the conservative Social Darwinists. It also had its critics in the reform Social Darwinists led by Lester Frank Ward and in the communists, socialists, anarchists, social gospelers, and a host of others. American Protestantism, by and large, defended the prevailing economic system.

The prosperity accompanying industrialization in the North became the envy of the poverty-stricken South, and the belief among Southerners that industrialization was the only solution to the South's economic ills gained wide acceptance through the New South Movement. Baptists, with near unanimity, welcomed industrialization. Expressions of approval appeared frequently in their state papers from 1865 to 1900. "The increasing rattle of looms and spindles in Georgia, Tennessee and Alabam[a], is the 'music of the future,' to which the South will keep harmonious step in the national march of progress," commented one editor.[26] A series of essays in the same paper recounted the advantages of industrialization and predicted that the South, because of its natural advantages—abundant water power, proximity to raw materials, plentiful and cheap labor supply, suitable climate, and inviting markets— would soon surpass the North as the textile center of the nation.[27] The North Carolina paper welcomed the appearance of every new mill in that state as a contribution toward economic recovery and happiness for everyone. The editor commented that factories would give employment, and "employment, wages; wages, comforts and education, and these last bring prosperity and happiness."[28]

Not all Baptists, however, were sanguine about the prospects of industrialization. Although few, if any, opposed industrialization altogether, a vocal minority warned against its undesirable consequences. In an article in the Georgia paper entitled "The South's Prosperity—A Matter of Joy —Then of Sadness—Now of Astonishment," a promoter of industrialization attempted to allay the rising apprehension among Baptists. He admitted that material progress was no substitute for spirituality, or "real" progress, but increased wealth could lead to better schools, more churches, and the furtherance of the gospel which did constitute true progress.[29]

The universal objection among Baptists to industrialization arose from the fear that industry would lead to rapid urbanization which in turn would corrupt morals and hinder the spread of Christianity. A committee at the Southern Baptist Convention in 1894 reported an alarming and increasing tendency among the people of the South to abandon the rural areas and "to overcrowd the cities." This condition, the report continued, "increases competition in standard business, creates an abnormal relationship between capital and labor, compels an unnecessary degree of poverty and, by reason of all these conditions, aggravates the temptations and evils peculiar to crowded communities."[30] "If we mean to take this

26. *Christian Index* (Atlanta), January 22, 1874, p. 5.
27. *Ibid.* (Atlanta), January 12, 1871, p. 8, January 26, 1871, p. 16.
28. *Biblical Recorder* (Raleigh, North Carolina), March 21, 1888, p. 1.
29. *Christian Index* (Atlanta), August 2, 1883, p. 2.
30. Southern Baptist Convention, *Proceedings, 1894,* p. 23.

country for Christ," said a similar committee in 1900, "we must make sure of the cities, for from them go forth those influences which bless or curse mankind." [31]

More frightening to Baptists than the migration of rural Southerners to the new urban centers was the prospect that industrialization would draw foreigners to Southern factory towns and industrial cities. Delegates at the Southern Baptist Convention in 1895 adopted a report describing the alarming consequences of immigration already apparent in the North:

Foreigners are accumulating in our cities, and hence our cities are the storm centers of the nation. But the great misfortune of all of this is that these foreigners bring along with them their anarchy, their Romanism, and their want of morals. We must evangelize them, or they will overwhelm us.[32]

This antipathy for immigrants in the 1890's is in marked contrast to the attitudes of Baptists in the late 1860's when they looked to Europeans to replace Negroes as agricultural laborers in the South.[33] Evidence is overwhelming, however, that Baptists opposed more than welcomed immigration.

The problems of industrialization were primarily academic for the denomination, for Baptists remained a predominantly agricultural people. Nevertheless, they expressed an avid interest in labor-management disputes and similar problems arising in other sections of the country. The many strikes which swept the industrial sections and occasionally invaded the South were the subject of numerous articles and editorials and occasionally received the attention of Baptist conventions.

Baptists consistently expressed sympathy for the working man, but they often criticized his efforts to improve his condition. They defended the right of labor to organize but set limits to which unions could go in pursuing their aims. They even accorded labor the right to strike as long as strikes did not jeopardize property and the public welfare. They opposed picketing and the efforts of strikers to prevent scabs from working during strikes. Concerning the railroad workers' strike against the Baltimore and Ohio Company in 1877, one editor commented:

We maintain the right of all men to enter into such combinations, and to adopt any means, not in contravention of law and justice, to secure their ends. Laborers have a right to strike for higher wages and capitalists for lower. To

31. Southern Baptist Convention, *Annual, 1900,* p. 39.
32. Southern Baptist Convention, *Proceedings, 1895,* p. 38.
33. *See* p. 128 for comments favoring European immigration.

strike for higher wages, and to prevent laborers from working at the established or lower rates, are quite different measures. All attempts to interfere with free individual or combined contracts to labor for wages, low or high, are in violation of the laws of men and of God, against the interests of society, and subversive of the very foundation of social order. If laborers, of any class, without or with cause of complaint, may break up the travel and trade on railroads, or arrest any other kind of business, at their own pleasure and for their own profit, then all right is disregarded, all laws are trampled in the dust, and all authority is overthrown. We are at the mercy of mobs.[34]

The Kentucky weekly was even more outspoken against the strike. Its editor called the strike "utterly unjustified . . . wrong in principle and a mistake in fact." Leaders of the strike and participants and their sympathizers were "entitled only to the consideration which is accorded public enemies." Workmen had the right to contract their labor, the editor conceded, and to stop work if they desired, "but there the right ends. They have no right to lift so much as a little finger to prevent others from working at rates and under conditions they refuse. . . . Law and order and the rights of property must be maintained whatever the cost," he continued. "Civilization, Christianity, even while they may weep over the cruel necessity which is forced upon them, have no alternative but to unite in the enforcement of law."[35]

Although Baptists deplored the use of violence by strikers against management, they sanctioned the use of force by management in defense of property. Commenting on the Homestead strike of 1892 and the Pullman strike of 1894, the Georgia paper declared:

The remedy for the state of things where violence interferes with the rights of other workers, applies the torch for the destruction of property or uses any other means to accomplish the same ends, and to jeopardize the lives of innocent people, is the bayonet and the bullet, promptly and fearlessly applied. Gentleness in dealing with such outlaws is simply cruel injustice to law abiding, peaceable citizens.[36]

The Mississippi paper argued that strikes hurt not only management and the public but also the strikers themselves:

Perhaps workingmen will learn after a while that even low wages and sure pay and constant employment is [*sic*] better than striking for higher wages,

34. *Religious Herald* (Richmond), July 26, 1877, p. 2.
35. *Western Recorder* (Louisville), July 26, 1877, p. 4.
36. *Christian Index* (Atlanta), July 19, 1894, p. 4.

with long intervals of idleness, bootless conflicts and a final return to work at the same old wage-rate. Such seems to be about the way all of the recent strikes have terminated or will most likely terminate. Let all of us hope that all of this experience, want, suffering and disappointment will serve to teach a little wisdom to all workingmen.[37]

With few exceptions Baptists defended management against the efforts of labor to secure a greater share of the new wealth of the industrial age.

Only rarely did the Baptist press give labor unqualified support. One such instance was a series of articles in the Kentucky paper by Arthur Yager, professor of history and economics at Kentucky Baptists' Georgetown College. Professor Yager defended labor and all its methods. He maintained that unorganized labor was at a disadvantage in its struggle with organized capital. Only by thoroughly organizing could labor overcome this disadvantage, and until organizations could be effected, labor was justified in strengthening its demands through strikes, boycotts and, when the cause demanded, through destruction of property.[38]

Yager was obviously at variance with his brethren, however. Alabama Baptists more accurately reflected Baptist thinking when they declared at their state convention in 1886 that Christianity was the remedy for labor-management difficulties:

As a power in civil, social and domestic life, Christianity must ever stand confessed as the most influential ever brought to bear upon human character and destiny. . . . Its language to capital is, "Do justly, love mercy, and walk humbly with thy God;" its language to labor is, "Be content with your wages." [39]

Baptists seemed totally unatuned to the realities of industrial America. At no time before the end of the century did the denomination admit the necessity of modifying its traditional approach in order to cope with the problems of the modern world. The simple preaching of the gospel was still the panacea for all the ills of mankind.

As suggested by their defense of capital in all labor-management disputes, Baptists considered the existing free-enterprise system the best possible of economic orders. They defended capitalism against all threats —communism, socialism, anarchy, old world "agrarianism," and all

37. *Baptist Record* (Jackson, Mississippi), July 5, 1894, p. 1.
38. *Western Recorder* (Louisville), April 15, 1886, p. 1; April 29, 1886, p. 1. Other articles appeared in subsequent issues.
39. Alabama Baptist Convention, *Minutes, 1886*, p. 12.

forms of statism. They ridiculed Dennis Kearney's Workingmen's Party on the West Coast by labeling it "California Communism." [40] They called Johann Most, the noted European socialist newly arrived in the United States, a "pestiferous fellow . . . modern Attilla . . . most consummate hambug." He was fit only for the penitentiary, "generally the Arcadia of his sort of gentry." [41] They condemned Eugene Debs for his part in the railroad strike of 1894, while they congratulated President Cleveland for his use of federal troops in defense of capital.[42] "The right of private property lies at the foundation of all social order," said one editor. "There can be no enterprise, no industry and no government without it." [43] "The maintenance of the rights of private property is absolutely essential to the existence of civilized society," the same editor said later. "Every attempt to overthrow the rights of private property is a war on civilization and human happiness." [44]

Although Baptists staunchly defended the American politico-economic system, they were not totally blind to its shortcomings. They defended the corporate form of business which had made possible the tremendous concentration of economic power, but they also criticized the abusive use of this power. The North Carolina paper blamed the impersonal corporation for a mine disaster which cost the lives of forty miners: "Not all corporations are soulless," said the editor, "but this one is, and its like have brought reproach upon the very name corporation." [45] "Corporations are necessary," said a contributor to another journal, "but it is also needful to remember that they are not soulless, irresponsible machines, but made up of living men with duties to God and the world, and what we need today is a better understanding of this psychology of corporations and a quickening of the sense of moral responsibility for their acts." [46]

Another evil in the economic order which Baptists singled out for criticism was the liaison between government and business. Baptists questioned the justice in protective tariffs, subsidies to business, land grants and loans to railroads, monopolistic franchises, the use of the

40. *Christian Index* (Atlanta), March 11, 1880, p. 5.
41. *Ibid.,* January 11, 1883, p. 11.
42. *Ibid.,* July 12, 1894, p. 2; *Baptist and Reflector* (Nashville), July 19, 1894, p. 1.
43. *Religious Herald* (Richmond), May 9, 1878, p. 2.
44. *Ibid.,* December 25, 1879, p. 2.
45. *Biblical Recorder* (Raleigh, North Carolina), February 5, 1896, p. 1.
46. *Religious Herald* (Richmond), May 21, 1891, p. 1.

armed forces in behalf of corporations, and the maintenance of a hard money system.[47] Criticism of this kind appeared only occasionally, however. Never did the denomination as a whole become concerned.

Baptists rarely questioned the basic soundness and essential goodness of the capitalistic system. Abusive practices and inequitable conditions in the economy were not faults of the system but rather reflections of weakness in human nature. The remedy for the flaws of capitalism was not to destroy or even to modify greatly the system but rather to reform the individuals responsible for operating the system. If businessmen and laborers would "adopt the law of justice as taught in the Scriptures," declared the Alabama paper, the flagrant abuses of capitalism would disappear. "We are all Standard Oil magnates," he said, "when it comes in our reach to pocket a dime at the expense of another." [48] The real problem was sinful man, not the economic order.

The most cogent criticism of American capitalism came from the pen of Professor Arthur Yager of Georgetown College. He not only criticized the obvious inequities of the economic order, but he also questioned some of its basic concepts. Some "new form of co-operative industry" would probably be necessary, he said, in order to ensure labor, capital, and the general public their proper interests.[49] "There is something wrong somewhere" when men like Jay Gould were accorded full rights of ownership and control over railroads which labor and public patronage helped build. Something was wrong in our society, he said, when

both law and universal custom give to the capitalist and the capitalist alone the *sole* ownership of the business, which capital and labor have jointly built up. . . . So accustomed have we become to this arrangement in the actual business world, that we have come naturally to think of it as both necessary and right; but as sure as there is truth in human reasoning there is a great injustice hidden away somewhere in the roots of the whole matter. . . . The present practice of granting these valuable public franchises to great corporations with almost unlimited privileges can not much longer be tolerated.

Government ownership of railroads and other great corporations concerned with the public interest might not be the best solution as some

47. *Ibid.*, October 16, 1873, p. 4; *Christian Index* (Atlanta), August 25, 1892, p. 4; *Biblical Recorder* (Raleigh, North Carolina), March 23, 1898, p. 1; *Alabama Baptist* (Montgomery), February 23, 1888, p. 1.

48. *Alabama Baptist* (Montgomery), July 22, 1897, p. 1.

49. *Western Recorder* (Louisville), April 29, 1886, p. 1.

reformers were advocating, he continued, but "it is to be doubted if a final solution of this great problem will ever be reached, until some sort of State control has been devised, which will amount to virtual ownership." [50]

In subsequent articles Yager criticized the government for permitting rugged individualists to operate unchecked. He described their methods as more extra-legal than legal, "a cross between bunko-steering and highway robbery." Modern industrial society had outgrown English common law, he maintained, and

not until the American people, fully awakened to the necessity of action, have thrown aside their old-fashioned *laissez faire* political economy, and have taken a firmer grasp upon the illusive forces of the commercial world, will these modern depredators be driven from their covers and forced to submit to the law.[51]

In the closing article of his series, Yager predicted that only changes of revolutionary proportions could correct society's economic ills. Current labor problems, he said, were

unmistakable signs that the present organization of industrial society is fundamentally wrong; that it is wrong in spite of the fact that our public economy, our political philosophy, jurisprudence, customs, traditions, all agree that it is right. . . . Nothing short of a complete revolution of social philosophy will ever bring theory and fact into harmony again. The world is now probably passing through this social revolution.

To prevent violent revolution, he continued, science, the state, and the church would have to co-operate in forming a new system and a new morality. What science dictated, the state should enforce and the church, sanction. Yager directed a parting blow at established religion for its support of the existing economic order. He concluded,

Now I assert, with all due reverence and humility, that the morality taught by the church at the present day is not a pure and perfect morality. It is a morality tainted by compromise with the existing economic order of things. . . . The spirit of modern business sums up these relations in the maxim, "Everybody must look out for himself," whereas Christ said love your neighbor as yourself. These two cannot be reconciled.[52]

50. *Ibid.,* May 6, 1886, p. 1.
51. *Ibid.,* May 13, 1886, p. 1.
52. *Ibid.,* May 20, 1886, p. 1.

Yager's views were unique among Baptists. Although Baptists were aware of the shortcomings of capitalism, they failed to see the fundamental conflicts which Yager pointed out and, consequently, they envisioned none of the drastic measures which he proposed. Basic reforms in the economic order would have to come from the masters of capital, who, being moved by the power of the gospel, would voluntarily correct the most flagrant abuses. Baptists approved industrial paternalism. They applauded factory owners who provided homes, schools, churches, parks, bath houses, and other factory-owned facilities for their employees. Pullman, Illinois, said one writer, was the ideal industrial community.[53] The South Carolina State Convention commended a certain Langley Manufacturing Company for donating to the State Mission Board a "beautiful house of worship, costing $3,000," and for promising to support a pastor "at $600 per year besides a parsonage." "Other corporations," the convention declared, "would find it to be to their interest to follow this noble example."[54]

Baptists rarely suggested means for improving the economic system which contravened the wishes of capital. Toward the end of the period some support arose among Baptists for child labor laws and for government arbitration in labor disputes, but Baptists, by and large, were staunch defenders of the status quo.[55]

Having given near unanimous support to the capitalistic system as it existed at the time, Baptists logically could be expected to defend the society which capitalism had produced. And defend it they did! Baptists subscribed to the Puritan concept of wealth and poverty. They accepted the unequal distribution of wealth as the natural and divine order of things. Gradation in wealth, commented one editor, "has its origin in natural and immutable laws," and any artificial effort to eliminate either wealth or poverty was contrary to natural order.[56] When a rich man acquired his wealth honestly and used it properly, said another editor, "it is perfectly fair to regard his financial success as a token of Divine favor; and increasing wealth may be evidence of increase in favor."[57]

53. *Religious Herald* (Richmond), December 4, 1884, p. 1.
54. South Carolina Baptist Convention, *Minutes, 1900,* p. 21.
55. *Christian Index* (Atlanta), November 23, 1899, p. 3; *Biblical Recorder* (Raleigh, North Carolina), November 7, 1900, p. 1.
56. *Religious Herald* (Richmond), May 2, 1878, p. 2.
57. *Christian Index* (Atlanta), November 21, 1878, p. 4. Reprinted in the *Baptist Courier* (Columbia, South Carolina), January 30, 1879, p. 1.

The power to acquire wealth was God-given, and one's failure to exploit his talents was a sin in the sight of God. "A man who has a talent for making money," one editor said, "is bound to employ it, as he is to use any other gift, for the glory of God."[58] Just as Paderewski and Tennyson excelled in music and poetry because of their superior abilities in these fields, so millionaires made their wealth because of their special talents for business. If injustices existed in the distribution of wealth, the fault lay with God who gave different degrees of ability, not with men who exercised their natural gifts. He continued:

That a business man should make a million, while the great mass can barely make a living, no more implies injustice than that one painter can sell a little picture for $10,000 while other artists live but one degree above starvation. . . . I must remain of the opinion that differences in the accumulation of wealth are, like differences in the accumulation of knowledge, a result merely of differences in personal gifts. . . . Wealth is for the greater part produced, not by the muscle labor of the workman, but by the brain labor of the employer . . . not by the men in the shop, who may have no idea what they are making, but by the employer in his office-chair, who thinks out what articles are most needed and how they can best be produced. . . . Wherein, then, is there an injustice if the increase of profit has mostly gone, not to the muscle laborer, but to the brain worker, who alone has brought about this increased production?[59]

The accumulation of wealth inevitably raised the question of the proper use of that wealth. The rich, according to Baptists, were required to use their money in a manner that would be pleasing to God, but the traditional virtues of frugality and thrift did not apply. It was the duty of the rich to spend. "If God has given a man wealth," said one writer, "it is an indication of providence that he ought to live like a rich man, and thus do his share of keeping up the high civilization of the world."[60] Commented another:

A rich man need not limit his personal and family expenditures to the mere necessaries of life. . . . Whatever tends to promote health, vigor, intelligence, refinement, comfort, innocent enjoyment and respectability, wealth may be legitimately used to secure. . . . God has placed us in a world, which he has benevolently furnished with the means of indulging our appetites and

58. *Religious Herald* (Richmond), April 4, 1872, p. 2.
59. *Ibid.,* May 24, 1894, p. 1.
60. *Christian Index* (Atlanta), October 27, 1887, p. 8.

gratifying our tastes; and he surely will not condemn the temperate and grateful use of his own bounties. To erect comfortable and tasteful dwellings, to supply them with neat and convenient furniture, to gratify the fondness for paintings and statuary, to spread a bountiful table, to be arrayed in good and tasteful apparel, to have handsome equipages for travelling, and to beautify grounds and gardens, are all lawful objects for the expenditure of money.[61]

Baptists praised the Vanderbilts for their lavish spending in developing Biltmore Estates near Asheville, North Carolina. "Mr. Vanderbilt," said one editor, "is illustrating the well-established principle of political economy, that money spent in luxury is not necessarily money wasted." Extravagant spending created employment for those engaged in service industries, stimulated the production of luxury goods, and in general improved the economy.[62]

If extreme wealth were divinely ordained, so was poverty. Just as wealth was inevitably limited to the few, so poverty was the inescapable lot of the many. One editor commented,

God has linked poverty with the whole system of truth. He has ordained it as a perpetual heritage of his people, as a condition of society as inevitable as society itself. . . . We must look at this matter, then, just as we look at any other of the divine enactments, as appealing to our Christian sensibilities. Poverty is not a mere accident, but a law of life . . . the normal state of society as God has constituted it.[63]

In another issue the same editor commented:

Poverty, when it comes upon a man as the natural consequences of his own faults or follies, may fairly be taken as an expression of Divine disfavor. When it arises from other causes, it may be regarded simply as the schooling of Providence.

When God withheld material blessings from some men's honest labors, he concluded, it may be "to keep them humble, and pure, and true, their nature being such that wealth would ruin them." [64] "If God has placed me [*sic*] in a state of poverty," added another editor, "and our honest, earnest exertions cannot extricate us from it, then that is the state which

61. *Religious Herald* (Richmond), April 4, 1872, p. 2.
62. *Ibid.*, May 21, 1896, p. 2. *See also* Georgia Baptist Convention, *Minutes,* 1892, "Report on Education," p. 24.
63. *Christian Index* (Atlanta), July 19, 1883, p. 8.
64. *Ibid.*, November 1, 1878, p. 4.

he has chosen for us, and if we humbly trust in him, and do his will, we shall find that it is best for us." [65] "Let the poor be able to say with Paul," admonished the Georgia paper, " 'I have learned in whatever state I am, therewith to be content.' . . . 'A good name is rather to be chosen than great riches, and loving favor rather than silver and gold.' " [66] Whatever one's station in life, Baptists believed, it could be considered the result of God's favor or disfavor, or man's own improvidence. In any event, man had no just complaint against the order of things.

The foregoing is a fair representation of "the Baptist" attitude toward wealth, although not all Baptists agreed. Dissent from the majority view appeared in the 1880's and increased in the next decade. Some Baptists held that possession of excessive amounts of wealth was wrong regardless of how the money might have been accumulated. The death of William H. Vanderbilt was the occasion for one editor to question the moral justification for the accumulation of so vast a fortune as the Vanderbilts possessed:

It is a question with us whether any man has a moral right to be the owner of property to the value of two hundred millions of of [*sic*] dollars. Of course, the legal right is not questioned; the point is, whether a man is doing his duty, either to God or his fellow-man, when he appropriates to himself ten thousand times as much as he can make any use of.

When did a man reach the point where he should begin to divide his wealth? "We answer in a word," the editor continued. "If a man has but a crust of bread, and sees his neighbor starving, he ought to break his crust in two and give half to his neighbor." [67]

A visit to New York in 1890 caused another editor to raise similar questions. He described for his Southern readers the contrasts between the palatial homes of the wealthy and the nearby squalid slums of industrial workers:

And not rarely by any means, the wealth which ministers to their pampered bodies has been squeezed out of the helpless wretches who drag out a miserable existence in the dirtiest quarter of the great city. Is it any wonder that men cry out against the existing order? [68]

65. *Religious Herald* (Richmond), April 4, 1872, p. 2.
66. *Christian Index* (Atlanta), October 27, 1887, p. 8.
67. *Ibid.,* December 17, 1885, p. 3.
68. *Religious Herald* (Richmond), July 17, 1890, p. 2.

The Georgia paper questioned whether large fortunes like that of Jay Gould's could be accumulated by honest means, while the Virginia paper reminded its readers that Christ's command to "lay not up for yourselves treasures on earth" was to be taken equally as seriously as "believe and be baptized." [69] In yet a more critical vein, the Virginia editor compared the bomb-throwing communist with the "wealthy communist"—the unscrupulous business man who took other people's money by legal but unfair means. Both were equally guilty, he said, but the latter was more reprehensible because he commanded the respect of society.[70]

The great majority of Baptists, however, failed to be disturbed by the apparent injustices in the distribution of wealth. Unequal possession of this world's goods was compatible with God's plan for men. The rich and the poor were obligated to each other, and each benefited from the existence of the other. One editor expressed it this way:

The interests of the rich and the poor, if not identical, are inseparable. The rich not only supply the wants of the poor, but furnish employment for them . . . and by their wages procure sustenance and comforts for themselves and their families. All the improvements made by the rich, all the luxuries they enjoy, and all the splendors by which they are surrounded, enure to the benefit of the laboring classes. . . . The manufacturer, who makes millions for himself, scatters millions among his employees.[71]

Furthermore, said another editor, the poor give the rich the opportunity to exercise the grace of benevolence, and the rich serve as examples for the poor to emulate. "The rich and the poor are not only a blessing to each other," he concluded, "but a necessity to each other. Society is a unit." [72]

When the comments of Baptists on economic matters are put in proper relation to their expressed opinions on other issues, it is apparent that the denomination was not greatly concerned with problems of the economy. They tended to accept the economy as they found it. They offered few criticisms and still fewer suggestions for improvement. In sum, they defended American capitalism as the best of all possible orders.

---

69. *Christian Index* (Atlanta), February 26, 1891, p. 9; *Religious Herald* (Richmond), February 23, 1893, p. 1.

70. *Religious Herald* (Richmond), September 21, 1893, p. 2. A few other articles hinted that excessive wealth was *ipso facto* ill-gotten. *See* for example, *Baptist and Reflector* (Nashville), September 25, 1890, p. 8, *Biblical Recorder* (Raleigh, North Carolina), September 27, 1893, p. 2.

71. *Religious Herald* (Richmond), May 2, 1878, p. 2.

72. *Christian Index* (Atlanta), October 27, 1887, p. 8.

6. Social Evils and Social Reform

H E slavery controversy and the sectional conflict which followed divided the nation's reformers and dissipated their energies. For almost a decade after the war, organized efforts for social betterment all but ceased. In the 1870's, however, survivors from the antebellum reform period united with a new generation of reformers to revive the crusading tradition. The last quarter of the century then became a period of intense reform activity.

The relationship of Southern Baptists to this reform movement was only tangential. For the most part they remained true to their historical mission of preaching the gospel and regulating the behavior of their own members. But as the century advanced, they became increasingly concerned with the conditions of society and lent their support to most phases of the secular reform crusade. Baptists usually approved those reform objectives for which they could find a precedent in the Bible or in traditional Christian morality, but they generally ignored or opposed those movements which lacked Biblical or moral sanction.

Upholding the Christian observance of the Sabbath was an objective of the reform movement which Baptists supported. They considered Sunday a day for worship, rest, and the performance of simple deeds of Christian benevolence. All unessential work should cease, and only those activities which contributed to the physical and spiritual improvement of individuals and the community should be permitted. These criteria were not difficult to observe in a simple agrarian society, but in the changing times of the postwar period, strict compliance was impossible. Rapid urbanization, the seven-day work week demanded by industry, the "continental Sabbath" introduced by the "new immigrants," and the loosening of theological dogma challenged the traditional ideals of the Puritan Sabbath.

For more than a decade after the Civil War, Baptists took cognizance of the increase in "Sabbath breaking" but considered the problem primarily the concern of churches and individual Christians. They upheld the

Protestant concept of Sunday as God's Holy Day and warned their members against making it a work day or a mere holiday. Before the end of the seventies, however, they admitted that churches and individual Christians no longer could cope with the problem. In an attempt to maintain the Puritan ideal, they projected their campaign to a larger audience beyond the church fold. In their journals and conventions, through secular societies and the secular press, and with the aid of the state, they sought to eliminate those Sunday activities which they considered to be desecrations of the Lord's Day—commercial entertainment and recreation, newspapers, parades, unnecessary civil functions, and business and industrial operations.[1]

Baptists criticized most severely industries and transportation companies which forced their employees to work seven days a week. The capitalistic system was worse than slavery, said one editor, for not even slaves worked on Sundays. Concerning the new industrial tyranny he continued:

It is a shame that our systems of labor are so exacting and so poorly remunerative as not to afford a larger liberty to our laboring classes. . . . A railroad is a bloodless and conscienceless thing, and in that respect it often bears a striking resemblance to the magnates who control it. The steamboat is the property of somebody, but that somebody is buried in the inaccessible mystery of a soulless company, and can hear no protest against its wrongdoings.[2]

The same editor said later,

If men are to have masters, in Heaven's name give us masters who have souls.[3]

Next to impersonal corporations, Baptists directed their strongest protest against fairs and expositions which opened on Sundays. They raised some objection to the Centennial Exposition in Philadelphia in 1876 and the several national and regional fairs which followed, but most vehemently they protested the Sunday opening of the Chicago World's Co-

1. *Christian Index* (Atlanta), August 24, 1876, p. 2; Kentucky Baptist General Association, *Proceedings, 1876*, p. 34; North Carolina Baptist Convention, *Minutes, 1878*, pp. 31, 37–38; Southern Baptist Convention, *Proceedings, 1879*, pp. 34–35 (This was the first such report at the Southern Baptist Convention.); *Religious Herald* (Richmond), March 4, 1880, p. 1; Arkansas Baptist Convention, *Proceedings, 1880*, p. 32.
2. *Religious Herald* (Richmond), April 6, 1882, p. 2.
3. *Ibid.*, March 8, 1883, p. 2.

lumbian Exposition in 1893. For three years before the fair began they used every means at their disposal to protest. They recommended flooding Congress and the managers of the fair with letters and petitions, and if this failed to close the fair on Sunday, they suggested boycott. "Let Christians give no countenance or encouragement to such wickedness by their presence or their money," advised one editor.[4] Because of the international character of the fair, Baptists considered the Sunday opening a disavowal of Christianity by "Christian America." The delegates to the Southern Baptist Convention in 1891 declared,

Be it resolved, that the Southern Baptists, in convention assembled, representing a constituency of 1,235,765 Baptists, respectfully petition the World's Fair management to close its gates on Sunday, thus giving due respect to the God of nations and to the Christian sentiment that underlies our civilization.[5]

In an article entitled "Awful," a contributor to one of the state papers predicted dire consequences to America for permitting the desecration of the Sabbath at Chicago:

This is more than a national sin; it is an international offence against God. . . . If God rebuked the personal sin of Moses by debarring him from entering into the promised land, and destroyed the nationality of the Jews because of their rejection of Christ, and drowned the antediluvians for their wholesale wickedness, shall not God avenge this high-handed affront from the modern world? I verily believe, that some awful judgment from heaven will mark the Almighty's displeasure at this audacious insult from the world at large.[6]

Coincidentally, a series of fires and storms swept the fair grounds in the summer of 1893 causing considerable damage, after which the management decided to close the fair on Sundays. "It is not affirmed," said one editor, "that the calamities are the logical consequence of their [the directors'] wickedness. Still, they are closely connected with the exhibition, and the directors did well to allow their full influence on their minds." Poor attendance and low gate receipts were the obvious reasons for closing the fair, he admitted, but regardless of the circumstances, the closing was a vindication of the ideals of Christian America.[7]

4. *Christian Index* (Atlanta), July 6, 1893, p. 4.
5. Southern Baptist Convention, *Proceedings, 1891,* p. 21.
6. *Religious Herald* (Richmond), May 25, 1893, p. 1.
7. *Christian Index* (Atlanta), August 3, 1893, p. 4.

In the last twenty-five years of the century, Baptists showed a decided change in attitude toward what they considered to be the proper means of combatting Sabbath desecration. From a policy of relying totally on church discipline and moral suasion, they began co-operating in the 1870's with nonsectarian sabbatarian organizations—the International Sabbath Association, the American Sabbath Union, and the Sunday League of America. And, in the last ten or fifteen years of the century, they came to agitate for state and federal laws to effect Sabbath reform. In 1887 Mississippi Baptists proposed a law which would prevent "running freight trains through the State on Sundays."[8] Alabama Baptists requested their legislature in 1892 to pass a law declaring "the hours of Saturday after 12m. duly authorized and set apart as a legal holiday" to enable industrial and other laborers to have time for recreation on Saturday afternoons so that the Sabbath could be reserved for worship.[9] Baptists in other states made similar requests.[10]

A few Baptists argued that the use of civil law to enforce a religious ideal violated the separation of church and state principle. "The New Testament affords the same authority for co-ercing [*sic*] men on Monday as it does on Sunday," argued one such objector, "and if it be scriptural to enact laws to prohibit vice, *as vice,* it follows that it is equally just and right to enact laws to compel men to holiness."[11] Advocates of Sunday laws maintained that such legislation did not contravene the separation principle. No religious creed was enacted in forcing industries, businesses, and recreational facilities to close operations on Sunday. Employees simply were protected in their right to exercise their own chosen religious convictions.[12] Furthermore, others argued, the law of the Sabbath transcended all man-made religious creeds. "Scientific experiment has shown," declared Texas Baptists, "that not only man and beast, but that machinery will do more work and last longer when the law is observed." Civil law for the observance of the Sabbath was merely legislation for the good of

8. Mississippi Baptist Convention, *Proceedings, 1887,* pp. 14, 35.

9. Alabama Baptist Convention, *Minutes, 1892,* pp. 34, 55.

10. *Christian Index* (Atlanta), September 26, 1878, p. 5; *Religious Herald* (Richmond), March 20, 1879, p. 1; Texas Baptist General Convention, *Proceedings, 1893,* p. 82; Tennessee Baptist Convention, *Proceedings, 1898,* p. 25; North Carolina Baptist Convention, *Minutes, 1900,* p. 47.

11. *Biblical Recorder* (Raleigh, North Carolina), March 17, 1875, p. 1.

12. *Religious Herald* (Richmond), April 13, 1876, p. 1; September 11, 1879, p. 2.

society and, therefore, wholly within the scope of the police powers of the state. That the law of the Sabbath was an adjunct to the Christian faith was only incidental.[13]

The introduction of a resolution at the Southern Baptist Convention in 1889 calling for the endorsement of the American Sabbath Union and its platform for a law to protect federal employees from Sunday work evoked what one observer called a "most interesting and able" debate. Opponents of the resolution labeled the proposed law a "Trojan horse . . . the thin edge of an entering wedge," and a step toward the "hateful union of church and state." "Government employees are not drafted," argued another; "let them go at something else and they would not have to violate the Sabbath." [14] The adoption of the resolution after prolonged debate was significant in clarifying the attitudes of Baptists on the question of Sabbath observance laws. Defenders of the separation of church and state principle continued to inveigh against Sunday legislation, but most Baptists showed little hesitancy toward the end of the century about petitioning either the national congress or state legislatures for assistance in promoting the Christian Sabbath. They continued to use church discipline and nonsectarian organizations, but they relied chiefly on legislative action.

Baptists showed unrelenting hostility to gambling in all its forms. Cards, dice, and other simple gambling devices designed specifically for the purpose were, like murder or adultery, so obviously contrary to Christian morality that Baptists devoted little attention to them. The more subtle forms, which enjoyed a degree of respectability, received the greater condemnation. State lotteries, church and charitable raffles, and betting on horse racing were the principal targets of the Baptist anti-gambling effort.

Baptists opposed the state lotteries chartered in Louisiana and several of the Southern states during Reconstruction. Although objecting to these devices from the first, the denomination became thoroughly aroused over them only in the late eighties when the Louisiana Lottery Company attempted to renew its franchise.[15] Baptists throughout the South, but

13. Texas Baptist General Convention, *Proceedings, 1896*, pp. 108–109.
14. *Religious Herald* (Richmond), May 23, 1889, p. 2; Southern Baptist Convention, *Proceedings, 1889*, p. 38.
15. The franchise of the Louisiana Lottery Company, chartered in 1867, was to expire in 1890. In the late 1880's the company launched a propaganda

especially in the states adjoining Louisiana from which the lottery drew its patronage, united with Louisiana Baptists in an effort of defeat the "enormous swindle . . . this immense engine of evil." [16] The state papers followed the progress of the re-charter bill in the Louisiana legislature. The bill passed both houses but was vetoed by Governor Francis T. Nicholls. The lottery forces then mustered sufficient strength to have it recommitted and passed over the governor's veto in the house. In the senate, however, the effort to override failed by one vote, a situation made possible only by the death of a pro-lottery senator. A contributor to the Mississippi paper appraised the incident as evidence of the "Singular Interference of Providence. . . . The Lord made bare his arm as in days of yore and saved Louisiana." [17]

Although they failed to secure a new charter in the legislature, the promoters of the lottery succeeded in pushing through the legislature and submitting to the voters a constitutional amendment which would have permitted their company to operate twenty-five years longer. Baptists again rallied to the support of Governor Nicholls and his "spartan band," and again the anti-lottery faction won. The Louisiana Baptist Convention commended its constituents for their part in defeating the lottery and claimed some credit for lending its moral support and prayers to the cause. [18]

The destruction of the Louisiana Lottery Company virtually ended the lottery question in the United States for the remainder of the century. The company attempted to establish operations in Florida, but federal laws, requested and supported by Baptists and other denominations, ended this attempt. The company then retreated to Latin America.

Baptists placed charitable lotteries, raffles, and other games of chance in the same category with professional gambling. No cause, however worthy, could justify gambling as a means of support. Georgia Baptists commended a group of ladies in Columbus for their worthy intentions but castigated them for employing a dishonorable means in attempting to raise money by lottery for the relief of Jefferson Davis while he was

---

campaign aimed at securing an extension of its charter and an amendment to the state constitution permitting its operation beyond 1895, the date set in the constitution for the discontinuance of public lotteries.

16. Mississippi Baptist Convention, *Proceedings, 1889*, p. 28.
17. *Southern Baptist Record* (Meridian, Mississippi), July 24, 1890, p. 2.
18. Louisiana Baptist Convention, *Minutes, 1891*, pp. 40–42; *1892*, p. 40.

imprisoned in Fortress Monroe.[19] Virginia Baptists opposed an association chartered by the state legislature for the purpose of raising money for charitable causes through lotteries and raffles. Later they condemned a raffle to raise money for needy Confederate veterans. Baptists even denounced church-sponsored games of chance, labeling them "religious sins." [20]

The organized gambling which Baptists, as a predominantly rural people, were likely to encounter most frequently was betting on horse races at county and state fairs. Baptists considered horse racing without betting harmless or even beneficial in stimulating interest in stock breeding, but betting made races "engines of evil and corruption . . . so grossly immoral and pernicious as to be condemned by all good men." [21] Because of the prevalence of betting at fairs, many Baptists counseled against attending fairs altogether.

Opposition to gambling at race tracks was constant though unorganized until the 1890's when Baptists in several states united with other churches and reform organizations in support of anti-gambling laws. The Virginia weekly was among the most active papers in supporting a bill to outlaw " 'pool-selling' and 'book-making' . . . [on] athletic games, [and] tests of speed or endurance of animals." [22] The editor reported step-by-step the movement of an anti-gambling bill through the Virginia legislature and exerted pressure by publishing the voting records of senators and representatives. He even suggested that Christians bolt the Democratic Party if the Democratic-controlled legislature failed to enact the anti-gambling law. When the bill passed, a contributor congratulated the editor for his part in the crusade and rejoiced that once again Christians could conscientiously patronize the agricultural fairs of the states.[23]

Baptists of Florida gave full support to a similar campaign in that state, and in Georgia and Alabama, Baptists were still engaged in anti-gambling crusades when the century ended. By 1900 Baptists had come to rely primarily on legislative action to curb organized gambling, al-

19. *Christian Index* (Atlanta), February 28, 1867, p. 38.
20. *Religious Herald* (Richmond), March 18, 1875, p. 2; *Christian Index* (Atlanta), August 30, 1894, p. 9.
21. *Biblical Recorder* (Raleigh, North Carolina), September 27, 1871, p. 3.
22. *Religious Herald* (Richmond), January 9, 1896, p. 1.
23. *Ibid.*, January 23, 1896, p. 2; April 2, 1896, p. 1.

though they continued to exercise church discipline against members who engaged in or encouraged the evil.[24]

Baptists expressed a great deal of concern for the low state of public morals as reflected in what they believed to be the mounting crime rate of the late nineteenth century.[25] They attributed the increase in crime and the growing disrespect for the law primarily to ineffective law enforcement and the uncertainty of punishment. They deplored the lengthy delays in bringing criminals to trial, the leniency of juries, the generous use of executive clemency, evasion of the law on technicalities, partiality shown by the courts to people of wealth and social standing, and the unethical practices of lawyers who showed more interest in fees than in justice.

Baptists considered the unsatisfactory functioning of the trial jury the most serious weakness in the legal structure. The *jury system* was not at fault, commented one editor, but good citizens had vitiated it by refusing to serve, leaving jury duty to the rabble who fell easy prey to cunning and unprincipled lawyers while justice went unheeded. This situation, this editor continued, "illustrates one of the secret causes of the boldness with which men commit crime." [26] The Georgia paper expressed the same lack of respect for juries: "It is a notorious fact, and a shameful one, that it is almost impossible to get a jury that will convict a man of murder, no matter what the evidence may be." [27]

The lax and uncertain administration of punishment not only encouraged crime, Baptists believed, but it also caused respectable citizens to lose confidence in the courts and to resort occasionally to lynching and other extra-legal methods of obtaining justice. "Very many of our best people have ceased to look to the action of a jury to punish a criminal as he deserves to be punished," observed the Alabama paper.[28] "If people felt

24. *Florida Baptist Witness* (Ocala), May 1, 1895, p. 2; *Alabama Baptist* (Montgomery), November 23, 1899, p. 1; *Christian Index* (Atlanta), July 6, 1899, p. 6.

25. Because comparative statistics are not available, it is impossible to determine whether or not crime was increasing. *See* Ronald H. Beattie, "Sources of Criminal Statistics," American Academy of Political and Social Sciences, *Annals,* CCXVIII (September 1941), 19–28. The crime incident rate was considerably higher in the South than in other sections of the nation, however. *See* Woodward, *Origins of the New South,* pp. 158–160.

26. *Alabama Baptist* (Selma), April 17, 1884, p. 2.

27. *Christian Index* (Atlanta), December 13, 1888, p. 9.

28. *Alabama Baptist* (Selma), April 17, 1884, p. 2.

that crime would be punished surely and speedily," declared another journal, "they would always be content to let the law take its course. The sole cause of mob law is the failure of the ordinary channels of justice." [29]

Although Baptists generally admitted that inappropriate punishment for crime contributed to mob action, they hardly agreed that it was the "sole cause." The most common cause of lynching, they contended, was the commission of that "unmentionable crime" by a Negro man against a white woman. A few Baptists defended lynching for rape, but the vast majority considered lynching even for rape unjustified, though perhaps *understandable*.[30] In answer to the argument that rape justified lynching, one editor commented:

We solemnly protest against all lawlessness. If anything could justify the act of killing a man by a mob, it is the crime mentioned; but even that falls far short of its justification. Manslaughter by a mob is murder. . . . No individual and no combination of individuals have any authority, from men or from God, to take the life of a person for any crime, private or public, except in self-defense. The best interests of society demand that all mob violence should be repressed or punished. . . . No man's property or life is safe, where mobs have sway.[31]

This remained the prevailing opinion of Baptists on the subject of lynching to the end of the century.

Criticism of the South by the Northern press prompted by the increase of lynching in the eighties and nineties evoked defensive responses from Baptists. They did not defend lynching per se, but they denied that lynching, as the North claimed, was peculiar to the South and that it was the result of racial prejudice. The crimes which caused most lynchings would have the same effect anywhere, Baptists averred, and to prove their contention they gave wide publicity to mob action in other sections of the country.[32]

As a remedy for this kind of lawlessness, Baptists suggested eliminating the causes, not enacting stricter laws against lynching. "Prompt arrest, expeditious trial, and speedy infliction of punishment in all crimes will do more to put an end to lynchings than all the legal enactments against the

29. *Baptist and Reflector* (Nashville), March 19, 1891, p. 8.
30. *See* pp. 111–113.
31. *Religious Herald* (Richmond), September 10, 1874, p. 2.
32. *Ibid.*, February 22, 1894, p. 2; *Christian Index* (Atlanta), May 10, 1894, p. 10; *Baptist and Reflector* (Nashville), May 30, 1895, p. 1.

lynchers that can be devised," commented a prominent Virginia Baptist.[33] Other Baptists stressed religious education, moral training, and the gospel of Christ. In homes, churches, and schools, the public (meaning whites, the potential mobsters) should be taught the value of human life and respect for law. As the most effective means of deterring lynching, Baptists proposed that the would-be Negro rapist whose crime caused most lynchings, be evangelized, taught Christian respect for womanhood, and impressed with the inevitable fact that his "nameless crime" would likely result in judgment by lynch law in the South for many years to come.[34] This last remedy was as much an apology for lynching as it was a condemnation of the practice.

To reverse the crime incident rate in general, Baptists advocated stricter parental control of children, certain enforcement of the law, more frequent administration of capital punishment, and a more concerted effort by the churches to spread the gospel. Baptists considered the loosening of family ties and the decline in paternal discipline to be a major cause of the increase in crime. Stern discipline in the home was the best school for responsible citizenship. A contributor to the Georgia paper expressed it succinctly: "We believe in 'home rule' and the hickory in the parent's hand." [35]

Baptists universally approved capital punishment and recommended its frequent use as a deterrent to crime. The objective of punishment, said one editor, was threefold—punitive, deterrent, and exemplary:

Capital punishment is the only kind which fulfills all of these conditions. It is the only adequate punishment for murder, the only sure deterrent from other crimes, and the only example powerful enough to exert any great influence upon others. Let it be continued. Let justice be done in each case. Let the innocent go free, but let the guilty be punished surely, swiftly. Then we should see less crime in our land.[36]

33. *Religious Herald* (Richmond), June 1, 1899, p. 4. One honest observer of Southern life made this argument sound ridiculous when he candidly asserted that no Negro who committed the "unmentionable crime" had ever escaped the supreme penalty of the law when tried before a jury of Southern whites. *See Christian Index* (Atlanta), May 31, 1883, p. 8.

34. Virginia Baptist General Association, *Minutes, 1897*, p. 34; *1900*, p. 32; Mississippi Baptist Convention, *Proceedings, 1897*, p. 12; *Christian Index* (Atlanta), May 11, 1899, p. 2; *Religious Herald* (Richmond), November 30, 1893, p. 1.

35. *Christian Index* (Atlanta), June 4, 1891, p. 8.

36. *Baptist and Reflector* (Nashville), March 6, 1890, p. 1.

A proposal to eliminate capital punishment in Georgia drew this comment from the editor of the state paper:

The abolition of capital punishment has been tried in other governments as well as in several of the States comprising this union, and in every case, so far as we now remember, a few years experience was sufficient to show the error. . . . If a murderer had been hanged at the beginning of this year, half a dozen valuable lives might have been saved.[37]

Baptists found Biblical justification for capital punishment. When Michigan reinstated the death penalty after having prohibited it for some time, one editor commented:

Thus history repeats itself. "Whoso sheddeth man's blood by man shall his blood be shed." Genesis 9:6. This is the law of God, which has never been repealed, and never will be.[38]

Baptists believed that hanging was the most effective method of administering the death penalty. The result was sure and its administration was calculated to deter potential criminals. Proposals in the latter part of the century to substitute execution by gas or electricity for hanging received little support from Baptists. There were too many unknowns about these new methods, commented one editor, but

we know all about a rope; it never fails, and operates equally on everyone. . . . Hanging has been a success for many years, and we do not believe that it will ever be improved upon.[39]

The chief deterrent to crime remained, however, the preaching of the gospel. Crime sprang from a depraved heart, Baptists believed, and its remedy was to be found only in the gospel which alone had power to change the heart. At a time when crime was threatening the very foundations of civilization, Baptists declared, preaching the gospel had become not merely a divine command which men could heed or ignore. It had become a matter of survival.[40]

Believing as they did that punishment for crime should be sure, swift, and harsh, Baptists quite logically showed little sympathy for the penal reform movement of the time. They rejected the basic premises of the

37. *Christian Index* (Atlanta), July 17, 1879, p. 5.
38. *Ibid.*, August 1, 1889, p. 1.
39. *Ibid.*, August 29, 1889, p. 9.
40. *Ibid.*, December 20, 1877, p. 2.

movement—that justice required no vindication other than reform of the individual offender and that penal institutions existed to reform, not to punish. An editorial in the Georgia paper entitled "A Lurking Heresy," denounced the National Prison Congress meeting in Atlanta in 1886. The whole program, the editor said, was ridiculous, unscriptural, and "misguided philanthropy . . . universalism, let us say, *un*disguised." Civil penal institutions should be modeled after God's system. "Is hell a school of reform?" he asked.[41] "The only objection which we have to our Georgia Penitentiary," the same editor added later, "is that its penalties are not severe enough to be deterrent of crime."[42] Still later he commented: "The fashionable idea of a penitentiary now-a-days is that it is a place where criminals are to be petted and coddled. It appears to us that a good many people have gone crazy on this line."[43]

Baptists generally agreed with the Georgia editor, although few of them were as harsh as he in criticizing penal reform. A contributor to the Virginia weekly called the Richmond city jail the "luxurious Valley Inn," where prisoners were treated with "soft and silly sentimentalism." The whipping post, he said, should be revived as a substitute for short jail sentences:

The lash vigorously laid on until the victim becomes supple and humble, and begs for mercy, would be a far more suitable punishment for at least three-fourths of those who are confined in our prisons, where they daily breathe the very atmosphere of crime, and, when they are turned out, are only more hardened in sin and more expert in evil arts.[44]

North Carolina Baptists opposed the organization of a prison association in that state. It was wrong in purpose, the state paper contended:

In the first place convicts are not unfortunates; they are criminals. A man who commits crime deserves to suffer. . . . Do the promoters of [prison reform] really think that convicts ought to have eiderdown quilts, electric conveniences, and meals to order? Would they have the convict enjoy penitentiary

41. *Ibid.*, December 2, 1886, p. 8.
42. *Ibid.*, July 7, 1887, p. 1.
43. *Ibid.*, March 7, 1889, p. 1. It would be interesting to know what influence, if any, Joseph E. Brown had on the policies of the *Christian Index*. Brown was a prominent Baptist who made a fortune from the use of convict leased labor in his Dade Coal Mines. *See* C. Vann Woodward, *Origins of the New South 1877–1913* (1951), p. 215.
44. *Religious Herald* (Richmond), December 23, 1886, p. 4.

life? Or are they making their high-sounding pleas just to get into the papers; organizing for want of ability to do something else? What is a penal institution? . . . It is a place of punishment, not a reformatory. . . . The penitentiary is not to reform him; but to punish. . . . Let the North Carolina Prison Association, now in its beginning, question seriously if it has a mission of good or evil.[45]

In the closing years of the century—and occasionally before then—Baptists came to support at least one phase of the prison reform movement. They joined actively in the movement to ameliorate the treatment of juvenile offenders. As early as 1880 they proposed separating juvenile prisoners from hardened criminals. In that year the Tennessee Baptist Convention adopted a resolution which read in part:

WHEREAS, A large number of children, especially in the towns and cities, are living in ignorance and vice, unrestrained by parental care, who, for petty offenses, are frequently imprisoned with older and hardened criminals, whose influence tends to confirm the wicked propensities of such children; therefore,

Resolved, That this Tennessee Baptist Convention respectfully recommend to our next Legislature the importance of providing suitable Reformatory Schools or Houses of Refuge for such children, where they can be controlled and educated.

2. That we heartily unite with other Christian bodies in urging this subject upon the attention of our Legislature, as a matter of great importance to our entire State.[46]

Agitation for the establishment of reformatories continued to mount until by 1900 Baptists in practically every state were behind the effort. Even the reactionary *Christian Index* of Georgia offered its support. In the same editorial in which the editor declared that "prison life must be made bitter and forbidding," he also approved a bill before the legislature to create a state reformatory:

We indulge in no weak sentiment for bad boys, but these escapades of youth are not always the indications of depraved hearts. Frequently there has been no instruction in childhood, and the crime is largely a matter of association. To send such criminals to the penitentiary is to make them forced associates of hardened criminals. Here they are taught new lessons in the trade of the

45. *Biblical Recorder* (Raleigh, North Carolina), November 13, 1895, p. 1.
46. Tennessee Baptist Convention, *Proceedings, 1880,* p. 37. This was the first such resolution passed by an assembly of Baptists.

criminal, and worse than this, take up the vulgar thoughts and indecent ideals of these men.[47]

The reluctance of Baptists to endorse the modern penal reform movement was a logical consequence of their close adherence to the Biblical view of evil and punishment and was indicative of their proclivity to view all social problems in the light of prescientific knowledge and theology. By 1900, however, their conservativism was beginning to give way. They had come to acknowledge that crime was, in part at least, a product of environment, that reclamation as well as punishment was a legitimate aim of penal institutions, and that the whole prison system needed revision. An editorial in the North Carolina paper in 1900 illustrates this changing attitude: "The theory of punishment in a Christian land," the editor said, "is that its purpose is to cure as well as prevent."[48] The contrast between this position and that expressed in the same paper just five years earlier is indicative of rapidly changing opinion.[49]

Baptists gave moral support, but little else, to the many humanitarian reform movements of the late nineteenth century. They accepted the deaf, dumb, blind, insane, indigent, and other victims of life's misfortunes as worthy objects of Christian charity, but they did little as a denomination beyond expressing sympathy for these hapless people. Besides the feeble and unsuccessful efforts of the North Carolina Convention to establish a home for mentally retarded children,[50] only the care of orphans and aged ministers and their families aroused Baptists sufficiently to move them to action.

Care of the fatherless was a charitable endeavor enjoined by Scripture, but the denomination failed to heed the command until the Civil War when the number of orphans in the South increased sharply. During the war and immediately thereafter, every state convention acknowledged its responsibility to war orphans, especially the duty of educating them. A committee report titled "On the Education of Indigent Children of Deceased Soldiers" adopted by the Louisiana Convention was typical of reports approved in every state. No part of the work of the convention

47. *Christian Index* (Atlanta), September 30, 1897, p. 6.
48. *Biblical Recorder* (Raleigh, North Carolina), November 7, 1900, p. 1.
49. See pp. 160–161.
50. North Carolina Baptist Convention, *Minutes, 1890*, pp. 23, 28, 31; *1897*, p. 64.

deserved greater consideration, agreed Louisiana Baptists, than "that of educating the poor children of our noble patriots, who have fallen in the defence of our common country." [51] The good intentions of Baptists in Louisiana and in other states seldom materialized, however, because of the economic prostration of the South.

Mississippi Baptists succeeded first in organizing a home for war orphans. During the war the state convention appointed agents to collect money for the project. One of the agents, Thomas C. Teasdale, planned to raise money by selling cotton in the North. He visited Richmond and Washington and made the necessary arrangements with "both governments." As he explained his scheme in 1866, he could have purchased cotton in the South for $.60 a pound Confederate money, sold it in New York for $1.00 a pound Federal money, and then exchanged each Federal dollar in the South for $10.00 Confederate money. A "few hundred bales" were exchanged in this way, Teasdale reported, but the "splendid arrangement" failed to produce sufficient funds to enable Mississippi Baptists to open an orphans home "only because it was undertaken too late." [52]

In spite of the earlier disappointment and the discouraging financial condition of the state following the war, Mississippi Baptists persisted. On October 1, 1866, they opened their home near Meridian with two children in residence. By the time the state convention met the following May, the home was caring for 136 children.[53] Financial difficulties and litigation over property made the home's existence precarious, but it remained open until 1874. The trustees made their last report to the convention in 1875 in which the conditions which necessitated the closing of the home were described:

The institution is without *money*, without *supplies*, without *credit*, and in this condition no other alternative is left. . . . The Home has performed its mission. It raised and educated hundreds of orphans of Confederate soldiers, and with that the people lost interest in it.[54]

Elsewhere in the South in the immediate postwar periods, Baptists shared the enthusiasm of Mississippi Baptists for caring for and educating

51. Louisiana Baptist Convention, *Minutes, 1863*, p. 15.
52. Mississippi Baptist Convention, *Proceedings, 1866*, p. 15.
53. *Ibid.*, 1867, p. 29.
54. *Ibid.*, 1875, p. 21.

war orphans, but with less tangible results. An "asylum" under Baptist auspices operated in Atlanta from 1871 to 1881,[55] and in all the other states Baptists contributed to the support of privately operated "Baptist homes" and assisted in a variety of ways in the education of hundreds of children of deceased or disabled Confederate veterans.

In the late eighties and nineties, another wave of enthusiasm for the care of orphans swept Southern Baptists, resulting this time in the founding of permanent orphanages in most of the states. North Carolina Baptists organized the first home completely under the control of their state convention in 1888. In the nineties, orphanages owned and operated by the state conventions opened in Virginia, Tennessee, South Carolina, Alabama, Arkansas, and Georgia. And in the remaining Southern states, Baptists had plans for the institutional care of the homeless well under way by 1900.[56]

Next to the care of orphans, the benevolent cause of greatest concern to Baptists was the care of aged ministers and their dependents. In journals and convention reports, Baptists continually acknowledged their obligation to support their "indigent and superannuated or worn-out Baptist ministers . . . and the widows and children of deceased ministers of the above character." [57] In the 1870's a number of state conventions undertook the establishment of ministerial aid funds, but few of these efforts bore any appreciable results. Virginia Baptists had the most success. Their plan, adopted in 1871, provided a board of nine trustees to collect funds and administer relief. One-third of all contributions was

55. Georgia Baptist Convention, *Minutes, 1871*, p. 16; *1882*, pp. 18–19.

56. North Carolina Baptist Convention, *Minutes, 1888*, pp. 21–22; Virginia Baptist General Association, *Minutes, 1892*, pp. 34–39; Tennessee Baptist Convention, *Proceedings, 1892*, p. 33; South Carolina Baptist Convention, *Minutes, 1891*, pp. 7–9, 13; Alabama Baptist Convention, *Minutes, 1893*, p. 52; Arkansas Baptist Convention, *Proceedings, 1896*, pp. 20–21; Georgia Baptist Convention, *Minutes, 1899*, pp. 56–57. Baptist supported homes in Kentucky and Texas, although ownership and control were not vested in the state organizations. *See* Kentucky Baptist General Association, *Proceedings, 1896*, p. 35; Texas Baptist General Convention, *Proceedings, 1900*, pp. 117–120; Louisiana Baptist Convention, *Minutes, 1900*, pp. 22–25; Florida Baptist Convention, *Minutes, 1900*, pp. 50–51. In 1897 the Mississippi Baptist Convention extended "sympathy and support" to a privately owned "Baptist Orphanage" in Jackson, but it did not assume control of the home until after 1900. *See* Mississippi Baptist Convention, *Proceedings, 1897*, pp. 11, 12, 20.

57. Kentucky Baptist General Association, *Proceedings, 1870*, p. 29.

deposited in a permanent fund, and the remainder, with the interest on the permanent fund, was used for current relief. The program developed slowly. In 1876 the fund paid out only $204.65, but by 1900 benefit payments had increased to $4,483.75.[58] Before the end of the century less successful plans were in operation in Kentucky, Texas, North Carolina, Georgia, Tennessee, Florida, and South Carolina. Baptists in Arkansas, Alabama, Louisiana, and Mississippi reported no organized work.

The lack of ministerial relief programs may be accounted for in part by the belief among many Baptists that such work was the proper function of local churches, not the state or South-wide conventions. The report of a committee on "Sustentation" at the Mississippi Convention in 1887 reflected this attitude. Most aged and indigent ministers and their dependents were supported by the people among whom they had labored, stated the report, and "this is the best way for the work to be done." [59] If Baptists were so unconcerned for the needy "within the household of faith," they were not likely to be greatly concerned with the unfortunates outside the fold—and, indeed, they were not.

One of the most militant crusades of the post–Civil War generation was the feminist movement. Its antecedents predate the Civil War, but it was not until after the war that American women mustered sufficient strength to breach significantly the double-standard tradition. The right to vote, equal educational opportunities, equal rights before the law, equal pay for equal work, wider opportunities in business, and equal rights in the marriage union were the most important objectives of the movement. The most radical feminists went even further and demanded the complete emancipation of women from all subordinate relations to men.

Southern Baptists opposed the organized feminist movement and all other efforts to effect any significant change in the traditional role of women in society. Their opposition rested basically on religious belief. They held that God had created women different from (and inferior to) men in physical strength, nervous stamina, and power of mind. Consequently, women were equipped by providential design and natural endowments for a station in life different from and subordinate to that of

58. Virginia Baptist General Association, *Minutes, 1871,* pp. 41–42; *1876,* pp. 29, 31; *1900,* pp. 33–36.
59. Mississippi Baptist Convention, *Proceedings, 1887,* p. 51.

men. Any effort, therefore, to elevate women to the level of men was contrary to God's will.[60]

Baptists recognized the implications for Southern women of the imbalance in the sex ratio resulting from the death of thousands of Confederate soldiers. A large number of Southern women who normally would have become housewives would be denied marriage and forced to earn their own livelihood. Also because of the man shortage, women of the South would have to do much of the work formerly done by men to enable the South to recover from the effects of the "late social disruptions." Women could find employment, Baptists believed, as teachers, seamstresses, domestic servants, day laborers in factories, and in other honorable occupations suitable to their physical strength. By so engaging in new occupational fields, the women of the South could hasten the return of prosperity and prove themselves "worthy daughters of the land of Washington and Lee, of Beauregard and Gordon."[61] To enable women to qualify for their new responsibilities, Baptists advocated a broader education for women, but not of the same kind as that available to men. Elementary courses in mathematics and economics could help equip women for jobs in post offices, retail shops, and other business establishments, but advanced training in the sciences, languages, and professions was unsuitable for the "weaker sex."[62]

Baptists showed only hostility toward organizations devoted to the furtherance of women's rights. Since Baptists assumed that the two sexes had been divinely ordained to fill roles in life—roles approximating those already existing—they considered any effort to change these rela-

60. *Religious Herald* (Richmond), February 20, 1868, p. 2; May 7, 1874, p. 15; *Christian Index* (Macon, Georgia), January 13, 1866, p. 9; *Biblical Recorder* (Raleigh, North Carolina), August 26, 1868, p. 1; *Western Recorder* (Louisville), January 7, 1886, p. 2. Only one definite statement to the contrary was noted in the course of research. A contributor to the Virginia paper called the idea that women were mentally inferior to men a "heathen notion." Even so, he concluded, women's place was in the home. See *Religious Herald* (Richmond), February 7, 1895, p. 1.

61. *Religious Herald* (Richmond), August 9, 1866, p. 2.

62. *Biblical Recorder* (Raleigh, North Carolina), August 26, 1868, p. 1; Mississippi Baptist Convention, *Proceedings, 1877*, pp. 48, 59–61; *Western Recorder* (Louisville), January 7, 1886, p. 2; South Carolina Baptist Convention, *Minutes, 1888*, pp. 20–23; East Tennessee Baptist General Association, *Proceedings, 1876*, p. 9.

tionships *ipso facto* wrong. They looked upon the feminist movement as an attempted invasion by women of areas providentially reserved for men. Efforts of women to gain greater rights and privileges were interpreted as a desire on the part of women to be like men. When women emulated men, commented one editor, they forsook their calling and became "mere unsexed paragons that call up within us as much repugnance as admiration." [63] "We are advocates of *woman's rights*," declared another editor, but "not of such rights as would convert her into a man." [64] Commenting on the female leaders of the feminist movement, a contributor to another journal asserted:

Eager for the fray, the unsexed women would plunge into the arena and mount the forum, to measure strength with men. . . . There is no genuine assertion of woman's rights; there is actually *abandonment* of these, with an unseemly claim for *man's* rights.[65]

"Our hope lies in woman the saint," declared another Baptist, "not in woman the amazon." [66]

The objective of the feminist movement which drew the loudest protest from Baptists was equal suffrage. The franchise could be the degradation of women and the destruction of the home and the nation, Baptists believed. Given the ballot, women might then logically demand and receive the right to hold office and be dragged into "that course of electioneering, demogogism, excitement and party trickery by which offices are secured." [67] If permitted to exercise the *privileges* of democracy, women might also expect (or even demand) a share in the *responsibilities* of democracy, even to serving in the armed forces.

Opposition to the women's rights movement continued throughout the period, but most Baptists were pessimistic about being able to prevent women from achieving some of their objectives, especially the right to vote. The best that Baptists hoped to do was to encourage the women of the South to resist the appeal of the "bold and unprincipled women" from the North who led the agitation. Thus, they hoped, those qualities

63. *Christian Index* (Macon, Georgia), January 13, 1866, p. 9.
64. *Religious Herald* (Richmond), February 9, 1871, p. 1.
65. *Christian Index* (Atlanta), May 28, 1885, p. 8.
66. *Religious Herald* (Richmond), February 6, 1868, p. 1.
67. *Ibid.*, February 11, 1869, p. 2.

of virtue and elegance which Southern womanhood had always represented could be preserved.[68]

Baptists persistently defended the traditional place of women as the homemakers in society. This attitude showed no appreciable change from the Civil War to the end of the century. "We have a profound respect for woman;" declared the Virginia paper in 1868,

and it is because we have, that we desire to see her moving in the sphere to which her Creator has assigned her, and for which her physical, intellectual and moral qualities eminently fit her. As the friend, companion and solace of man, all her rights and interests are secure. . . . Every honorable man will do her reverence. As the rival of man, in the struggle for place, power and preeminence, she, as the "weaker vessel," is doomed to defeat. From such a contest, she must inevitably come forth, not with modesty, delicacy and loveliness which impart a charm and influence to her sex, but soiled, dishonored and disappointed.[69]

Thirty years later the same paper expressed the same sentiment:

When . . . woman becomes *emancipated* from the care of the young and the making of the home, she has entered into the worst of all bondage, which comes always to every one who disregards the law of his own life. They only "walk at liberty" who have learned to obey the divine precepts, as written in their very being.[70]

Although Baptists opposed the women's rights movement, they welcomed the expanding role of women in behalf of benevolent and religious causes. They encouraged the participation of women in the temperance crusade and in similar movements as long as these efforts remained dissociated from the feminist agitation and from politics.[71] They also granted women a larger and freer sphere of action in the expanding denominational program, especially in the promotion of missions.

The privileges of women in local churches expanded significantly

68. *Working Christian* (Columbia, South Carolina), March 7, 1872, p. 1; *Florida Baptist Witness* (Ocala), June 24, 1891, p. 2; *Western Recorder* (Louisville), June 21, 1894, p. 1.

69. *Religious Herald* (Richmond), February 20, 1868, p. 2.

70. *Ibid.,* January 5, 1899, p. 1.

71. *See* pp. 193–194. R. P. Johnson, "Prohibition and Woman's Suffrage," *Seminary Magazine,* I (November 1888), 201–203; *Alabama Baptist* (Montgomery), August 23, 1888, p. 2; *Florida Baptist Witness* (Ocala), November 26, 1890, p. 2.

during the period, although some freedoms granted women in other denominations continued to be denied in Baptist churches. Whether women should preach, teach Sunday school classes, serve as deaconesses, and administer the business and benevolent affairs of the churches remained debatable questions in different sections of the South. For twelve or fifteen years after the war considerable sentiment existed among Baptists for creating the office of "deaconess," but evidently the tradition of male control of church affairs was too strong to permit so radical an innovation. After about 1880 little was said about the new office.[72]

The question of permitting women to preach was even more widely discussed than the deaconess question, but few Baptists genuinely favored it. Most of the discussion was nothing more than condemnation of the practice aimed at Methodists and other churches which permitted it. St. Paul's injunction to "let the women keep silent in the church" was rigidly applied to keep women out of the pulpit. Most Baptists agreed with the North Carolinian who said:

We do not propose to be persuaded, cajoled, or drawn by the force of public or private opinion, into adopting this unscriptural and foolish practice. . . . Let *all* our people *positively* refuse the use of our churches to such an unscriptural and dangerous innovation. . . . "From womanly men, and from manly women, good Lord deliver us." [73]

In other phases of local church life, however, women were doing much of the work by the end of the century. They were the teachers in most of the Sunday school classes (except adult male classes), they were conducting most of the benevolent work of the churches, and they were promoting the mission program of the churches with very little assistance from men. In spite of the vital role of women, however, control of church affairs remained in the hands of men.

At the state level in the denominational organization, women received more and more privileges as time passed except for a brief period of reaction during the 1880's. Beginning with Kentucky in 1869, women sat as messengers in all the state conventions by the end of the century

---

72. *Christian Index* (Macon, Georgia), April 13, 1865, p. 2; *Religious Herald* (Richmond), April 13, 1871, p. 1; *The Baptist* (Memphis), February 22, 1879, p. 5; Texas Baptist Convention, *Minutes, 1884,* p. 53.

73. *Biblical Recorder* (Raleigh, North Carolina), February 10, 1892, p. 2.

except in Virginia, Georgia, South Carolina, and Alabama.[74] Membership in the conventions entitled the women to vote on business matters, and before 1900 a few women began serving on committees and even addressing the conventions.[75]

Women received fewer privileges at the South-wide convention than at the state meetings. At least one woman, Mrs. Myra E. Graves, was accepted as a delegate to the Southern Baptist Convention in 1877 and again in 1882, although she was listed by the credentials committee as "M. E. Graves," perhaps with the intention of concealing her sex.[76] In 1885, however, two women representing the Arkansas convention were refused seats at the convention. This action provoked a discussion lasting four days after which the constitution of the convention was amended by substituting the word "brethern" for the word "member" in the section defining membership, thus eliminating the possibility of women delegates for the remainder of the century.[77] Discussion over the constitutional amendment continued for several months after the convention, but the preponderance of opinion supported the change.

Although Southern Baptist men surrendered very little authority to the women of the denomination, they welcomed their assistance in support of home and foreign missions and gradually granted them almost complete freedom in leading and conducting their own mission programs. Women's missionary "mite societies" and "sewing circles" had been known and accepted in the denomination since the early nineteenth century, but it was not until the last quarter of the century that co-ordinating agencies appeared throughout the association, the state, and the South.[78] South

74. If women attended the state-wide meetings in Virginia, Georgia, South Carolina, and Alabama, their names were not listed among the delegates. Women delegates to the North Carolina Convention represented "sewing circles" and Sunday schools, not churches. *See* North Carolina Baptist Convention, *Minutes, 1876*, p. 10.

75. Tennessee Baptist Convention, *Proceedings, 1885*, p. 27; Arkansas Baptist Convention, *Proceedings, 1896*, p. 35; Florida Baptist Convention, *Minutes, 1899*, p. 20; *1900*, pp. 16–17.

76. William Wright Barnes, *Southern Baptist Convention, 1845–1953* (1954), p. 148.

77. Southern Baptist Convention, *Proceedings, 1885*, pp. 14, 30; *Religious Herald* (Richmond), May 14, 1885, pp. 2–3; June 25, 1885, p. 1. *Christian Index* (Atlanta), July 2, 1885, p. 3. Changes in the constitution were made in Article III which stipulated the conditions of membership. *See Proceedings, 1885*, p. 3.

78. Barnes, *Southern Baptist Convention*, pp. 140–143.

Carolina Baptist women organized the first "Central Committee of Woman's Missions" in 1876, and in the following decade similar organizations were formed in almost all the other states.[79]

The efforts of Baptist women to create a South-wide co-ordinating missionary agency under their own control met firm resistance from many of the leading ministers of the denomination. They feared that a separate missionary union was contrary to Scripture and church tradition, and, more important, they suspected the women of desiring to use such an organization as a front for the feminist movement. "An independent organization of women," cried Tiberius G. Jones of Virginia, "naturally tends toward a violation of divine interdict against women's becoming a public religious teacher and leader—a speaker before mixed assemblies, a platform declaimer, a pulpit proclaimer, street preacher, lyceum lecturer, stump orator, *et id omne genus.*"[80]

Notwithstanding the opposition, Baptist women succeeded in perfecting their South-wide organization in 1888. They chose to call their agency the "Woman's Missionary Union, Auxiliary to the Southern Baptist Convention," a name which no doubt did much to allay opposition among the older ministers. By the turn of the century virtually all opposition to the women's missionary work had ceased.[81]

Another minor "evil" of late nineteenth-century society which Baptists opposed was the growth in professional and amateur athletics. They deplored the craze over professional baseball and boxing and the increasing popularity of amateur football. They considered baseball an excellent game for boys, but when grown men organized themselves into clubs and traveled around the country staging exhibitions for money, the game became a disgrace. "It is a shame," said one editor, "that well-developed muscular power should be employed for a purpose so ignoble. The whole tendency of the amusement is to idleness and vice."[82] Baptists criticized

79. South Carolina Baptist Convention, *Minutes, 1876,* p. 16; *1877,* pp. 11–12.

80. Virginia Baptist General Association, *Minutes, 1888,* p. 42. The most vocal objectors to women's work were, like Jones (1821–1895), elderly ministers whose attitudes toward the place of women in the church were formed in antebellum times.

81. *Religious Herald* (Richmond), May 17, 1888, p. 1; May 24, 1888, p. 1; Southern Baptist Convention, *Proceedings, 1890,* pp. V–VI, XII–XXIII; Barnes, *Southern Baptist Convention,* pp. 150–156.

82. *Religious Herald* (Richmond), May 20, 1875, p. 2.

spectators and newspapers for encouraging the profitless pastime and advised church members to avoid commercial baseball, either as spectators or as participants. Church discipline was seldom recommended, however.[83]

Baptists denounced football even more vigorously than baseball. Like baseball, it could be wholesome recreation for boys, but when college men played it at the risk of life and limb and to the neglect of their studies, it became a definite evil. The editor of the Virginia paper agreed with another editor in failing to see what pleasure cultured ladies and gentlemen and university professors could derive from "that dirtily clad, bare and frowsy headed, rough-and-tumble, shoving, pushing, crushing, pounding, kicking, ground-wallowing, mixed-up mass of players, of whom any might come out with broken limbs, or be left on the ground writhing with ruptured vitals." [84] Because of the brutality of the game, some Baptists favored abolishing it completely. The Virginia General Association called for the elimination of the sport, at least in Baptist-supported colleges. The editor of the Georgia paper appealed to the legislature to abolish football throughout the state after the death of a player from an injury sustained in a game between the University of Georgia and the University of Virginia.[85]

Professional prize fighting received the unmitigated condemnation of Baptists. The opinion of the Virginia paper soon after the Civil War remained the consensus of Baptists: "This barbarous and loathsome sport is the disgrace of the age," [86] and "in the name of humanity, of civilization and of our country, to say nothing of Christianity, we solemnly protest against the practice of glorifying the low combatants of the ring." [87] In the 1890's, when boxing was becoming respectable, Baptists exerted considerable effort to prevent it from being recognized as a legitimate sport. The Georgia paper condemned the Corbett-Dixon fight in New Orleans in 1892 as "more degrading than dog-fights," and the

83. *Christian Index* (Atlanta), August 22, 1867, p. 132; *Religious Herald* (Richmond), December 8, 1870, p. 2. The Tennessee Convention was unable to agree on a resolution condemning football and baseball. *See* Tennessee Baptist Convention, *Proceedings, 1895,* p. 28.

84. *Religious Herald* (Richmond), February 25, 1897, p. 1.

85. Virginia Baptist General Association, *Minutes, 1897,* p. 53; *Christian Index* (Atlanta), November 4, 1897, p. 7.

86. *Religious Herald* (Richmond), October 14, 1869, p. 2.

87. *Ibid.,* August 27, 1874, p. 2.

betting which attended the fight as equally reprehensible. "All these things," said the editor, "present a sickening spectacle, and show rapid downward strides in the moral tone of society." [88] Another editor described the Mitchell-Corbett fight in Jacksonville, Florida, in 1894 as

a brutal and degrading spectacle. . . . The only difference between a modern prize fight and the old gladiatorial combats of Rome is that the gladiators frequently killed each other, and the prize fighters unfortunately do not always succeed in doing so.[89]

Baptists castigated fight promoters and complimented citizens who attempted to prevent the staging of fights. They especially praised several Southern governors who prevented fights within their states by legal action.[90]

Notwithstanding their frequent criticism of baseball, football, and boxing, Baptists failed to be stirred to crusading action. The lack of opportunity in the South to witness or engage in professional and collegiate sporting events perhaps prevented the question from becoming much more than purely academic.

Southern Baptists as a denomination generally remained apathetic toward organized reform movements during the last third of the nineteenth century. Except for the temperance crusade [91] and a few other movements which could be supported by Scripture, Baptists offered little assistance to reform effort directly. Within the denomination, however, a significant trend was apparent. By the close of the century Baptists were becoming aware of their responsibility to society and were exerting some influence in eradicating social evils through co-operation with other churches and with secular reform movements.

88. *Christian Index* (Atlanta), September 15, 1892, p. 4.
89. *Baptist and Reflector* (Nashville), February 1, 1894, p. 1.
90. *Alabama Baptist* (Montgomery), March 10, 1892, p. 2; *Religious Herald* (Richmond), September 29, 1892, p. 2; *Christian Index* (Atlanta), January 25, 1894, p. 4; Florida Baptist Convention, *Minutes, 1894,* p. 17; Louisiana Baptist Convention, *Minutes, 1895,* p. 13; Texas Baptist General Convention, *Proceedings, 1895,* pp. 41, 44; Alabama Baptist Convention, *Minutes, 1895,* p. 43.
91. *See* Chapter 7.

7. Temperance

HE manufacture, sale, and consumption of intoxicating beverages are practices as old as the settlement of America. In colonial times and for half a century thereafter, drinking was universal. Americans of both sexes and of all ages and levels of society consumed quantities of rum, cider, gin, whiskey, brandy, and smaller amounts of wine and beer. Laymen and clergy alike drank for nourishment, for medicinal purposes, and for pleasure. Any public gathering was likely to be enlivened by the liberal consumption of spirits. A house-raising, a husking bee, a wedding, a funeral, and even an ordination—all were occasions for drinking. With drinking so prevalent, drunkenness inevitably resulted, and drunkenness often led to quarreling, fighting, sexual irregularities, and occasionally killings.

The evils of drink were apparent in early America, but reformers emphasized the moderate or "temperate" use of alcoholic beverages as the primary remedy, not prohibition nor even strict regulation. Colonies and states and local units of government frequently employed regulatory laws and ordinances to control the liquor traffic, but only Georgia, from 1735 to 1742, attempted total prohibition, and that without success.

Protests against the evils of alcohol increased rapidly after the middle of the eighteenth century. Much of the new momentum came from clergymen. The promotion of temperance through organized societies began in the last ten or fifteen years of the eighteenth century, and by 1820 temperance societies existed in all the states. In the next two decades a number of state and national organizations were perfected, and several temperance journals began publication. More important, however, in furthering the temperance cause, the churches joined the crusade. Church congregations offered ready-made audiences for temperance lectures, and temperance meetings, in churches and elsewhere, acquired the characteristics of revival meetings. The church's influence heightened the emotional appeal of the temperance crusade and added the prospects of

eternal damnation to the growing list of woes which awaited the unre-
pentant drunkard. It is doubtful, however, that the threat of hell-fire was
any more effective in scaring drunkards into sobriety than the weird
accounts by secular lecturers of "spontaneous conbustion" and other
bizarre consequences of alcoholism.

Until about 1830 temperance societies relied almost completely on
"moral suasion" for attaining their objectives, but in the thirties temperance promoters began agitating for liquor controls by legislation. Rhode
Island and New Hampshire adopted local-option laws, a number of other
states prohibited the sale of liquor by the drink, and in 1851 Maine
adopted the first state-wide prohibition law since Georgia's abortive
effort. Before the Civil War, a total of sixteen states and territories
adopted various forms of prohibitive legislation.

The antebellum crusade reached a peak in the early 1850's and declined rapidly thereafter. Immediately before and during the Civil War
and for several years thereafter both the beer and distilled liquor businesses boomed, and the cause of temperance correspondingly declined.

The revival of interest in temperance after the Civil War must be
attributed to the efforts of temperance-minded women. In the early
seventies, a sometime physician, lecturer, and publicist, Dr. Dioclesian
Lewis, inspired large numbers of women in the Midwest to attack open
saloons directly. The hundreds of saloons closed by these zealots soon
reopened, but the temperance movement had acquired a new force which
played a significant role in the ultimate achievements of the crusade. Out
of this "Whirlwind of the Lord," as Frances Willard called the women's
crusade, emerged the less spectacular but more effective Woman's Christian Temperance Union. From its inception in 1874, the W.C.T.U.
advocated the legal prohibition of all intoxicating beverages. The enactment of nationwide prohibition more than a generation later must be
credited to a considerable degree to the energetic women who led this
organization.

A serious handicap to the temperance movement in the post–Civil
War generation was the failure of its many factions to agree on a single
course of action. Dozens of organizations advocated as many different
schemes for eliminating the liquor evil. Amendments to the federal
Constitution, amendments to state constitutions, state prohibition laws,
local-option laws, and moral suasion were a few of the most common
remedies.

The crescendo of temperance effort begun in the early 1870's reached a climax in the mid-eighties and declined for a decade or more. Rhode Island and South Dakota repealed their prohibition amendments, and statutory prohibition was reversed in several states. By 1902 only Maine, Kansas, and North Dakota were still dry, but even in these states enforcement was a farce. Only in the final thrust of temperance effort which culminated in the Eighteenth Amendment to the national Constitution was the momentum of the eighties regained.

The great need of the temperance movement throughout the nineteenth century was a well-financed and ably led organization to unify the efforts of all the divergent factions. The Anti-Saloon League of America proved to be such an organization. Precedents of the League can be traced to the woman's crusade in Ohio in the decade of the seventies, although the nationwide organization was not perfected until 1895, and a well-directed program was not under way until about 1900. From the turn of the century until national prohibition became a reality, the Anti-Saloon League was the prime mover. It effectively employed all the known media for influencing public opinion and wisely refused to endorse any political party—even the Prohibition Party—but concentrated on electing the right men. Pulpits and Sunday schools of the country proved to be among the most powerful media for spreading the League's objectives. With few exceptions, the churches of the land sanctioned the League and contributed to its support.

The foregoing survey of the temperance movement in the United States is applicable to the South only in a general way, for the South failed to keep pace with the rest of the nation in promoting temperance. Some of the reasons for this are obvious. First, drinking was a well-established custom in the South. Between the heyday of rum drinking in New England and the "beer invasion," the South was the heaviest-drinking section of the country. Second, the difficulty of communication in the sparsely settled South hindered the dissemination and acceptance of any idea, especially one which contravened an established custom. Third, and most important, Southerners regarded the temperance movement with suspicion because of its association in their minds with abolitionism, Negro rights, women's rights, and other unpopular isms emanating from New England. Individual Southerners might be as zealous for the *cause* of temperance as Northerners, but they lagged behind in the development of methods of promoting the cause. Moral suasion, the oldest and most personal technique of the temperance crusaders, remained the principal method employed by Southern reformers until the turn of the century, and in promoting temperance in this manner Southerners were unexcelled. In the flurry of temperance activity in the eighties, however, Southerners began co-operating with each other and with temperance forces outside the region, and by 1900 the South was a vital part of the nationwide movement.

The history of temperance effort among Southern Baptists after 1865 closely approximates the development of the movement in the South at large. Baptists were slow in achieving a united front. Besides the conviction that drunkenness was wrong and that conversion was the best method of combatting the evil, there was little agreement among them. They argued over many questions relating to the total problem: What did the Bible teach about strong drink? Was the moderate use of hard liquor and other alcoholic beverages commensurate with Christian conduct? Should whiskey be used as medicine? Should a Christian sell liquor or rent property to be used for that purpose? Were the churches obliged to fight the liquor evil, or was soul-winning their only task? And finally, should fermented wine be used in the communion service? By the end of the century, however, Baptists had threshed out their major differences and had come to be an integral part of the nationwide attack on alcohol. The in-fighting among Baptists, while greatly weakening their usefulness to the total temperance movement, nevertheless provides a revealing insight into the development of temperance consciousness within the denomination.

The common ground for the development of a temperance movement among Southern Baptists was the conviction that drunkenness was the cardinal sin of the land. The liquor traffic increased throughout the country during and immediately following the Civil War, and the South was perhaps more vitally affected than any other section. Drunkenness and its attendant evils were reported to be common among all classes in the South, church members as well as others. Referring to the drink evil, the delegates to the Virginia General Association in 1866 declared:

The alarming prevalence of intemperance among all classes of our people demands of Christians renewed zeal in countering and crushing this monster vice, it being assuredly on the increase, the fruits, in some respects, of the late war, when even professing Christians were (and still are) engaged in selling or drinking the intoxicating fluid, frought as must be conceded, with so much danger to body and soul, exciting blasphemy, insult, crime, and loathsome pestilence.[1]

Other sins were not overlooked by Baptists in their crusade for righteousness, but strong drink was considered the most

destructive curse of the 19th century, imperiling our homes, hostile to our churches, a constant menace to society, the prolific mother of vice and crime, the corrupter of politics, a breeder of anarchy in our government, and in all its dark record the offspring of the devil.[2]

An emotional discourse like this could always arouse enthusiasm for temperance among Baptists.

From the very beginning of the period under consideration, many Baptists advocated total abstinence as the only safe practice for church members, but most Baptists refused to accept this principle until many years later. In the first issue of the Virginia paper after the war, a correspondent warned the young men of the South that "teetotalism" was the only security against intemperance.[3] Baptists were slow to embrace teetotalism, however, because the use of strong drink was a custom of long standing and, more important, the Bible seemed to sanction—or at least did not condemn—the moderate use of alcoholic drink. The Virginia paper criticized the advocates of total abstinence who attempted to find justification in the Bible:

Total abstinence from intoxicating liquors, with certain limitations, is commended by expediency, the experience of multitudes, the opinion of many wise and good men, and by a fair application of certain scriptural principles. . . . [But] the Bible contains no prohibition of the use of wine and strong drink, and all attempts to draw such a prohibition from it is a perversion of Scripture, and injurious to the cause which it is intended to subserve.[4]

Another contributor to the same paper argued that total abstinence was not only contrary to the Word of God, but also was in conflict with nature. No appetite was evil within itself; only overindulgence constituted evil. Without a specific command to abstain totally from the use of

1. Virginia Baptist General Association, *Minutes, 1866,* p. 22.
2. Florida Baptist Convention, *Minutes, 1895,* p. 69.
3. *Religious Herald* (Richmond), October 19, 1865, p. 1.
4. *Ibid.,* August 18, 1870, p. 2. An occasional defense of this position was noted as late as 1887. *See ibid.,* September 1, 1887, p. 1.

strong drink, it could be presumed that moderation was approved by God, who gave the appetite. For man to condemn what God evidently approved was tantamount to presuming more wisdom than God, he concluded.[5]

Baptists, who liked their spirits and who looked for distinct "thou shalt not's" to shape their conduct, had to be convinced that a basis for total abstinence existed in the Bible before changing their views. Not until the middle eighties did they generally concede that the Scriptures condemned the consumption of hard liquors in any quantity whatever. This position was supported by inferences drawn from a number of Bible passages, the most important of which was the warning that no drunkard could enter the Kingdom of Heaven. From this, Baptists reasoned that the moderate use of liquor might lead to excessive use or, by example, might cause a weaker brother to succumb to the habit. Also, by the decade of the eighties, many Baptists were convinced that the drinking of hard liquor was contrary to the "spirit" of the Bible. Total abstinence was therefore the only policy for the dedicated Christian.[6]

Even after the principle of total abstinence was accepted by Baptists, considerable disagreement over what constituted "total" abstinence continued until the end of the century. That the use of distilled liquors should be prohibited was conceded by the 1880's, but whether the same proscription should apply to wine, cider, beer, and other malt drinks remained debatable. Until the mid-eighties, in fact, the proposal that intemperance might be curbed by *encouraging* the consumption of wine and beer appeared frequently in Baptist papers. These suggestions were always answered promptly, however, usually by citing conditions in Europe to show that excessive drinking of wine and beer could also result in drunkenness.[7]

Promoters of teetotalism encountered their greatest difficulty in at-

5. *Ibid.*, November 21, 1872, p. 1.

6. The arguments against the moderate use of hard liquor were common from the 1860's but did not gain ascendancy until the 1880's. The last major exchange of views for and against the moderate use of hard liquor noted in the course of research occurred in the *Religious Herald* (Richmond) in November and December 1882. The last defense of the moderate use of hard liquor appeared in the *Western Recorder* (Louisville), February 14, 1884, p. 3.

7. *Religious Herald* (Richmond), October 27, 1881, p. 1; March 18, 1886, p. 2; April 19, 1888, p. 1; *Biblical Recorder* (Raleigh, North Carolina), September 13, 1876, p. 2; *Baptist Record* (Meridian, Mississippi), April 29, 1886, p. 6.

tempting to proscribe the use of wine. Wine was considered the least harmful of alcoholic beverages, and its use in moderation was widespread in the rural South. The farm columns of many Baptist journals contained recipes for making wine, and numbers of articles encouraged farmers to diversify their crops by raising grapes, scuppernongs, blackberries, and strawberries for the express purpose of stimulating wine manufacturing in the South.[8] More important still, wine-drinking was apparently approved in the Bible. St. Paul admonished young Timothy to "take a little wine" for his stomach's sake, and Christ Himself condoned the practice in performing His first miracle by turning water into wine. "We fully believe," said one writer, "that the wine made by Christ at the marriage in Cana was intoxicating, if drunk to excess"—otherwise there was no miracle.[9] "That Christ drank wine during His stay on earth, no one can doubt," said another. Condemning wine-drinking, therefore, would be denouncing an act of Christ.[10]

Professor John A. Broadus of the Southern Baptist Theological Seminary admitted that Christ drank wine when He was on earth, but warned Christians against following this practice literally. Christ drank wine because it was the custom of His times. Had He lived nineteen centuries later, He would have drunk tea or coffee. It was unthinkable, Broadus concluded, that Christ would have lent His influence to a practice which encouraged debauchery as wine-drinking did in the nineteenth century.[11] "Now if our temperance men could be persuaded to put their advocacy of total abstinence on the ground of present facts and present dangers . . . and abandon all attempts to find an explicit Bible command," commented one editor, "what a relief it would be to them and to the cause!"[12] This common-sense approach was advanced by a number of others and was important in leading Baptists to condemn the use of wine in spite of Biblical examples to the contrary.

The controversy over wine-drinking led Baptists to question their long-established practice of serving fermented wine in communion. Communion—or the Lord's Supper as they preferred to call it—and baptism by immersion were the two "ordinances" which Baptists believed Christ

8. *Christian Index* (Atlanta), May 24, 1866, p. 88; December 6, 1883, p. 14.
9. *Religious Herald* (Richmond), July 3, 1879, p. 2.
10. *Ibid.*, November 21, 1872, p. 1.
11. *Ibid.*, April 8, 1875, p. 1.
12. *Ibid.*, April 26, 1888, p. 1.

had commanded His followers to observe. Although they considered both ordinances as symbolic only in meaning, they nevertheless attempted to observe them as literally as possible. They practiced immersion as the only valid baptism and logically should have used fermented wine in the communion service. "If we must have real water for baptism and not some substitute for it, why not have real wine for the supper?" questioned one editor.[13] If Christ used real wine, commented another, Baptists might as well "substitute sprinkling for baptism" as to use grape juice for wine.[14] This was a powerful argument among immersing Baptists!

The controversy was ironic in that the same staunch Baptists who insisted most vehemently on following the examples of Christ as closely as possible were also the individuals who opposed the use of fermented wine. In an effort to resolve their dilemma, these literalists advanced the "two wine" theory which held that both fermented and unfermented wines were in common use in the time of Christ, and that Christ drank only the unfermented variety.[15]

Arrayed against the advocates of the two-wine theory was a large number of prominent Baptists—among them the scholarly and highly respected John A. Broadus—whose arguments were decidedly more cogent. Citing the work of scholars of all faiths, ancient and modern, secular and sacred, they marshaled an incontrovertible amount of evidence to prove that as far as could be determined, Christ used only fermented wine. This did not mean, however, that Baptists were compelled to use fermented wine in their communion services. Considering that the Lord's Supper was symbolic only and that wine-drinking would cause offense to many total abstainers, these "liberals" argued that grape juice could be substituted for wine and none of the truths embodied in the communion symbols would be lost.[16]

The argument raged most intensely from about 1887 to about 1890 and then ceased almost entirely. The years of controversy did not lead to unanimity on the question, but Baptists seem to "agree to disagree" and

13. *Christian Index* (Atlanta), October 13, 1887, p. 1.
14. *Alabama Baptist* (Selma), April 2, 1885, p. 1.
15. *Working Christian* (Columbia, South Carolina), April 12, 1877, p. 3; *Baptist Record* (Meridian, Mississippi), September 18, 1884, p. 1; *Alabama Baptist* (Selma), February 19, 1885, p. 1.
16. *Religious Herald* (Richmond), April 8, 1875, p. 1; *Alabama Baptist* (Selma), April 2, 1885, p. 1; *Baptist Record* (Meridian, Mississippi), July 9, 1885, p. 1; *The Baptist* (Memphis), May 19, 1888, p. 8.

avoid further discord. At their convention in 1891, for example, Tennessee Baptists promptly tabled the following motion: "*Resolved,* That in the observance of the ordinance of the Lord's Supper, the unfermented juice of the grape should be used and not alcoholic wines." [17] An article in the Virginia paper in 1900 entitled "A Plea for Unfermented Wine," failed to produce an editorial comment or a letter of rejoinder. An editorial in another journal in the same year advising the use of grape juice instead of "saloon wine which intoxicates" and suggesting the name of a company which bottled unfermented juice specifically for communion services also failed to raise an argument.[18] The controversy seems to have been settled, or perhaps suspended, as a matter of expediency. Whether Christ used fermented or unfermented wine in the first century was of less importance to temperance-conscious Baptists in the late nineteenth century than the encouragement which the use of fermented wine would give the liquor business.

The growth of temperance sentiment among Baptists is graphically revealed in the increasing severity of church discipline against members accused of trafficking in strong drink. At the close of the Civil War, only drunkenness and operating open saloons were universally considered "churchable" offenses, but by 1900 any activity which aided and abetted the liquor business subjected the offender to church action. This is the more significant in view of the fact that church discipline as a general practice was declining among Baptists during this time.

The changing attitudes toward liquor dealers is revealing. Throughout the whole period from 1865 to 1900, saloon-keepers—who, as Baptists believed, existed for the express purpose of getting people drunk—were subject to church discipline, but for much of the time druggists and grocerymen who sold liquor as a legitimate item of trade were absolved of wrongdoing.[19] One paper defended the honest, Christian grocer who

17. Tennessee Baptist Convention, *Minutes, 1891*, p. 35.

18. *Religious Herald* (Richmond), April 26, 1900, p. 3; *Alabama Baptist* (Montgomery), May 17, 1900, p. 4.

19. Most Baptists made this distinction although the belief that all liquor dealers should be disciplined was not uncommon in the 1860's and 1870's. See *Religious Herald* (Richmond), February 23, 1865, p. 2; *Christian Index* (Atlanta), February 4, 1869, p. 17; Georgia Baptist Convention, *Minutes, 1870*, p. 14; *Working Christian* (Charleston), August 9, 1870, p. 4; *The Baptist* (Memphis), September 7, 1872, p. 2; Florida Baptist Convention, *Minutes, 1872*, p. 16.

sold liquor: "Many such Christian merchants have we known. . . . We would that all our churches were entirely in their hands." Every liquor dealer should be judged on his own merits, the editor continued. If a dealer were "temperate, honest, a lover of good men, a reprover of vice, interested in the cause of Christ, liberal, devout . . . maintains his Christian character in his business . . . his influence on the whole, favorable to piety," then such a man should be retained in church fellowship. Contrary to the opinion of some, a dealer could not be held responsible for drunkenness resulting from the sale of his goods. The person who drank to excess was alone responsible, the editor concluded, for

the man who sold him the liquor which made him drunk, simply as an article of legitimate traffic, is no more responsible for the crime than the farmer who grew the grain of which the liquor was distilled, or the cooper who manufactured the barrel in which it was stored, or the mechanic who made the still by which it was extracted.[20]

The South Carolina paper agreed. Selling liquor was a legitimate business and to discipline a liquor dealer simply for plying his trade was the "subversion of a great moral principle." [21]

During and after the 1870's, however, the churches exercised their disciplinary powers more and more frequently against members engaged in any way in the liquor business. The only remedy for the liquor evil, said a contributor to the Virginia paper was

to exclude from the church every man, woman and child who gives aid and comfort to this crying evil by making, buying, selling or using as a beverage any intoxicating liquor whatever. If the writer could, *he would do it tonight. Amen.*[22]

Two incidents in the 1890's involving disciplinary action against liquor dealers and distillers attracted South-wide attention and indicate the growth of temperance sentiment among Baptists. The first developed from a personal feud between James B. Cranfill, editor of the Texas *Baptist Standard* and vice-presidential candidate on the Prohibition Party

20. *Religious Herald* (Richmond), October 13, 1870, p. 2. For many years the *Religious Herald* continued to defend liquor dealers and to oppose discipline except in cases involving drunkenness.
21. *Working Christian* (Charleston), November 8, 1870, p. 2.
22. *Religious Herald* (Richmond), October 19, 1876, p. 1.

ticket in 1892, and Thomas T. Eaton, editor of the Kentucky *Western Recorder* and pastor of the Walnut Street Baptist Church in Louisville. In 1895 Cranfill lauched a crusade in his paper against churches which retained liquor dealers as members. In the course of his attack he singled out the Walnut Street Church and its pastor for pointed criticism. In his paper Eaton defended the "distillers" in his church and countercharged Cranfill with misusing missionary funds while the latter was state missions secretary of Texas. The controversy erupted on the floor of the Southern Baptist Convention in 1896 when Cranfill introduced a resolution condemning churches which refused to expel liquor dealers. Eaton was absent from the convention at the time, but his son, Joseph, an attorney, rose to defend his father, against whom the resolution obviously was directed. Joseph Eaton introduced a substitute motion to the effect that churches exclude missionary secretaries who failed to give full account of funds entrusted to them. "Around these resolutions there raged a most excited and exciting debate," commented one journal. Eaton's motion was finally tabled and the Cranfill resolution adopted, "but the whole incident was extremely unpleasant." [23]

The other incident attracting wide attention involved a member of the First Baptist Church of Athens, Georgia, who was appointed manager of the local state-owned whiskey dispensary. The Sarepta Baptist Association, to which the First Church belonged, voted to withdraw fellowship from the church unless or until the manager of the dispensary was dismissed. The church argued that all good was mixed with evil and that the dispensary was better than open saloons. Consequently, until complete prohibition became a reality, the church would support the dispensary system and retain its manager in fellowship. After several months of controversy, however, the church dismissed the dispensary manager and the denomination at large approved its action. [24]

These two controversies helped solidify Baptist opinion against "fellowshipping" liquor dealers. Although conclusive evidence is lacking, the

23. *Ibid.,* May 21, 1896, p. 2; *Western Recorder* (Louisville), May 14, 1896, p. 13; June 4, 1896, p. 4; *Baptist Courier* (Greenville, South Carolina), May 14, 1896, p. 2; Southern Baptist Convention, *Proceedings, 1896,* pp. 44–45. As far as could be determined, the liquor dealer remained in the Walnut Street Church.

24. *Christian Index* (Atlanta), October 13, 1898, pp. 1–2; October 20, 1898, pp. 1–2; October 27, 1898, p. 12; September 28, 1899, p. 6; February 15, 1900, p. 6.

probability is that liquor dealers felt ill at ease in Baptish churches after these incidents.

The increasing frequency with which associations and conventions urged disciplinary action by their churches against users of and dealers in alcoholic beverages is indicative of the mounting concern among Baptists for the temperance cause. During the seventies and thereafter, these bodies, which traditionally had exercised no authority whatever over local churches, presumed more and more to advise and even to coerce their constituent churches. In 1872 the Florida convention recommended that all its member churches "withdraw fellowship from all members who habitually indulge in the use of intoxicating beverages, or sell the same as beverages." [25] The following year the Georgia convention advised its churches to "cut off" all members who continued to "hold their bottles." [26] The Texas convention adopted a similar resolution in 1876, Mississippi in 1878, and the remaining states, except North Carolina, before the end of the century.[27] After years of debate the Southern Baptist Convention finally adopted a strong resolution in 1896:

We announce it as the sense of this body that no person should be retained in the fellowship of a Baptist church who engages in the manufacture or sale of alcoholic liquors, either at wholesale or retail, who invests his money in the manufacture or sale of acoholic [*sic*] liquors, or who rents his property to be used for distilleries, wholesale liquor houses, or saloons. Nor do we believe that any church should retain in its fellowship any member who drinks intoxicating liquors as a beverage, or visits saloons or drinking places for the purpose of such indulgence.[28]

The adoption of this resolution by the South-wide convention may be considered the symbolic triumph of the temperance movement within the denomination.

Although Baptists as a denomination strongly supported prohibition by 1900, they nevertheless refrained from condemning the use of whis-

---

25. Florida Baptist Convention, *Minutes, 1872*, p. 16.
26. Georgia Baptist Convention, *Minutes, 1873*, p. 22.
27. Church discipline was discussed at the Louisiana Convention in 1880 but not specifically recommended in a resolution. News items of churches and associations which adopted total abstinence as a test of church membership appeared frequently in the state papers during the 1870's and later.
28. Southern Baptist Convention, *Proceedings, 1896*, p. 45.

key for medicinal purposes when taken on the advice of a physician. The use of whiskey as medicine was a custom of long standing and consequently difficult to change. Some Baptists opposed the practice throughout the period under consideration, but most comments on the custom were little more than admonitions of caution. An association in Virginia rather humorously warned that the use of liquor as a medicine could easily get out of control since every man was his own physician when it came to prescribing it.[29] As medical science developed more and better remedies for specific ailments and doctors relied less on whiskey as a panacea, Baptists more frequently denounced "medicinal drinking." The practice continued among Baptists into the twentieth century.

The growing concern for temperance among Baptists was accompanied by an increasing degree of agreement on the best methods of combatting the liquor evil. Although never reaching complete accord, they nevertheless achieved a practical working agreement by 1900. True to their belief in the total depravity of man and the necessity for a divine remedy, they consistently held forth the gospel of personal salvation as the only certain and permanent cure for intemperance and all its attendant evils. But as the century drew to a close, they leaned more and more on "man-made" remedies, including secular societies, governmental restraints, and education.

The fundamental premise on which Baptists based their temperance effort was that intemperance was sin and the cure, therefore, was the same as that for all man's sins—the gospel of Christ. Although they accepted all temperance effort as limited good, they consistently relied on the reform of the individual through a changed heart as the only permanent solution. Whether the problem were drunkenness, wine-bibbing, dram-drinking, or dealing in the traffic, "nothing but grace" could give sufficient strength to overcome the evil. "The work of Temperance Reform and the heart's conversion should be prosecuted conjointly, in order to attain the greatest possible triumph," commented one editor.[30] The Bible treated intemperance as sin and not as "an amiable weakness or incurable disease," declared a temperance committee at the Florida convention in 1884, and nothing "but the saving grace of Christ" could effect a permanent cure.[31] Baptists in other states endorsed a similar position. When

29. *Religious Herald* (Richmond), August 11, 1870, p. 2.
30. *Christian Index* (Atlanta), April 5, 1877, p. 1.
31. Florida Baptist Convention, *Minutes, 1884*, p. 10.

efforts to further temperance through political action and other means failed, Baptists were quick to re-emphasize the necessity of conversion. The Georgia Baptist Convention very clearly expressed this sentiment after the defeat of a temperance measure at the polls in 1891:

Intemperance is more a *personal* than a *social* evil. It deals more with individuals than with the masses. The simple statement of this principle should suggest to us a method of action. It is a truth of wide application that men are not to be redeemed from any wrong or won to any good by wholesale. One by one we must seek out the weak, the tempted, the fettered—one by one we must present to them the gospel of sympathy, help, liberty and duty.[32]

Although they relied primarily on personal conversion to effect temperance reform, Baptists welcomed all "proper methods" in behalf of the cause. An ever-increasing number advocated regulation or prohibition by law, for example. Some objected, however, on the ground that temperance was a moral and religious issue and of no concern to the government, while others opposed—or at least refused to support—governmental action out of a sense of futility or because of objections to specific laws or plans. Before 1900, however, practically all objection to legal restraints ceased.

A greater problem among Baptists than whether or not the powers of government *should* be employed in the temperance cause was the disagreement over *how* governmental powers could be used and how Baptists, individually and collectively, could best exert their influence to this end. That individual Baptists should use the power of the franchise against the liquor traffic was conceded, but whether or not and to what extent churches, associations, and conventions should involve themselves in politics were questions of grave concern. State conventions began adopting resolutions and petitions calling for legislative action in behalf of temperance in the early 1870's, although opposition to such action remained strong for a number of years.[33] The usual objection was that such action violated the separation of church and state principle. A special committee reported to the North Carolina Convention in 1879:

We heartily sanction every effort calculated to lesson [*sic*] the evils of intemperance, and as citizens of the commonwealth we will co-operate with

32. Georgia Baptist Convention, *Minutes, 1891*, p. 33. Responses were similar in other states where political action failed.
33. Mississippi Baptist Convention, *Proceedings, 1872*, p. 38.

our fellow-citizens, or secular organizations, to influence public opinion in that direction.

But, on account of our well-known principles in regard to any connection of Church and State, we deem it inexpedient for us, as a denomination, in our associated capacity, to memorialize the Legislature on this subject.[34]

In 1880 the Georgia Convention adopted a resolution memorializing the general assembly on behalf of a certain temperance law, but after strong objections and lengthy discussion they rescinded the resolution.[35] The weekly papers, whose relationship to the denomination permitted freer discussion, showed less reticence about calling on the government for aid, especially after 1880. The Southern Baptist Convention avoided memorials and petitions on the subject until after the turn of the century.

After accepting the principle of regulation and control of liquor by the state, Baptists still disagreed over the best specific method, although they showed a willingness to support almost any method which gave promise of success. Tennessee Baptists expressed the sentiment which prevailed throughout the denomination toward the end of the century:

We would recommend as suitable methods prayer, a right example, moral suasion, strict discipline in our churches, and the adoption of any measure which seems practicable and effective, such as prohibition, local option, or anything else which will accomplish the results desired. But whatever methods may be adopted for securing the end, one thing is certain—THE SALOON MUST GO! DOWN WITH THE SALOON! [36]

Baptists generally questioned the value of responsibility laws which would make the seller of strong drink liable for damages resulting from the sale of his liquor and laws which made drunkenness a penitentiary offense. They also overwhelmingly opposed a "high license" system for controlling the liquor traffic. Commented one editor:

When considered, as it should be, in connection with the evils of whisky, high license is an open insult to the common sense of mankind. It is but a tribute paid by whisky for the privilege of ruining men temporily and eternally. No

34. North Carolina Baptist Convention, *Minutes, 1879*, p. 35. The 1880 convention reversed this action and petitioned the legislature for a state-wide prohibition law. See *Minutes, 1880*, p. 41.

35. Georgia Baptist Convention, *Minutes, 1881*, pp. 12–13, 15, 16, 17, 24, 27–28.

36. Tennessee Baptist Convention, *Proceedings, 1897*, p. 25.

kind of tax, no amount of money, no amount of legislation, can ever compensate for the evils of whisky.[37]

Various state conventions called the high license system an "iniqui- tous . . . partnership between the saloon and the State," a "crime by the state," a "compromise with sin," and a league with "hell and the devil." [38] The South-wide convention denounced the license system as "an offense against God and a crime against humanity," a system "through which men buy the right to destroy human hope and happiness, and blight human souls." [39] The Georgia paper condemned licensing as a "low policy of intemperance" by which the liquor business sought to buy respectability and legality and to silence demands for total prohibition.[40]

Somewhat contradictory to their attitude toward the high license system as a compromise with evil, Baptists generally approved state- owned dispensaries, not as an ultimate good, but as an improvement over the open saloon. The difference between liquor bought at the state dis- pensary and that purchased at an open saloon, commented the South Carolina paper, was the difference between a "killing and a savage butchery. Both are murder, but the latter adds fiendish ferocity to the crime. The dispensary is a murderous business, but barrooms are some- thing a little worse." [41] Most comments on the dispensary system were more charitable. Several Baptist papers actively supported bills proposing the establishment of state-owned or locally owned dispensaries. The

37. *Tennessee Baptist* (Memphis), May 28, 1887, p. 5. The high license system was an effort to regulate the liquor traffic by levying the liquor retail license so high (as high as $2,000 per year in Massachusetts) that only a few dealers in a community could afford to operate. Nebraska adopted the first state- wide high license law in 1881, and several other states followed in the next few years. Wherever the system was adopted it reduced the number of saloons and made them more respectable but failed to reduce the consumption of liquor. By 1890 prohibitionists had come to oppose the high license system, while liquor manufacturers usually favored it. *See* John G. Woolley and William E. Johnson, *Temperance Progress in the Century* (1903), pp. 177–200.

38. Mississippi Baptist Convention, *Proceedings, 1890,* p. 25; Alabama Bap- tist Convention, *Minutes, 1891,* p. 48; South Carolina Baptist Convention, *Min- utes, 1891,* p. 10; Georgia Baptist Convention, *Minutes, 1897,* p. 41.

39. Southern Baptist Convention, *Proceedings, 1889,* p. 39; *1892,* p. 45.

40. *Christian Index* (Atlanta), May 29, 1890, p. 1; September 11, 1890, p. 6. Only two articles supporting regulation by licensing were noted, and both of these were quotations from other publications. *See Religious Herald* (Richmond), April 23, 1891, p. 1; December 17, 1891, p. 2.

41. *Baptist Courier* (Greenville, South Carolina), May 25, 1893, p. 21.

Tennessee paper reflected the attitude of Baptists generally: "For our part we prefer the complete prohibition of the traffic, but still a half a loaf is better than no loaf, and if this is the best that we can get, we shall have to be satisfied with this and thank the Lord for it." [42] Until complete prohibition could be enacted, therefore, Baptists considered the dispensary system the least objectionable way of handling the liquor traffic. Complete opposition to the system was rare. [43]

Throughout the period under consideration many Baptists advocated total prohibition rather than regulation as the most satisfactory method of dealing with the liquor traffic, and the number holding this view increased constantly. "I am fully persuaded," said one editor, "not only that governments have a right to pass stringent prohibitory laws, but that the solution of this momentously great question lies in this very principle of prohibition." [44] By the mid-1880's total prohibition was *the* Baptist position. Thereafter, the problem was simply to agree on the best method of achieving this end. Whether prohibition could be best attained by local option, state prohibition, or nationwide prohibition remained a debatable question until the end of the century. Although the prohibition movement was not uniform among Baptists in different parts of the South, indications are that they preferred first (in point of time) local option, then state prohibition, and finally, at the end of the century, nationwide prohibition. Whether state and national prohibition should be effected through legislative action or constitutional amendment was of no particular importance.

Prohibition by local option was most popular among Baptists in the seventies and early eighties. This method was best, they believed, because it placed the responsibility for enforcing the law on local citizens. Local option, said one editor, "is the only plan that can succeed; for when the prohibitory law is not sustained by public opinion it cannot be enforced." [45]

42. *Baptist and Reflector* (Nashville), December 6, 1894, p. 1.

43. It is surprising, perhaps, that no one raised objection to the dispensary system on the ground that it put the government in the liquor business. The system must have been considered a vast improvement over the open saloon.

44. *Biblical Recorder* (Raleigh, North Carolina), January 7, 1880, p. 2. Significantly, the Mississippi Convention changed its "Temperance" committee to "Prohibition" committee. *See* Mississippi Baptist Convention, *Proceedings, 1895,* p. 24.

45. *Christian Index* (Atlanta), August 31, 1882, p. 8.

As temperance sentiment increased, however, local option came to be considered only a halfway measure, better than open saloons and the dispensary, but inferior to total prohibition. Delegates to the Louisiana convention in 1888 pledged themselves to support "all honorable and legitimate measures for the complete extermination of the liquor traffic, either by the *temporary* method of local option or by the *more permanent and effective* means of complete prohibition." [46] After agitating for local option for two decades, the Georgia paper rather abruptly in the 1890's began calling it only an "entering wedge" for total prohibition, and, before the end of the decade, the editor was condemning the system. In an editorial entitled "Local Option in Murder Laws," he pointed out the inconsistency in legalizing liquor in one city or county and prohibiting it in others. By this logic, he argued, murder could be legalized in some areas. If the liquor traffic were wrong anywhere, it was wrong everywhere.[47]

Local option continued to be preferred in some sections of the South for the remainder of the century, but its popularity declined in favor of state-wide prohibition after the mid-eighties. Agitation for state-wide prohibition by law or by constitutional amendment appeared as early as 1880, and about 1890 it became the primary objective of Baptist temperance promoters.[48] In the nineties Baptists entered energetically into the crusade, but they found the movement for state prohibition a discouraging endeavor. The loosely arrayed temperance forces were hardly a match for the better organized liquor men who seemed to be in league with the courts, the established political parties, and law enforcement agencies. Constitutional amendments and laws, once adopted, could be and often were rendered ineffective by judicial interpretation and apathetic enforcement. Baptists attributed the ineffectiveness of state prohibition to the perfidy of public officials, the apathy of church members, and the Negro

46. Louisiana Baptist Convention, *Minutes, 1888,* p. 18. Emphasis added.

47. *Christian Index* (Atlanta), November 16, 1899, p. 6. A month later, however, after a bill in the legislature providing for total prohibition failed, the editor again reversed his opinion and admitted that "the local option law is the best prohibition movement ever devised." See *ibid.,* December 14, 1899, p. 6.

48. This emphasis on state-wide prohibition by Baptists was part of a larger movement which was sweeping the country during the eighties. *See* Ernest H. Cherrington, *The Evolution of Prohibition in the United States of America* (1920), pp. 176 ff. From the number of articles, editorials, letters, reports, and resolutions, it would appear that Baptists favored state prohibition by *legislative enactment* rather than by constitutional amendment.

vote.[49] Texas Baptists blamed the defeat of a prohibition amendment in their state on an open letter by Jefferson Davis in which he opposed the amendment as an abridgment of personal liberty. One Texas Baptist called the letter the "unkindest cut of all. . . . If our cause is crushed to the earth," he said, "it must be remembered, in the dark years to come, that the honored name of Jefferson Davis helped to crush it. God help us to carry Prohibition, and to forgive the error of that great man." [50] The Davis letter was used again by the liquor forces in Tennessee a month later and helped defeat—or so Baptists believed—a prohibition amendment in that state. The letter, commented the editor of the Tennessee paper, "was a shameful prostitution of his great name in supporting the greatest evil that afflicts our land." [51]

The lack of success of the prohibition movement at the state level was instrumental in causing many Baptists to turn to the federal government for assistance in controlling the liquor traffic. Agitation for national prohibition was extremely rare among Baptists until the 1890's, and then it was only sporadic and unorganized. The first Baptist body to recommend specifically that prohibition be achieved by national authority was the Alabama Convention, which adopted the following report in 1883:

Your [temperance] committee beg permission . . . to say that they believe this Convention, as a body of *Christian men who are citizens of the State of Alabama,* ought to commit themselves to labor for Constitutional Prohibition as a *final* aim, and to labor for anything now which may be best in our respective sections, and which looks to State and United States Constitutional Prohibition.[52]

Although Baptists offered more and more support to the movement for national prohibition after this time, they failed to close ranks in a united effort before 1900. As the century closed Baptists were searching still for that one best method of promoting prohibition.

In propagating the gospel and in promoting other good causes, Baptists have been reluctant to co-operate with other religious and secular groups.

---

49. *The Baptist* (Memphis), October 8, 1887, p. 7; Mississippi Baptist Convention, *Proceedings, 1891,* p. 20; *Christian Index* (Atlanta), December 1, 1887, p. 9; January 29, 1891, p. 5; Georgia Baptist Convention, *Minutes, 1900,* p. 52.
50. Reported in the *Western Recorder* (Louisville), August 4, 1887, p. 8.
51. *The Baptist* (Memphis), September 10, 1887, p. 4.
52. Alabama Baptist Convention, *Minutes, 1883,* p. 23.

This proclivity was evident in the early stages of the temperance crusade, but with the passage of time they came to co-operate with other denominations and societies to an extent never before known in their history. The temperance cause, in fact, initiated the loosening of Baptist exclusiveness and opened the way for all subsequent co-operative action for social and humanitarian betterment.

Throughout the late nineteenth century, Baptists generally sympathized with temperance societies, although they often questioned the value of any temperance effort outside the churches. "I have long been convinced that the church of Christ is the right place to look for a *real temperance society,*" declared a Virginia Baptist in 1865.[53] The general association of the state echoed this view a year later, but added: "We greet with pleasure the revival of temperance organizations, and recommend such worthy enterprises to the personal co-operation and assistance of 'them that love the Lord.' "[54] These statements reflect the thinking of a considerable segment of Baptists until the end of the century.

In their journals and at their general meetings, Baptists usually gave moral and sometimes financial support to all the well-known temperance societies—the Order of Good Templars, the Sons of Temperance, the National Temperance Society, the National Bureau of Reform, the Woman's Christian Temperance Union, the Anti-Saloon League, and even the Catholic Total Abstinence Society. Their approbation of the Catholic Total Abstinence Society and other temperance efforts by Catholics was a significant departure from precedent. Baptists were highly critical of Roman Catholics and often accused them of supporting the liquor traffic. A contributor to one state paper declared that members of the "Roman hierarchy . . . encourage the drinking habit," and delegates at a state convention described strong drink as one of Satan's most potent agents and "one of Rome's greatest allies."[55] Nevertheless, Baptist opposition to strong drink was sufficiently strong—for a brief period at least—to overcome their traditional antipathy for everything Catholic.

The one notable exception to the general Baptist practice of supporting temperance societies was their attitude toward the W.C.T.U. Baptists sanctioned the participation of women in the postwar temperance move-

53. *Religious Herald* (Richmond), February 23, 1865, p. 2.
54. Virginia Baptist General Association, *Minutes, 1866,* p. 22.
55. *Christian Index* (Atlanta), November 26, 1885, p. 3; Arkansas Baptist Convention, *Proceedings, 1895,* p. 26.

ment and approved the activities of the W.C.T.U. as long as it adhered solely to temperance reform. But as the union became enmeshed in politics and expanded its interests to include women's rights, Baptists withdrew their support. One paper denounced the W.C.T.U. for its political agitation and its "fanatical zeal . . . to nullify one of the sacred ordinances of God's house," by permitting women to speak in public, and also "its sanctimonious pretensions to purify the Lord's Supper," by substituting grape juice for fermented wine.[56] A more damning article in another paper denounced the W.C.T.U. as

anti-Christian [in] spirit and aim. . . . The whole spirit of the "W.C.T.U." is to turn Christianity into a set of "reforms"—anti-liquor, anti-tobacco, "social purity," "female suffrage," and what not. Where these ideas thoroughly prevail New Testament Christianity must necessarily perish.

Furthermore, the writer continued, the *"Jesuitical manner"* and objectives of the union were

a menace to true womanhood. A woman political, voting or trying to vote, fanatical on all "reform," ready to face a mixed audience and address it, ready to talk in public and in private about fornication, rape, "age of consent," &c., scoffing at the idea of subordination to man, or of obeying her husband (if she has one), as the Bible commands—this is the style of woman that the "W.C.T.U." is trying to manufacture, and has to some extent manufactured. . . . Do our Baptist women at the South wish to surrender the gospel; to attack the communion in most unwomanly fashion; to encourage orations by women in mixed assemblies; to promote female preaching and female suffrage; to put before their precious daughters the most odious examples and teachings; in general, under the guise of zeal for temperance, to open the door for every soul-destroying and home-destroying "ism" to enter in; and to throw away the peerless crown of Southern womanhood? If they do, let them go into this "W.C.T.U." movement.[57]

A lively exchange of letters followed this article. Many writers took exception to the ideas expressed, but more stated approval. Never after this time did Baptists support the W.C.T.U. enthusiastically.

The secular temperance society to which Baptists gave their greatest support was the Anti-Saloon League of America. Organized nationally

56. *Tennessee Baptist* (Memphis), November 28, 1885, p. 6.
57. *Religious Herald* (Richmond), June 6, 1889, p. 1.

only in 1895, the League was by 1900 the principal agency through which temperance forces were unified into a victorious movement. In view of the historical tendency of Baptists to avoid "entangling alliances," the aid which they rendered the League was little short of revolutionary. State conventions authorized collections for the League's support, publicized its literature, and appointed messengers and delegates to the national meetings of the League. The older, conservative element of the denomination protested these innovations, but the denomination at large concurred.[58] Conditions were changing. Baptists were losing their separateness and becoming more conscious of their responsibility to society. Eradicating the evils of intemperance was more important than denominational traditions. In the successful drive of the Anti-Saloon League toward national prohibition through constitutional amendment, Southern Baptists lent valuable support.

As already indicated, Baptists believed in promoting temperance reform through political action, but their dedication to temperance was not sufficiently strong to cause them to make it the organizing principle of their politics. As a denomination, Baptists never supported the Prohibition Party. Three prominent Southern Baptists were candidates on the national Prohibition ticket between 1872 and 1900—Green Clay Smith, presidential candidate in 1876, James B. Cranfill, vice-presidential candidate in 1892, and Joshua Levering, presidential candidate in 1896—but Baptists refused to endorse them. Baptists more often denounced than supported the Prohibition Party because of its endorsement of women's rights and, more important, because of their fear of splitting the Solid South. Supporting the Prohibition Party, warned the South Carolina paper,

would imperil white supremacy, and this is sufficient reason alone on which to base our opposition, as the moral and religious welfare of this State is best subserved by the maintenance of honest, upright government, under the control of its native white people, and we have only to recall our past experience to demonstrate the truth of this assertion. . . . Temperance is not a political question, but is simply a moral one. . . . We do not believe a

58. Alabama Baptist Convention, *Minutes, 1895*, p. 33; South Carolina Baptist Convention, *Minutes, 1896*, p. 17; Tennessee Baptist Convention, *Proceedings, 1897*, p. 36; Virginia Baptist General Association, *Minutes, 1897*, p. 42.

greater misfortune could happen to the temperance-movement than to lug it into politics.[59]

The Baptist way of effecting temperance reform through politics was essentially the same as that advanced by most Southern Populists for achieving agricultural reform—by gaining control of the Democratic party machinery or by voting for candidates most sympathetic to the cause. "We can only express the wish," declared Alabama Baptists, "for a larger influence exerted at the polls, believing that only sober men and officers who are in sympathy with prohibition, should receive the support of Christian voters. We can expect nothing better out of the ballot box than we put in." [60] The admonition to "vote as you pray" sounded repeatedly in Baptist circles. "The man who prays 'Thy kingdom come,' and votes for an old soaker, is not for Christ," declared a North Carolina minister, and most Baptists agreed.[61]

Southern Baptists lagged behind other major denominations in supporting the temperance crusade between 1865 and 1900. With the passage of time, however, their interest increased until by the end of the century they were fast drawing abreast of the most aggressive religious groups. The first half of the decade of the eighties was a time of rapid growth in temperance concern among Baptists. During these years they awakened to the seriousness of the liquor problem and assumed a share of the responsibility for its solution. With the adoption of the first temperance resolution by the Southern Baptist Convention in 1886, Baptists symbolically dedicated themselves to the ultimate destruction of the drink evil.[62] The contribution of Baptists to the cause of temperance cannot be measured precisely, but indubitably it was considerable.

59. *Baptist Courier* (Greenville, South Carolina), May 3, 1888, p. 2. A number of articles appeared in the journals suggesting that Baptists insist on a dry plank in the Democratic platform and, if their demands were refused, bolt the party. See *Western Recorder* (Louisville), November 30, 1882, p. 3; *Baptist Record* (Meridian, Mississippi), April 23, 1885, p. 2; *Alabama Baptist* (Montgomery), June 3, 1886, p. 1; *The Baptist* (Memphis), May 19, 1888, p. 15; *Texas Baptist Standard* (Waco), June 4, 1896, p. 4.

60. Alabama Baptist Convention, *Minutes, 1895,* p. 33.

61. *Biblical Recorder* (Raleigh, North Carolina), October 2, 1895, p. 1.

62. Southern Baptist Convention, *Proceedings, 1886,* p. 33. In reference to this report, the *Religious Herald* (Richmond) commented: "The discussion indicated entire unanimity in opposition to the liquor traffic, and it required the vigorous use of the gavel to prevent the Convention from frequently bursting out in applause."—*See* issue of May 20, 1886, p. 2. Two years later, however, Dr.

James P. Boyce, president of the convention, ruled out of order two delegates who attempted to introduce resolutions on temperance. *See* Southern Baptist Convention, *Proceedings, 1888,* pp. 33, 34. Dr. Boyce's ruling did not stem from any sympathy with the liquor business; rather, he considered temperance a social and political question and thus outside the "purview of the Constitution" of the convention. The convention upheld Dr. Boyce's ruling out of respect for him, but the debate which ensued indicated that the majority of the denomination disagreed. *See Baptist Courier* (Greenville, South Carolina), May 24, 1888, p. 1; *Religious Herald* (Richmond), July 12, 1888, p. 1; William Wright Barnes, *Southern Baptist Convention, 1845–1953* (1954), p. 246.

8. Personal Morality

HE Southern Baptist faith remained an intensely personal matter throughout the period from 1865 to 1900. Not only in its emphasis on personal redemption in preparation for the *next* life but also in matters of conduct in *this* life, the denomination stressed the responsibility of the individual. The world could be made better only as individual Christians exemplified the ideals of their faith in their daily living. Personal purity, not social betterment movements, could create a better world. The role of the church in this process was that of keeping its members consistently walking in the heavenly way through admonition, reproof, and, as a final resort, church discipline.

In exercising its leavening influence on society, the denomination was more concerned with the leisure-time activities and personal habits of its members than with the moral and ethical implications of their workaday existence. Any action or activity which contravened a Biblical command or failed to contribute to the individual's spiritual edification was likely to be condemned or at least questioned. Gambling, lying, stealing, adultery, and other actions clearly proscribed by Scripture were uniformly condemned; but dancing, horse racing, smoking, card playing, novel reading, patronizing the theater, and other worldly amusements were practices about which Baptists showed a variety of opinion.

Judging from the amount of discussion devoted to the subject, dancing (next to drinking) was the cardinal sin among Christians. Dancing was always listed among the "worldly amusements" from which church members were admonished to abstain on pain of excommunication. This "hugging institution," as one writer called dancing, was "not only unscriptural but anti-scriptural . . . a sinful pleasure . . . wounding to the feelings of all the truly pious . . . [and] destructive of the religious influence of those who practice it."[1] Stories of the tragic consequences of

1. *Religious Herald* (Richmond), November 29, 1866, p. 1.

dancing often accompanied tirades against the "devil's pastime." One such story in one of the papers recounted the frightful end of a young man who collapsed from exhaustion and died on the dance floor. "Alas!" commented the editor. "What a place is the ball room from which to receive the last dread summons!"[2]

The kind of dance which drew the severest criticism from Baptists was the "modern round dance." Some Baptists defended the old-fashioned square dance as harmless recreation. Arguments over the two kinds of dance appeared in the weekly papers and occasionally erupted in denominational meetings. Following a discussion at an associational gathering in Virginia, a delegate introduced a resolution to the effect that the "square dance be sanctioned and the round dance be forbidden," to which another delegate replied: "Ah! brethren, I mightily fear, if we authoritatively permit the square dance, that some people may soon *pinch off the corners* and make it the round *dance*."[3] The resolution failed, and, as a rule, Baptists condemned dancing regardless of its geometric appellation.

The principal objection among Baptists to dancing arose from their abnormal fear of the intimate association of the sexes. Dancing might not be wrong but it tended toward evil. "Dancing, we judge, is not sinful *per se*," commented one editor, but "it requires no prophet to perceive that the ardor and inconsiderateness of youth, the excitement of music, and the frivolities engendered by association, would be likely to lead to unwarrantable familiarities between the sexes."[4] "Sex is the spirit of the dance," declared one writer.[5] "Young men and young women may dance alone," said a Tennessee Baptist, "but you cannot get them to do it, and the reason why they will not, is the reason it is wrong."[6] "Three-fourths of the female cases of disgrace and ruin originated in the dance," commented another writer.[7] Baptists considered the damage to the reputation of Christians who participated in this "hugging set to music" to be incalculable.[8]

Baptists condemned dancing as an evil pastime not only for their own members but also for those outside the church. The Mississippi Conven-

2. *Christian Index* (Macon, Georgia), January 20, 1866, p. 15.
3. *Religious Herald* (Richmond), June 9, 1881, p. 1.
4. *Ibid.*, March 16, 1876, p. 1.
5. *Ibid.*, April 23, 1885, p. 1.
6. *The Baptist* (Memphis), November 27, 1880, p. 289.
7. *Religious Herald* (Richmond), May 9, 1878, p. 1.
8. *Western Recorder* (Louisville), July 14, 1881, p. 1.

tion, for example, protested the annual balls sponsored by the state university and the agricultural and mechanical college. These affairs, stated a petition of protest to the presidents and boards of trust of these institutions, were "a source of trouble to our Churches and of dissipation to our boys and girls."[9] Other protests followed and as a result—or so Mississippi Baptists claimed—the annual dance at the A. and M. College was discontinued.[10] The North Carolina paper also objected to the annual graduation dances at the tax-supported university and the technological college of that state. The editor pointed out the hypocrisy of giving the graduates a Bible at commencement exercises and then "honoring" them with a soul-destroying dance an hour later.[11]

The opposition of Baptists to dancing varied little between 1865 and 1900. They devoted less attention to the subject in the last decade of the century, but denunciations, when expressed, were no less severe.[12]

Baptists inveighed against other "worldly amusements," though not as fervidly as against dancing. Cards, billiards, novels, skating, chess, and even occasionally checkers and croquet were adjudged outright sinful or, at best, time consuming and unprofitable. Quite often Baptists lumped these practices together as "innocent amusements . . . falsely so-called," and warned church members against them.[13] Novel reading received a great deal of attention. Few Baptists were as narrow as the one who declared:

I am fully convinced, both by observation and experience . . . that novel-reading to *any* extent, by *any* one, and particularly by a professing Christian, is in many respects deeply injurious to the reader, and hurtful to the cause of Christ.[14]

But most Baptists agreed that novels and all other secular reading matter should be selected carefully and read in moderation. They condemned the writings of the "godless" Tolstoy, Zola, and Whitman and the popular

9. Mississippi Baptist Convention, *Proceedings, 1885,* pp. 22, 25.

10. *Ibid., 1892,* p. 31; *1893,* p. 20.

11. *Biblical Recorder* (Raleigh, North Carolina), June 9, 1897, p. 2.

12. *Religious Herald* (Richmond), November 1, 1894, p. 1; *Christian Index* (Atlanta), February 24, 1898, p. 6.

13. Alabama Baptist Convention, *Minutes, 1866,* p. 16; *Religious Herald* (Richmond), December 20, 1866, p. 1.

14. *Religious Herald* (Richmond), May 2, 1872, p. 1.

Police Gazette and the "dime novel." Baptists approved the works of Sir Walter Scott, however, and religious novels generally.[15]

Baptists viewed with alarm the growing popularity of the theater, opera, circuses, and other kinds of commercial entertainment. Some argued that the theater, like the dance, was not necessarily wrong within itself, but that the American stage, as it existed, was productive of evil. An occasional contributor to the state papers defended a particular play or argued that the best theatrical productions, like the best novels, could be enjoyed by adult Christians without harmful effects. A professor at a denominational school expressed the dilemma of many educated Baptists by pointing out the inconsistency in kindling an interest in the theater by teaching classical and Shakespearean drama and then condemning those who patronized the theater. But, he confessed, he had no solution to offer since he could not conscientiously approve the modern stage, nor would he give up reading and teaching the great dramas.[16]

Although a few Baptists defended the theater, the majority clearly opposed it and all related forms of entertainment. A Christian could attend the theater "only at the peril of his soul," commented one writer,[17] while another denounced modern plays because, he said, "we have a profound conviction that they are demoralizing and dangerous to Christians or anybody else who patronizes them."[18] "If the Scriptures are to be obeyed," wrote another, "the theater must be avoided."[19] The Louisiana paper accurately expressed the Baptist position:

No Christian can follow Jesus, and, then be found in a Circus. He that denies himself, takes up his cross, and walks in the foot-prints of our Lord, can not go into Shows, Theatres and such like.[20]

One of the chief objections to the theater was the immoral display of the feminine figure which characterized many dramas. One paper de-

15. *Ibid.,* July 23, 1874, p. 2; November 16, 1893, p. 1; November 21, 1895, p. 1; *Christian Index* (Atlanta), January 20, 1876, p. 1.
16. *Religious Herald* (Richmond), July 21, 1892, p. 1.
17. *Christian Index* (Atlanta), February 24, 1870, p. 33.
18. *Baptist Record* (Meridian, Mississippi), November 25, 1886, p. 1.
19. *Christian Index* (Atlanta), October 17, 1895, p. 2.
20. *Baptist Chronicle* (Ruston, Louisiana), November 24, 1892, p. 2. Baptists objected less to circuses than to the legitimate stage, although they usually included circuses among wordly amusements which Christians should avoid

scribed two successful plays of the time as the "apotheosis of the female leg. . . . The astonishing success of these impure exhibitions," said the editor, "ought to awaken genuine alarm among all who have the slightest wish to preserve society from going down into decay." [21] Baptists struck at the evil by recommending church discipline against members who persisted in the habit, and some Baptists even considered the theater sufficiently detrimental to public morals to justify regulation or prohibition by the state in the interest of the general welfare.[22]

Within the area of personal conduct, one of the most controversial subjects among Southern Baptists was the tobacco habit. Attitudes ranged from a forthright condemnation of the use of tobacco as a sin second only to drunkenness to a spirited defense of its use as beneficial in soothing the nerves, aiding digestion, and preventing "local scurvy." [23] The opponents of tobacco were more vocal than its defenders, but smoking, chewing, and dipping were customs of long standing in the South, and the purists who so caustically condemned tobacco were decidedly in the minority.

In the absence of specific Biblical commands against tobacco, the principal scriptural arguments against its use were based on several Bible verses concerning influence and abstinence from the appearances of evil. "Do you 'glorify God in your body and spirit, which are his,' by the use of tobacco?" asked one writer. "If you do not, then you are solemnly bound by your Christian profession to give it up. For 'whatsoever ye do in word or deed, do all in the name of the Lord Jesus.' " [24] Baptists were reminded often that the Christian's body was the temple of the Holy Spirit which could be desecrated by the use of tobacco.

Far more frequently, however, arguments against tobacco rested on "scientific" evidence rather than on Biblical commands. Opponents of tobacco cited eminent medical authorities to prove that tobacco was the causal agent in a long list of physical, nervous, and mental disorders. "Intermission of the action of the heart [or] narcotism of the heart," "tremors," "insomnia," and inflammation of the "excretory organs," were

21. *Christian Index* (Atlanta), February 13, 1868, p. 28. Quoted from the *Christian Intelligencer* (n.p., n.d.).

22. *Christian Index* (Atlanta), October 24, 1872, p. 165; *Alabama Baptist* (Montgomery), January 3, 1889, p. 1; *The Baptist* (Memphis), January 7, 1888, pp. 4–5.

23. *Religious Herald* (Richmond), May 9, 1878, p. 1.

24. *Ibid.*, April 7, 1870, p. 1.

among the physical and nervous ailments traced to tobacco.[25] Even more serious, tobacco could produce deleterious effects on the mind. The "uniform testimony" of leading physicians, said one editor, is that "diseases of the lungs and heart are the almost sure result" of smoking and that "the brain is weakened, and the nervous system shattered, and the general health undermined by it . . . while the effects on children and children's children is to entail on them nervousness, weakness and shattered constitutions, which will go on and down to coming generations."[26] Smoking among the young, declared the same editor later, "leads to a species of imbecility. . . . This ought to decide the question, and make the tobacco-habit an impossibility for the young."[27] The medical profession, said another editor, attributed to tobacco the stimulation of an appetite for strong drink: "The way that leads down to a drunkard's grave and to a drunkard's hell is strewn thick with tobacco leaves," he concluded.[28]

These extreme views by no means represented the opinions of any appreciable number of Baptists. Some of the same issues of papers which contained scathing denunciations of the tobacco habit also carried advertisements of various brands of tobacco. Farm columns in many journals offered advice frequently to farmers about tobacco culture and market conditions. One editor achieved the *ultimum absurdum* when he advised his readers to abstain from the use of tobacco; but, he concluded, "if they decline from following our advice, they cannot do better than to procure their supplies from J. B. Bland & Co. [one of the paper's advertisers]."[29]

The opponents of tobacco failed to secure the unqualified endorsement of the denomination because, no doubt, of the prevalent use of tobacco among the clergy. That tobacco was in general use among Baptist ministers is quite evident. A letter to the North Carolina paper suggesting that churches dismiss their preachers who refused to give up tobacco was answered with the quip that such a policy would "unchurch, and depose two thirds of the most pious, learned and, efficient and consistent minis-

25. *Biblical Recorder* (Raleigh, North Carolina), August 29, 1866, p. 4; *Alabama Baptist* (Marion), January 6, 1876, p. 4; *Religious Herald* (Richmond), December 19, 1895, p. 1; May 30, 1878, p. 1; *Christian Index* (Atlanta), June 18, 1896, p. 3.
26. *Christian Index* (Atlanta), April 13, 1882, p. 10.
27. *Ibid.*, September 1, 1892, p. 4.
28. *Religious Herald* (Richmond), December 17, 1896, p. 1.
29. *Ibid.*, June 27, 1869, p. 3.

ters not only in N.C. but in other States." [30] Smoking and chewing were common practices among ministers at denominational gatherings. The president of the Georgia Convention, meeting in the First Baptist Church of Augusta in 1885, requested the delegates—mostly ministers—to refrain from spitting on the newly carpeted floors of the church sanctuary, although, he said, smoking would be permitted in the conference rooms. [31] A Northern visitor to the Southern Baptist Convention in 1889 commended the delegates on the excellent manner in which they conducted their meeting; but, he said, they had their faults: " 'They fill the lecture-room with smoke. They bedaub the vestry floors with tobacco.' " [32] A Southern editor agreed with this criticism: "It is true that the tobacco nuisance is disgusting, and when it desecrates the house of God it is wicked." [33]

Chewing tobacco during church services and spitting on the floors were evidently common practices. "Can people kneel down in ambeer and tobacco cuds, and be decent?" queried one woman. "I ask," she continued, "what kind of a heaven would it be if the use of tobacco were permitted there?" [34] Another observer of the custom commented:

Somehow or other, I cannot keep from thinking that if Jesus had been there as He was in the Temple eighteen hundred years ago, He would have chided the brethren severely, if He would not have driven them out for making His house a tobacco chewer's spitbox. [35]

Some churches provided spittoons for their tobacco-chewing worshipers, which led one observer to comment that cuspidors might help keep the churches clean, but they merely encouraged the obnoxious habit which had best be discontinued all together. [36]

The use of tobacco continued among Baptists until the end of the century, but indications are that it was becoming less prevalent. The Texas convention took an oblique blow at tobacco in its temperance

30. *Biblical Recorder* (Raleigh, North Carolina), February 21, 1872, p. 2.
31. *Christian Index* (Atlanta), May 7, 1885, p. 8; May 21, 1885, p. 2. When the president made his request, a lengthy debate ensued over whether the request should be included in the minutes. It was not.
32. *Ibid.,* May 23, 1889, p. 1. Quoted from the *Christian Inquirer* (New York), n.d.
33. *Christian Index* (Atlanta), May 23, 1889, p. 1.
34. *Religious Herald* (Richmond), October 29, 1874, p. 3.
35. *Biblical Recorder* (Raleigh, North Carolina), June 28, 1876, p. 1.
36. *Ibid.,* July 30, 1884, p. 3.

report as early as 1878, and the Arkansas Convention forthrightly condemned the "poisonous weed" in 1890.[37] In response to an inquiry in 1888, a professor at Richmond College estimated that the proportion of ministerial students who smoked at his institution had declined from 50 percent to 20 percent in the previous fifteen to twenty years.[38] And, without appealing to the emotions or abusing Scriptures, a contributor to the *Seminary Magazine* in 1890 calmly developed his arguments and arrived at the conclusion that ministers should refrain from the use of tobacco in any and all forms.[39] Less emotion and more considered reasoning generally characterized the arguments against the use of tobacco in the last decade of the century.

Without Biblical command and incontestable scientific evidence to support them, the opponents of tobacco failed to win a sweeping victory for their cause within the denomination as the temperance crusaders had done. The majority of Baptists exhibited little enthusiasm over the issue. To them tobacco was neither demonstrably harmful nor prohibited by Scripture. It was unnecessary, expensive, and often offensive and nauseating to nonusers, and, withal, an undesirable habit from which the dedicated Christian should abstain. At the end of the century, however, Baptist ministers and laymen alike continued to smoke, chew, and dip, though perhaps with a slightly uneasy conscience.

Another problem which Baptists viewed as a matter of personal morality but with implications for society at large was the changing attitude in America toward marriage and the family. Baptists considered marriage an institution of divine origin, initiated by God in the Garden of Eden and validated by Christ at the marriage feast in Cana. The increasing divorce rate in the late nineteenth century was therefore of grave concern to Baptists.[40] To combat this trend they stressed the absolute necessity of strict compliance with God's marriage laws. In contrast to some religious denominations, Baptists did not consider the marriage bonds insoluble,

37. Texas Baptist Convention, *Minutes, 1878,* p. 15; Arkansas Baptist Convention, *Proceedings, 1890,* p. 43.

38. *Religious Herald* (Richmond), February 23, 1888, p. 1.

39. John C. Young, "Is It Appropriate for a Minister to Use Tobacco?" *Seminary Magazine,* III (February 1890), 63–65.

40. The divorce rate (number of divorces per 1,000 estimated midyear population) increased steadily from 0.3 in 1867 to 0.7 in 1900. *See* U.S. Bureau of the Census, *Historical Statistics of the United States, 1879–1945* (1949), p. 49.

although they disagreed about what constituted just grounds for divorce. Some held that the Bible condemned *divorce,* but permitted *separation;* others contended for two scriptural grounds for divorce, infidelity and desertion. By the middle 1880's most Baptists had come to accept only one scriptural cause, variously called "conjugal infidelity," "fornication," and "adultery." [41]

A point of even greater contention than what constituted legitimate grounds for divorce was the disagreement over the rights of divorced persons to remarry. Many Baptists considered remarriage by any divorced person wrong, but most came to agree that the innocent party in a scripturally dissolved marriage could remarry. Remarriage by the guilty party, however, was tantamount to adultery, and the person who married an unlawfully divorced person was guilty of perpetual adultery. Furthermore, declared the delegates to the Southern Baptist Convention in 1885, the minister who performed the ceremony for a person unjustly divorced "makes himself *particeps criminis.*" [42]

Baptists made little effort to bring society at large into conformity with their views on marriage and divorce. They condemned the liberal divorce laws of most of the states as anti-Christian and detrimental to society. States had no right to ignore God's marriage laws and encourage what one editor called "legalized adultery" and "consecutive polygamy," but Baptists agitated surprisingly little for strengthening these laws. [43]

Baptists relied primarily on church discipline and moral suasion to uphold the Christian ideal of the home and marriage. Few were as harsh as the editor who declared: "Let all persons who are divorced on slight pretences, and from lawless desires, be treated as debauchees and prostitutes, and excluded from decent society"; but as a denomination, they approved church disciplinary action against those who broke their marriage vows. [44]

Baptists maintained a strict Victorian attitude toward sex and the display of the female figure. They criticized newspapers for their candid

41. Southern Baptist Convention, *Proceedings, 1885,* pp. 30–31; *Christian Index* (Atlanta), July 27, 1887, p. 8; *Baptist Courier* (Greenville, South Carolina), March 21, 1885, p. 2.

42. Southern Baptist Convention, *Proceedings, 1885,* p. 31. *See also Christian Index* (Atlanta), July 7, 1887, p. 8; *Religious Herald* (Richmond), March 21, 1889, p. 1.

43. *Christian Index* (Atlanta), January 4, 1872, p. 1.

44. *Religious Herald* (Richmond), December 8, 1870, p. 2.

reporting of sex crimes and novels which treated sex lightly. They inveighed against "the freedom of modern social life" which sanctioned kissing and permitted "girls [to be] handled too much." [45] They protested the use of the feminine figure in advertising: "The beautiful form of woman," lamented one editor, "is prostituted to do the work of advertising a brand of cigars or soap." [46] Most vociferously they condemned the nude in art. Nude figures in paintings and sculpture at the Chicago Exposition in 1893 touched off a nationwide protest which Baptists supported. The lightly clad female form had a place in art, admitted one editor, but the line between decent and indecent exposure was not easy to determine. To aid his readers in making the distinction he proposed the following criterion: A woman might raise an objection to the exposure of the female figure in art without being excessively prudish "in every contingency in which she would object to the exposure of her own figure undraped;" while a man might object

in every contingency in which he would object to have the undraped figues [*sic*] of his mother or sister or wife or daughter subject to exposure. Or in view of the fact that this nude in art is always drawn from a nude model— from a living female figure undraped, let us state the rule of judgment this way:—objection [may be raised] by any woman when she would herself object to sitting, and by every man when he would object as her father or brother or husband or son to having her sit, as the nude model for it.[47]

Baptists raised a mild protest also against women's fashions, not on the ground of indecent exposure, however, but on the ground that the inordinate pursuit of fashion was sinful and that the fashionable practice of tight corseting was detrimental to the health of women and possibly to their unborn children. Commenting on a news item concerning the stillbirth of a child and the serious condition of the mother, one editor said:

That mother, I truly believe, is the *murderer of her child;* and if *she* dies, will be the murderer of herself. How? . . . It is brief, but portentous; *Tight lacing.* . . . O, Pride! thou hast sent more souls to hell than even the drunkard's cup, or the sword. . . . We pray God that, if these lines should meet

45. *Christian Index* (Atlanta), February 4, 1870, p. 32.
46. *Ibid.*, November 8, 1877, p. 4.
47. *Ibid.*, June 29, 1893, p. 4.

the eye of any daughter of the South who may thus be destroying herself, that
she may take warning, and forever abandon the criminal practice.[48]

Obviously, Baptists opposed all kinds of personal conduct which Scripture and law defined as sin and crime—lying, stealing, murder, adultery,
etc.—and many other forms of deviant behavior not so clearly defined.
They heaped condemnation upon dueling, the dying Southern "code of
honor," which one editor called *"honorable murder."*[49] They agreed with
the objectives of Anthony Comstock's Society for the Suppression of
Vice, although they never gave it their active support.[50] Baptists occasionally called for the assistance of government in promoting personal
purity through restrictive laws, but they relied primarily on personal
conversion, moral suasion, and church discipline to achieve and maintain
a high level of personal morality.

48. *Ibid.,* December 8, 1870, p. 192.
49. *Working Christian* (Charleston), August 30, 1870, p. 2.
50. *Religious Herald* (Richmond), February 6, 1890, p. 2.

Conclusion

HE most obvious conclusion that can be drawn from this study is that Southern Baptists were relatively unconcerned about the problems of society during the period from 1865 to 1900. As a denomination they attempted to remain true to what they believed to be the primary mission of the church—preaching the gospel—and they relegated social reform to a position of secondary importance. An excerpt from an article in the Virginia paper in which the writer attacked the "civic Church" and the whole philosophy of the social gospel is typical of the thinking of most Baptists on the subject of social problems and social reform. The true church, the writer said:

is not to deal directly with communities, States and nations, but with the individual. . . . Our future and eternal interests are as far above our present fleshly interests as the heavens are above the earth. The great question is not how to get ready to live here, but to live hereafter; to go to be with Jesus when we die and to stand acquitted in the day of final judgment. . . . [Christ favored social reform but] he waited for it as a necessary fruit of the blessed gospel received into men's hearts. . . . If we follow the teachings and example of Christ and the apostles, instead of the instruction and example of many modern reformers, we will act upon the principle that the regeneration of men by the Holy Spirit through the preaching of the word is the basis and surety of all true reform. It is of little use to make the outside of the platter clean when the inside is corrupt. . . . "Glory to God in the highest" first, and then "Peace on earth, good-will among men." [1]

The more socially minded Christians of other sections of the country considered this narrow view of the function of religion a fault, but Baptists considered it a mark of distinction. They took pride in the belief that they were fulfilling the true purpose of Christianity as indicated by Christ Himself and by His first-century followers. And, indeed, in re-

1. *Religious Herald* (Richmond), January 11, 1894, p. 1.

fusing to digress from the preaching of the gospel, Baptists were more faithful to the precedents of historical Christianity than those individuals and denominations that busied themselves with social reform and neglected the task of "making disciples." [2]

The failure of Southern Baptists to develop a greater degree of social consciousness was the logical consequence of certain characteristics of the denomination and of the region in which it flourished. Social Christianity was a highly sophisticated innovation in American religion and a radical departure from tradition. It was initiated by scholarly clerics and forced upon Northern churches by cataclysmic changes in society. Southern Baptists in the late nineteenth century were common people, poorly educated, and drawn from the lower- and lower-middle classes of rural society. People of such status accept change slowly.

Also, Baptists were Biblical literalists and self-proclaimed descendants of first-century Christians. Through denominational publications and from the pulpit they were constantly reminded that they were the heirs and defenders of the unchanging truths of primitive Christianity. Being a people, therefore, who consciously emulated the message and methods of the past, they looked askance at any suggested changes in beliefs and practices. For Baptists to resist a departure from tradition like that of social Christianity was an expected conditioned response.

Baptist ministers also contributed to the conservatism of the denomination. Provincial in outlook, and for the most part lacking the advantages of formal education, they were hardly better prepared than their followers to accept and promulgate a major change of emphasis in the denominational program.

Furthermore, the congregational structure of Baptist church government which granted to each member an equal share in determining denominational policy tended to depress the general level of thought and action of the denomination. The relatively few ministers who embraced some of the liberal social theories of the times seldom found their congregations in sympathy with their views.

One final observation on the nature of Baptists which hindered the development of social awareness: Baptists in the late nineteenth century were intensely "Southern" in outlook. They had defended slavery, justified secession, supported the Confederacy, and opposed Radical Recon-

2. Ernst Troeltsch, *The Social Teaching of the Christian Churches,* trans. Olive Wyon (2 vols., 2nd impression, 1949), I, 40–89.

struction. Until very late in the century everything Northern was anathema. The very fact that social Christianity was of Northern origin was reason enough for most Southern Baptists to view it with suspicion—if not wholly to disavow it. Northern-born social Christianity had first to overcome Southern sectionalism before it could find acceptance among Southern Baptists.

In addition to the characteristics of Southern Baptists militating against the acceptance of social Christianity, conditions in the South at large made the growth of social Christianity illogical. Industrialization and its attendant evils which had forced a re-thinking of Christian social values in the North were almost totally lacking in the South. In the absence of these environmental factors, Baptists would have been remarkable indeed if they had forsaken "proven ways" for novel means of propagating the faith which bore little or no relevance to existing conditions. To criticize Southern Baptists, therefore, for not embracing social Christianity is really to criticize them for not educating their ministers and members better; it is to censure the South for continuing its poor agrarian economy and not industrializing; it is, in short, to condemn a people for not accepting an innovation for which they felt no need and for which there was little apparent need. The old-time gospel seemed quite adequate for the rural South.

Although the denomination exhibited relatively little interest in applying their religion to social problems, a number of individual ministers and laymen gave evidence of strong leanings toward social Christianity. The influence of these men was not sufficient, however, to change substantially the course of denominational development. Neither the South-wide convention nor any state convention endorsed social Christianity, no editor of any state paper approved it, and none of the several individuals who showed sympathy for the new idea were ever elected to a high position of leadership in the denomination.[3]

A second conclusion—and perhaps of more significance than the first—is that Baptists *did* develop a degree of social consciousness during the late nineteenth century. Herein is a contradiction between Baptist theory

3. Among the prominent Baptists who seemed to lean toward social Christianity were: Arthur J. Barton, Clinton C. Brown, Charles S. Gardner, Victor I. Masters, Sr., Edwin McN. Poteat, Sr., William L. Poteat, and Arthur Yager. A study of the sermons of individual ministers and of local church activities would in all probability reveal the names of many others.

and practice. While openly refusing to admit any deviation from tradition, Baptists nevertheless modified their denominational program to accommodate in many practical ways the new emphasis on socialized religion. By their actions—if not by their preaching—Baptists, like other elements of Protestantism, admitted that social service was a legitimate goal of Christianity.

The contention of some historians that churches of the South were totally devoid of interest in social conditions is not corroborated by this study of Southern Baptists.[4] In comparison with denominations of the North, Southern Baptists appear reactionary; but a comparison of Southern Baptist activities in 1900 with those in 1865 or 1870 evinces a significant change of emphasis. This change is illustrated in no way better than in the steadily enlarging programs of the state and South-wide conventions. At the beginning of the period these bodies were concerned almost exclusively with preaching the gospel; by 1900, they were engaged in temperance reform, anti-gambling crusades, campaigns for the elimination of political corruption and the promotion of public morality, care of orphans and the aged, and other projects of social significance. In view of the fact that Baptist conventions had been organized for the promotion of rather narrow denominational objectives, the inclusion of these objects in the denomination's program is a significant indication of an increase in social concern.

A developing awareness of the denomination's responsibility to society is also clearly discernible in convention reports and in the weekly journals. "It is a one-sided Gospel," declared North Carolina Baptists in 1891, "when we preach only the spiritual side of the Gospel. The Savior came into the world to save souls, but spent a great part of His time in caring for the bodies of people."[5] In discussing the relationship of the Christian minister to social reform, a contributor to the Alabama paper in 1895 asked,

But is it his duty to address himself to society in its corporate capacity and affect the individual through the organism? I am persuaded that it is. . . . Jesus taught a sociology as truly as a theology. He was a great teacher of Social Dynamics, and altogether a most powerful social reformer.

4. C. Vann Woodward says, "One searches vainly for important manifestations" of an increasing emphasis on "socialized Christianity" in the South. *See* his *Origins of the New South, 1877–1913* (1951), p. 450.

5. North Carolina Baptist Convention, *Minutes, 1891,* p. 42.

Churches, like ministers, "have a function in society," he concluded, "and to fail to perform it is to be faithless to the Lord who so ordained." [6] Expressions like these were still comparatively rare at the end of the century, but they were appearing with increasing frequency.

The social issues over which Baptists were most concerned were those which had some moral or religious implication for the individual or some significance for the denomination. Baptists continued to be oriented toward the individual and his *spiritual* needs. They failed to see that "giving a cup of cold water" in the name of their Founder was an end within itself or that it could be a means to a spiritual end. Thus, for example, Baptists could be moved to tears over preaching the gospel to Negroes in Africa and remain completely apathetic toward political, social, and economic discrimination against Negroes in the South. They could be thoroughly aroused over the intemperate use of alcohol but completely unmoved by the injustices of an economic system which sanctioned the pitiless exploitation of sharecroppers and cotton-mill hands. Although Baptists developed an increasing interest in social conditions between 1865 and 1900, the contrast of this concern with their greater emphasis on otherworldly matters and with the rapid rise of social Christianity in the North dramatizes their relative apathy for the needs of mankind.

A final conclusion is that Southern Baptists defended the status quo. Their attitudes toward political, social, economic, and other problems of Southern society coincided with the prevailing attitudes of Southerners in general. The degree of influence which Baptists exerted on society cannot be measured, but whatever influence they had was overwhelmingly in support of existing conditions. Is this to suggest that society molded Baptists? Or that Baptists molded society? It would be a serious indictment indeed to hold Baptists responsible for fashioning Southern society as it was in the late nineteenth century. Granted that morals and mores are relative to time and place, by any standard—either in comparison with the best thinking of that day or of a later day—the society of the South between 1865 and 1900 hardly conformed either to high ethical standards or to Christian principles. The conclusion then must be that

6. *Alabama Baptist* (Montgomery), October 10, 1895, p. 1. *See also Christian Index* (Atlanta), May 6, 1897, p. 3; *Religious Herald* (Richmond), April 30, 1896, p. 1; Symposium on "The Place of the Pulpit in Moral Reform," *Seminary Magazine*, VI (May 1893), 458–462.

Baptists conformed to the society in which they lived. Their significance in Southern life consisted not in their power to mold their environment to conform to their standards. Rather their importance as a social force was in supporting and perpetuating the standards prevailing in society at large. Only on matters involving personal conduct or narrow religious principles did Baptists diverge noticeably from prevailing Southern views. This study, therefore, verifies the sociologists' contention that institutionalized religions respond more amenably to social pressures than to their "heavenly visions."[7] Christ said of His disciples, "These are in the world. . . . [But] not of the world."[8] But in their attitudes toward social conditions in the South, Baptists insisted on being both *in* and *of* the world.

7. Thomas Ford Hoult, *The Sociology of Religion* (1958), pp. 3–15.
8. John 17: 11, 14.

Bibliographic Note

THE most valuable sources for this study were the weekly papers published by Baptists in the twelve states of the South. Although privately owned and controlled, each of these papers was approved by the Baptist convention (or general association) of the state in which it was published. The next most valuable sources were the minutes and other annual reports of the state conventions and the Southern Baptist Convention. Extant files of papers, minutes, and reports are scattered throughout the South, but the Historical Commission of the Southern Baptist Convention has microfilmed all available records and deposited copies in the Dargan-Carver Library of the Baptist Sunday School Board, Nashville, Tennessee. The Baptist seminaries in Louisville, Kentucky, and Fort Worth, Texas, also have copies of most of the Historical Commission's microfilm holdings as well as files of other valuable materials. Most of the research for this study was done in the microfilm collection of the Dargan-Carver Library. The remaining research was completed in the libraries of the two seminaries mentioned above and of Baylor University, Waco, Texas. The seminary in Louisville has the best collection of minutes and papers.

The sheer quantity of weekly papers necessitated the employment of a sampling scheme. The *Religious Herald* (Richmond, Virginia), representing the liberal thinking of Baptists in the Upper South and the *Christian Index* (Macon and Atlanta, Georgia), representing the conservative views of Baptists in the Lower South were read in their entirety for the years 1865–1900. The scheme for examining newspapers published in the remaining states was to read only every tenth issue. However, for reaction to specific events known to be germane to this study—as, for example, the disputed election of 1876—all the appropriate issues of all the papers were examined.

Minutes of the state and Southern conventions usually recorded only the order of business and the disposition of matters brought up for discussion. The state papers reported convention deliberations in more detail than the minutes. Resolutions and reports of the various agencies of the conventions were carried in the minutes or attached as appendixes. Speeches during convention debates and resolutions framed in the heat of discussion often revealed the unmasked feelings of the delegates.

Other Baptist publications contributed very little to this study. The *Seminary Magazine* (Louisville, 1888–1900), edited and published monthly during the eight-month school term by students of the Southern Baptist Theological Seminary, Louisville, Kentucky, contained a number of articles of interest. The periodical literature (Sunday school lessons, etc.) of the denomination was largely of negative value, demonstrating only a lack of interest in social matters. Temperance lessons became a regular part of the Sunday school lesson series before 1900, but there was little else of social significance. Southern Baptists had no publishing house of their own until 1891. Before that time several publishers enjoyed quasi-approval of the denomination. Even after 1891 Southern Baptists continued to rely heavily on literature from the American Baptist Publications Society (Northern) which maintained branch offices in several Southern cities.

Memoirs, reminiscences, and autobiographies by denominational leaders proved to be of little value in this study. Biographies of prominent Baptists also contributed very few insights into the social development of Baptists.

The names of papers and convention minutes used in this study are here listed by states. The names of papers changed frequently. Only the major variations are indicated here. In parentheses after the name of each paper are the city (or cities) in which the paper was published, the date the paper began publication, and the inclusive dates indicating the years the paper actually was read. The names of the state-wide Baptist organizations also varied. Only the most commonly used names are cited here. The first date in parentheses is the year the organization was formed; the inclusive dates are the years the minutes were read. No sampling process was employed in examining minutes.

ALABAMA. *Alabama Baptist* (Marion, Selma, and Montgomery. 1873, 1873–1900). Alabama Baptist State Convention, *Minutes* (1823, 1860–1920). The editors of the state paper changed frequently as did the format.

ARKANSAS. The *Arkansas Baptist* began publication in 1881, but no files of the paper were available for this study. Arkansas Baptist State Convention, *Proceedings* (1848, 1869–1900). Files of the *Proceedings* were very sketchy.

FLORIDA. *Florida Baptist Witness* and *Florida Witness* (Lake City, DeLand, and Ocala. 1883, 1885–1900). Baptist Convention of the State of Florida, *Proceedings* or *Minutes* (1854, 1866–1900). The state papers were generally of inferior quality and both papers and minutes have been poorly preserved.

GEORGIA. *Christian Index* (Macon and Atlanta. 1821, 1865–1900). Baptist Convention of the State of Georgia, *Minutes* (1822, 1860–1900). The *Christian Index* was one of the largest and most prosperous religious papers in the South. It was better edited than most other papers and was consistently conservative on all questions.

KENTUCKY. *Western Recorder* (Louisville, 1825, 1860–1900). General Association of Baptists in Kentucky, *Minutes* or *Proceedings* (1837, 1860–1900). The *Western Recorder* was one of the most liberal papers in the South.

LOUISIANA. *Baptist Chronicle* (Shreveport, Ruston, and Alexandria. 1886, 1888–1900). Louisiana Baptist Convention, *Minutes* (1848, 1860–1900). The state paper was poorly edited, and the files are in bad condition.

MISSISSIPPI. *Baptist Record, Southern Baptist Record,* and *The Baptist* (Meridian and Jackson. 1877, 1880–1900). Mississippi Baptist State Convention, *Proceedings* or *Minutes* (1836, 1860–1900). The state papers were decidedly inferior. They were conservative, argumentative, and unresponsive to social problems.

NORTH CAROLINA. *Biblical Recorder* (Raleigh, 1833, 1865–1900). Baptist State Convention of North Carolina, *Proceedings* or *Minutes* (1830, 1860–1900). During the 1890's the *Biblical Recorder* devoted a great deal of attention to social matters.

SOUTH CAROLINA. *Southern Baptist* (Charleston, 1846, 1860); *Confederate Baptist* (Columbia. 1862, 1862–1865); and *South Carolina Baptist, Working Christian,* and *Baptist Courier* (Anderson, Yorkville, Charleston, Columbia, and Greenville. 1866, 1866–1900). State Convention of the Baptist Denomination in South Carolina, *Minutes* (1821, 1860–1920).

TENNESSEE. *The Baptist, Tennessee Baptist,* and *Baptist and Reflector* (Memphis and Nashville. 1867, 1867–1900). General Association of Baptists of East Tennessee, *Proceedings* (1844, 1868–1885); West Tennessee Baptist Convention, *Proceedings* (1835, 1860–1874); Tennessee Baptist Convention, *Proceedings* (1875, 1875–1900). Baptist work in Tennessee suffered from the same geographical and political sectionalism which afflicted the state generally. Also, frontier theological factionalism persisted in Tennessee throughout the nineteenth century. Until 1889 the state paper was owned by James R. Graves, the most contentious and—unfortunately for the denomination—the most influential polemicist ever to plague Southern Baptists. Graves used his paper to further his own interests rather than the denomination's. Graves's influence extended also into Kentucky, Mississippi, Arkansas, Louisiana, and Texas. When *The Baptist* underwent reorganization in 1889 and Graves lost his dominate position, the new paper, the *Baptist and Reflector,* showed decided improvement. It devoted more space to social questions and less to controversial theological matters.

TEXAS. *Texas Baptist, Texas Baptist and Herald, Baptist Standard,* and *Texas Baptist Standard* (Dallas, Austin, San Antonio, and Waco. 1874,

1884–1900). Baptist State Convention of Texas, *Minutes* (1848, 1860–1885); and Baptist General Convention of Texas, *Proceedings* (1886, 1886–1900). Texas papers tended to be conservative and argumentative.

VIRGINIA. *Religious Herald* (Richmond. 1828, 1865–1900). Baptist General Association of Virginia, *Minutes* (1822, 1860–1900). The *Religious Herald* was generally of higher quality than any other papers used in this study.

SOUTH-WIDE. Southern Baptist Convention, *Proceedings* (1845, 1845–1897); and *Annual* (1898, 1898–1920). In comparison with state conventions and general associations, the Southern Baptist Convention was more cautious in taking positions on social questions. The adoption in 1886 of the first temperance resolution was a turning point toward more involvement in social matters.

Information used in compiling the introductory portions of each chapter was drawn from a variety of published works. See the Bibliography for full bibliographic information. The best history of Baptists in America is Robert G. Torbet's *A History of the Baptists* (1963). Southern Baptists have produced few histories of real merit. The two works of most significance for this study are: William Wright Barnes, *The Southern Baptist Convention, 1845–1953* (1954), well written and factual but uncritical; and *Encyclopedia of Southern Baptists* (1958). The *Encyclopedia* is a composite work by hundreds of writers containing 4,349 articles on every phase of Southern Baptist life, including biographical sketches of hundreds of Baptist leaders. Although the articles are of uneven quality and generally uncritical, they constitute a valuable storehouse of information about the denomination.

The following four volumes in *A History of American Life* (1927–1948), edited by Arthur M. Schlesinger and Dixon Ryan Fox, give an excellent account of the social history of the times: Allan Nevins, *The Emergence of Modern America, 1865–1878,* vol. VIII (1928); Ida M. Tarbell, *The Nationalizing of Business, 1878–1898,* vol. IX (1936); Arthur Meier Schlesinger, *The Rise of the City, 1878–1898,* vol. X (1933); Harold Underwood Faulkner, *The Quest for Social Justice, 1898–1914,* vol. XI (1937). Harvey Wish presents an excellent treatment of social thought and social movements in his *Society and Thought in Modern America,* vol. II of his *Society and Thought in America* (1952). Merle Curti's *The Growth of American Thought* (1951) and Stow Persons's *American Minds: A History of Ideas* (1958) are standard general treatments of intellectual trends in America. Richard Hofstadter's *Social Darwinism in American Thought* (1955) is the classic statement of the impact of social Darwinism.

Francis Butler Simkins's *The South Old and New: A History, 1820–1947* (1947) is a good general history of the South during the late nineteenth century. E. Merton Coulter's *The South During Reconstruction, 1865–1877* (1947) and C. Vann Woodward's *Origins of the New South, 1877–1913* (1951) are excellent on Southern politics. Woodward's book is particularly good—not only on politics, but on all phases of Southern history during the period treated. These books are volumes XIII and IX, respectively, of *A History of the South,* edited by Wendell Holmes Stephenson and E. Merton Coulter (1947, 1951). Paul H. Buck's *The Road to Reunion, 1865–1900* (1938) and C. Vann Woodward's *Reunion and Reaction: The Compromise of 1877 and the End of Reconstruction* (1951) are the best treatments of the problem of re-establishing national comity after the sectional conflict. *Southern Politics in State and Nation* (1949) by V. O. Keys, Jr., is a perceptive treatment of the Negro in Southern politics. Charles A. and Mary R. Beard in *The Rise of American Civilization* (1956) and Samuel Eliot Morison and Henry Steele Commager in *The Growth of the American Republic* (1962) have outstanding brief treatments of the South and the nation during the years 1865–1900. The economic problems of the South are vividly treated in Woodward's *Origins of the New South* and the general histories already cited. *The Ills of the South* (1894) by Charles H. Otkin is an authoritative though ponderously written account of Southern farm tenancy by one who witnessed its development.

On the subject of religion and society between 1865 and 1900, the starting point is Arthur Meier Schlesinger's article, "A Critical Period in American Religion, 1875–1900," in the Massachusetts Historical Society, *Proceedings,* LXIV (June 1932), 523–547. Charles Howard Hopkin's *The Rise of the Social Gospel in American Protestantism, 1865–1915* (1940) and Henry F. May's *Protestant Churches and Industrial America* (1949) are among the best studies of the critical period, but both slight the South—justly so, perhaps. In *The Circuit Rider Dismounts* (1938) Hunter Dickinson Farish has done for Southern Methodists what the present study purports to do for Southern Baptists. His conclusions, however, differ frequently from those drawn from this study. Winthrop S. Hudson has suggested in fast-moving and trenchant style the causes of the decline of American Protestantism in his *American Protestantism* (1961). In *American Christianity: An Historical Interpretation with Representative Documents,* vol. II (1963), H. Shelton Smith, Robert T. Handy, and Lefferts A. Loetscher have written incisive summaries to accompany their collection of documents relating to the period 1865–1900.

Most of the studies of the South already cited touch on the race problem. *From Slavery to Freedom* (1947) by John Hope Franklin and *The Negro in the United States* (1949) by Edward Franklin Frazier are two standard histories of the Negro in America. The subject of Negro religion is covered in *The Negro's Church* (1933) by Benjamin Elijah Mays and Joseph William Nicholson and in *The History of the Negro Church* (1945) by Carter G. Woodson. *The Northern Teacher in the South, 1862–1870* (1941) by Henry Lee Swint is a basic study in the area suggested by the title. The amount of literature on the subject of race relations is enormous. M. F. Ashley Montagu's *Man's Most Dangerous Myth: The Fallacy of Race* (1952) and Oscar Handlin's *Race and Nationality in American Life* (1957) are among the best studies of racism. Gunnar Myrdal's *An American Dilemma: The Negro Problem and Modern Democracy* (1944) is the most comprehensive study of the Negro in America. It is concerned with the Negro problem in the late 1930's primarily but also treats the problem historically. Statements of the Southern views of racism in the late nineteenth century are found in Thomas Pearce Bailey's *Race Orthodoxy in the South: And Other Aspects of the Negro Question* (1914) and C. Vann Woodward's *The Strange Career of Jim Crow* (1957). A few of the articles most pertinent to this study from the vast quantity of periodical literature on the race question are: Ulrich B. Phillips, "The Central Theme of Southern History," *American Historical Review,* XXXIV (October 1928), 30–43; Charles H. Wesley, "The Concept of the Inferiority of the Negro in American Thought," *Journal of Negro History,* XXV (October 1940), 540–560; Francis Butler Simkins, "Ben Tillman's View of the Negro," *Journal of Southern History,* III (May 1937), 161–174; Stanley J. Folmsbee, "The Origin of the First 'Jim Crow' Laws," *Journal of Southern History,* XV (May 1949), 235–247; George B. Tindall, "The Campaign for the Disfranchisement of Negroes in South Carolina," *Journal of Southern History,* XV (May 1949), 212–234; Joseph H. Taylor, "The Fourteenth Amendment, the Negro, and the Spirit of the Times," *Journal of Negro History,* XLV (January 1960), 21–27; John G. Van Deusen, "The Exodus of 1879," *Journal of Negro History,* XXI (April 1936), 111–129; and Guion Griffis Johnson, "The Ideology of White Supremacy, 1876–1910," in *Essays in Southern History,* ed. Fletcher Melvin Green, vol. XXXI of *The James Sprunt Studies in History and Political Science,* eds. Albert Ray Newsome, *et al.* (1949), pp. 124–156.

On the topics of individual and public morality and social reform the three volumes already cited by Nevins, Schlesinger, and Faulkner in *A History of American Life* and Wish's *Society and Thought in Modern America* are good general treatments. The most spectacular social reform movement after the abolition effort was the temperance crusade. Literature on the history of this movement is voluminous, but much of it is highly partisan. The most reliable, objective, and sprightly written account is Herbert Asbury's *The Great Illusion: An Informal History of Prohibition* (1950). Other worthy studies include Ernest H. Cherrington, *The Evolution of Prohibition in the United*

States of America (1920) and D. Leigh Colvin, *Prohibition in the United States: A History of the Prohibition Party and of the Prohibition Movement* (1926). Foster Rhea Dulles in *America Learns to Play: A History of Popular Recreation, 1607–1940* (1952) discusses amusement during the period and occasionally notes the reaction of churches to popular pastimes.

The shortcoming of most of these general treatments of American society is their neglect of the South.

Bibliography

Alabama Baptist (Marion, Selma, and Montgomery). 1873–1900.

Alabama Baptist Convention. *Minutes.* 1860–1920.

Arkansas Baptist Convention. *Proceedings.* 1869–1900.

Asbury, Herbert. *The Great Illusion: An Informal History of Prohibition.* Garden City, New York: Doubleday and Company, 1950.

Ashley Montagu, M. F. *Man's Most Dangerous Myth: The Fallacy of Race.* New York: Columbia University Press, 1942; 2nd ed., rev. and enl., New York: Columbia University Press, 1945; 3rd ed., rev. and enl., New York: Harpers, 1952; 4th ed., rev. and enl., Cleveland: World Publishing Company, 1964.

Bailey, Thomas Pearce. *Race Orthodoxy in the South: And Other Aspects of the Negro Question.* New York: The Neale Publishing Company, 1914.

Baker, Robert Andrew. *Relations Between Northern and Southern Baptists.* [Fort Worth]: privately printed, 1948.

The Baptist (Jackson, Mississippi). 1898–1900.

The Baptist (Memphis, Tennessee). 1867–1882; 1887–1889.

Baptist and Reflector (Nashville, Tennessee). 1889–1900.

Baptist Chronicle (Shreveport, Ruston, and Alexandria, Louisiana). 1888–1900.

Baptist Courier (Columbia and Greenville, South Carolina). 1878–1900.

Baptist Record (Meridian and Jackson, Mississippi). 1880–1887; 1892–1898.

Baptist Standard (Dallas and Waco, Texas). 1892–1893.

Barnes, William Wright. *The Southern Baptist Convention, 1845–1953.* Nashville, Tennessee: Broadman Press, 1954.

Baughn, Milton L. "Social Views Reflected in Official Publications of the Cumberland Presbyterian Church, 1875–1900." Unpublished Ph.D. dissertation, Vanderbilt University, 1954.

Beard, Charles A. and Mary R. *The Rise of American Civilization.* 2 vols., New York: Macmillan Company, 1927; 1 vol. ed., New York: Macmillan Company, 1930; New ed., rev. and enl., 2 vols. in 1, New York: Macmillan Company, 1933; New ed., rev. and enl., New York: Macmillan Company, 1949; New ed., rev. and enl., New York: Macmillan Company, 1956.

Beattie, Ronald H. "The Sources of Criminal Statistics, *Annals* of the American Academy of Political and Social Science, CCXVII (September 1941), 19–28.

Biblical Recorder (Raleigh, North Carolina). 1865–1900.

Buck, Paul H. *The Road to Reunion, 1865–1900.* Boston: Little, Brown and Company, 1937; New York: Vintage Books, 1959. Boston: Little, Brown and Company, [1964].

Butts, R. Freeman, and Lawrence A. Cremin. *A History of Education in American Culture.* New York: Henry Holt and Company, 1953; New York: Holt, Rinehart, and Winston, 1961.

Cable, George W. "The Freedman's Case in Equity," *The Century Magazine,* XXIX (January 1885), 409–418.

Cherrington, Ernest H. *The Evolution of Prohibition in the United States of America.* Westerville, Ohio: The American Issue Press, 1920.

Christian Index (Macon and Atlanta, Georgia). 1865–1900.

Colvin, D. Leigh. *Prohibition in the United States: A History of the Prohibition Party and of the Prohibition Movement.* New York: George H. Doran Company, 1926.

The Confederate Baptist (Columbia, South Carolina). 1862–1865.

Coulter, E. Merton. *The Confederate States of America, 1861–1865,* Vol. VII of *A History of the South,* eds. Wendell Holmes Stephenson and E. Merton Coulter. [Baton Rouge]: Louisiana State University Press, 1951.

————. *The South During Reconstruction, 1865–1877,* Vol. VIII of *A History of the South,* eds. Wendell Holmes Stephenson and E. Merton Coulter. [Baton Rouge]: Louisiana State University Press, 1947.

Curti, Merle Eugene. *The Growth of American Thought.* New York: Harper and Brothers, 1943; 2nd ed., New York: Harper and Brothers, 1951; 3rd ed., New York: Harper and Row, 1964.

Dulles, Foster Rhea. *America Learns to Play: A History of Popular Recreation, 1607–1940.* New York: Peter Smith, 1952.

East Tennessee Baptist General Association. *Proceedings.* 1868–1885.

Edwards, Newton, and Herman G. Richey. *The School in the American Social Order: The Dynamics of American Education.* Boston: Houghton Mifflin Company, 1947.

Elkins, Stanley M. *Slavery: A Problem in American Institutional and Intellectual Life* [Chicago]: University of Chicago Press, 1959.

Encyclopedia of Southern Baptists. 2 vols., Nashville, Tennessee: Broadman Press, 1958.

Farish, Hunter Dickinson. *The Circuit Rider Dismounts: A Social History of Southern Methodism, 1865–1900,* Richmond, Va.: The Dietz Press, 1938.

Faulkner, Harold Underwood. *The Quest for Social Justice, 1898–1914,* Vol.

XI of *A History of American Life,* eds., Arthur M. Schlesinger and Dixon Ryan Fox. New York: The Macmillan Company, 1931, 1937.

Florida Baptist Convention. *Minutes.* 1866–1900.

Florida Baptist Witness (Lake City, De Land, and Ocala). 1883–1900.

Folmsbee, Stanley J. "The Origin of the First 'Jim Crow' Laws," *Journal of Southern History,* XV (May 1949), 235–247.

Franklin, John Hope. *From Slavery to Freedom: A History of American Negroes.* New York: A. A. Knopf, 1947; 2nd ed., rev. and enl., New York: Knopf, 1956.

Frazier, Edward Franklin. *The Negro in the United States.* New York: Macmillan Company, 1949; Rev. ed., New York: Macmillan Company, 1957; Rev. and abridged, Chicago: University of Chicago Press, 1966.

Georgia Baptist Convention. *Minutes.* 1860–1900.

Gobbel, Luther L. *Church-State Relations in Education in North Carolina Since 1776.* Durham, North Carolina: Duke University Press, 1938.

Handlin, Oscar. *Race and Nationality in American Life.* Boston: Little, Brown, and Company, 1957; Garden City, N.Y.: Doubleday & Company, 1957.

Hawk, Emory Q. *Economic History of the South.* New York: Prentice-Hall, Inc., 1934.

Hesseltine, William B. *A History of the South, 1607–1936.* New York: Prentice-Hall, Inc., 1936.

————. *The South in American History.* New York: Prentice-Hall, 1943; 2nd ed., with David L. Smiley, Englewood Cliffs, N.J.: Prentice-Hall, 1960.

Hofstadter, Richard. *Social Darwinism in American Thought.* Philadelphia: University of Pennsylvania Press, 1944; Rev. ed., Boston: Beacon Press, 1955; Rev. ed., Boston: Beacon Press, 1958; Rev. ed., New York: G. Braziller, 1959.

Hopkins, Charles H. *The Rise of the Social Gospel in American Protestantism, 1865–1915.* New Haven: Yale University Press, 1940.

Hoult, Thomas Ford. *The Sociology of Religion.* New York: The Dryden Press, 1958.

Hudson, Winthrop S. *American Protestantism.* Chicago: University of Chicago Press, 1961.

Jameson, J. Franklin. *The American Revolution Considered as A Social Movement.* Princeton: Princeton University Press, 1926; Boston: Beacon Press, 1956; New York: P. Smith, 1957; Boston: Beacon Press, 1960.

Johnson, Guion Griffis. "The Ideology of White Supremacy, 1876–1910," pp. 124–156 in *Essays in Southern History,* ed. Fletcher Melvin Green, Vol. XXXI of *The James Sprunt Studies in History and Political Science,* eds.

Albert Ray Newsome, *et al.* Chapel Hill: The University of North Carolina Press, 1949.

Jones, John William. *Christ in the Camp: Or Religion in Lee's Army.* Richmond, Va.: B. F. Johnson & Company, 1887.

Kentucky Baptist General Association. *Proceedings.* 1860–1900.

Key, Valdimer Orlando, Jr. *Southern Politics in State and Nation.* New York: A. A. Knopf, 1949.

Krout, John Allen. *The Origins of Prohibition.* New York: Alfred A. Knopf, 1925.

Kull, Irving S. and Nell M. *A Short Chronology of American History, 1492–1950.* New Brunswick, N.J.: Rutgers University Press, 1952.

Lewis, Abram H. *A Critical History of Sunday Legislation From 321 to 1888 A.D.* New York: D. Appleton and Company, 1888.

Louisiana Baptist Convention. *Minutes.* 1860–1900.

Lunden, Walter A. *Statistics on Crime and Criminals.* Pittsburgh, Penn.: Stevenson and Foster Company, 1942.

May, Henry F. *Protestant Churches and Industrial America.* New York: Harper & Brothers Publishers, 1949; New York: Octagon Books, 1963.

Mays, Benjamin Elijah, and Joseph William Nicholson. *The Negro's Church.* New York: Institute of Social and Religious Research, 1933.

Mississippi Baptist Convention. *Proceedings.* 1860–1920.

Morison, Samuel Eliot, and Henry Steele Commager. *The Growth of the American Republic.* New York: Oxford University Press, 1930; Rev. and enl. ed., New York: Oxford University Press, 1937; 3rd ed., rev. and enl., New York: Oxford University Press, 1942; 4th ed., rev. and enl., 2 vols., New York: Oxford University Press, 1950; 5th ed., rev. and enl., 2 vols., New York: Oxford University Press, 1962.

Murphy, Edgar Gardner. *The Basis of Ascendancy: A Discussion of Certain Principles of Public Policy Involved in the Development of the Southern States.* New York: Longmans, Green, and Company, 1910.

———. *Problems of the Present South: A Discussion of Certain of the Educational, Industrial and Political Issues in Southern States.* New York: Longmans, Green, and Company, 1909.

Myrdal, Gunnar. *An American Dilemma: The Negro Problem and Modern Democracy.* 2 vols., New York: Harper and Brothers Publishers, 1944; 20th anniversary ed., New York: Harper and Row, 1962.

Nevins, Allan. *The Emergence of Modern America, 1865–1878,* Vol. VIII of *A History of American Life,* eds. Arthur M. Schlesinger and Dixon Ryan Fox. New York: The Macmillan Company, 1927.

North Carolina Baptist Convention. *Minutes.* 1860–1900.

Norton, Herman A. "The Organization and Function of the Confederate

Military Chaplaincy, 1861–1865." Unpublished Ph.D. dissertation, Vanderbilt University, 1956.

Olmstead, Clifton E. *History of Religion in the United States.* Englewood Cliffs, N.J.: Prentice-Hall, Inc., 1960.

Otkin, Charles H. *The Ills of the South: or Related Causes Hostile to the General Prosperity of the Southern People.* New York: G. P. Putnam's Sons, 1894.

Pendleton, James Madison. *Christian Doctrines: A Compendium of Theology.* Philadelphia: American Baptist Publication Society, 1878.

———. *Church Manual: Designed for the Use of Baptist Churches.* Philadelphia: American Baptist Publication Society, 1867.

Persons, Stow. *American Minds: A History of Ideas.* New York: Holt, 1958.

Phillips, Ulrich B. "The Central Theme of Southern History," *American Historical Review,* XXXIV (October 1928), 30–43.

Porter, Kirk Harold. *A History of Suffrage in the United States.* Chicago: University of Chicago Press, 1918.

Randall, James G. *The Civil War and Reconstruction.* Boston: D. C. Heath and Company, 1937; 2nd ed., with David Donald, Boston: Heath, 1961.

Religious Herald (Richmond, Virginia), 1865–1900.

Schlesinger, Arthur Meier. "A Critical Period in American Religion," Massachusetts Historical Society, *Proceedings,* LXIV (June 1932), 523–547.

———. *The Rise of the City, 1878–1898,* Vol. X of *A History of American Life,* eds. Arthur M. Schlesinger and Dixon Ryan Fox. New York: The Macmillan Company, 1933.

Seminary Magazine (Louisville, Kentucky). 1888–1900.

Silver, James W. *Mississippi: The Closed Society.* New York: Harcourt, Brace & World, Inc., 1964.

Simkins, Francis Butler. "Ben Tillman's View of the Negro," *Journal of Southern History,* III (May 1937), 161–174.

———. *The South Old and New: A History, 1820–1947.* New York: Alfred A. Knopf, 1947; 2nd ed., rev. and enl., under title, *A History of the South,* New York: Alfred A. Knopf, 1953; 3rd ed., New York: Alfred A. Knopf, 1963.

Smith, H. Shelton, Robert T. Handy, and Lefferts A. Loetscher. *American Christianity.* 2 vols., New York: Charles Scribner's Sons, 1960, 1963.

South Carolina Baptist (Anderson). 1866–1868.

South Carolina Baptist Convention. *Minutes.* 1860–1920.

The Southern Baptist (Charleston, South Carolina). 1860.

Southern Baptist Convention. *Proceedings.* 1860–1897.

Southern Baptist Convention. *Annual.* 1898–1920.

Southern Baptist Handbook, 1951. Nashville, Tennessee: Broadman Press, 1951.

Southern Baptist Record (Meridian and Jackson, Mississippi). 1887–1891.

Stampp, Kenneth M. *The Peculiar Institution.* New York: Alfred A. Knopf, 1956.

Strong, Josiah. *Our Country: Its Possible Future and Present Crisis.* New York: Baker and Taylor for the American Home Missionary Society, 1885; New York: Baker and Taylor, 1886; rev. ed., New York: Baker and Taylor, 1891; rev. ed., New York: Baker and Taylor [1896]; edited by Jurgen Herbst, Cambridge, Mass.: Belknap Press of Harvard University Press, 1963.

Sweet, William Warren. *The American Churches: An Interpretation.* London: Epworth Press, 1947; New York: Abingdon-Cokesbury Press, 1948.

Swint, Henry Lee. *The Northern Teacher in the South, 1862–1870.* Nashville, Tennessee: Vanderbilt University Press, 1941.

Tarbell, Ida M. *The Nationalizing of Business, 1878–1898,* Vol. IX of *A History of American Life,* eds. Arthur M. Schlesinger and Dixon Ryan Fox. New York: The Macmillan Company, 1936.

Taylor, Joseph H. "The Fourteenth Amendment, the Negro, and The Spirit of the Times," *Journal of Negro History,* XLV (January 1960), 21–27.

Tennessee Baptist (Memphis). 1882–1887.

Tennessee Baptist Convention. *Proceedings.* 1874–1900.

Texas Baptist (Dallas). 1884–1886.

Texas Baptist and Herald (Dallas, Austin, and San Antonio). 1886–1891.

Texas Baptist Convention. *Minutes.* 1860–1885.

Texas Baptist General Convention. *Proceedings.* 1886–1900.

Texas Baptist Standard (Waco). 1893–1900.

Thompson, Edgar T., and Everett C. Hughes, eds. *Race: Individual and Collective Behavior.* Glencoe, Ill.: The Free Press, 1958.

Tindall, George B. "The Campaign for the Disfranchisement of Negroes in South Carolina," *Journal of Southern History,* XV (May 1949), 212–234.

Torbet, Robert G. *A History of the Baptists.* Chicago: The Judson Press, 1950; rev. ed., Valley Forge: The Judson Press, 1963.

Townsend, Leah. *South Carolina Baptists, 1670–1805.* Florence, S.C.: The Press of the Florence Printing Company, 1935.

Troeltsch, Ernst. *The Social Teaching of the Christian Churches.* Translated by Olive Wyon. New York: The Macmillan Company, 1931; 2nd imp., 2 vols., New York: The Macmillan Company, 1947; London: Allen and Unwin, 1950; London: Allen and Unwin, 1956.

Tyler, Alice Felt. *Freedom's Ferment: Phases of American Social History to 1860*. Minneapolis: The University of Minnesota Press, 1944; Torchbook ed., New York: Harper, 1962.

U.S. Bureau of the Census. *Eighth Census of the United States: 1860. Population*, [Vol. IV]. Washington, D.C.: Government Printing Office, 1866.

———. *Historical Statistics of the United States, 1789–1945*. Washington, D.C.: Government Printing Office, 1949.

———. *Ninth Census of the United States: 1870. Population*, Vol. I. Washington D.C.: Government Printing Office, 1872.

———. *Religious Bodies: 1906*, Part II, *Separate Denominations: History, Description, and Statistics*. Washington, D.C.: Government Printing Office, 1910.

Van Deusen, John G. "The Exodus of 1879," *Journal of Negro History*, XXV (April 1936), 111–129.

Vedder, Henry C. "Journalism of the Baptist Church in the United States," *The Chautauquan*, XXI (August 1893), 602–609.

Virginia Baptist General Association. *Minutes*. 1860–1900.

Wesley, Charles H. "The Concept of the Inferiority of the Negro in American Thought," *Journal of Negro History*, XXV (October 1940), 540–560.

West Tennessee Baptist Convention. *Proceedings*. 1860–1874.

Western Recorder (Louisville, Kentucky). 1860–1900.

Wish, Harvey. *Society and Thought in Modern America*, Vol. II of *Society and Thought in America*. New York: Longmans, Green, and Company, 1950–1952; 2nd ed., New York: D. McKay Company, 1962.

Woodson, Carter G. *The History of the Negro Church*. Washington, D.C.: Associated Publishers, 1921; 2nd ed., Washington, D.C.: The Associated Publishers, 1945.

Woodward, C. Vann. *Origins of the New South, 1877–1913*, Vol. IX of *A History of the South*, eds. Wendell Holmes Stephenson and E. Merton Coulter. [Baton Rouge]: Louisiana State University Press, 1951.

———. *Reunion and Reaction: The Compromise of 1877 and the End of Reconstruction*. Boston: Little, Brown, and Company, 1951.

———. *The Strange Career of Jim Crow*. New York: Oxford University Press, 1955; new and rev. ed., New York: Oxford University Press, 1957; 2nd rev. ed., New York: Oxford University Press, 1966.

Woolley, John G., and William E. Johnson. *Temperance Progress in the Century*. Philadelphia: The Linscott Publishing Company, 1903.

Working Christian (Yorkville, Charleston, and Columbia, South Carolina). 1869–1877.

Appendix A

BAPTIST BODIES IN THE UNITED STATES, 1906 [a]

White Baptist Bodies:
Northern Baptist Convention
General Six Principle Baptists
Seventh-Day Baptists
Free Baptists
Freewill Baptists
General Baptists
Separate Baptists
United Baptists
Duck River and Kindred Associations of Baptists (Baptist Church of Christ)
Primitive Baptists
Two-Seed-in-the-Spirit Baptists
Southern Baptist Convention

Negro Baptist Bodies:
Colored Primitive Baptists
United American Freewill Baptists (Colored)
National Baptist Convention (Colored)

[a] U.S. Bureau of the Census, *Religious Bodies: 1906*, Part II. *Separate Denominations: History, Description, and Statistics* (1910), p. 45.

Appendix B

BAPTIST BODIES IN THE UNITED STATES, 1906 [a]
NUMBER OF CHURCHES

	South [b]	Other [c]	Total
White Baptist Bodies, Totals	21,763	13,520	35,283
Northern Convention	0	8,272	8,272
General Six Principle	0	16	16
Seventh-Day	7	70	77
Free	216	1,130	1,346
Freewill	542	66	608
General	179	339	518
Separate	36	40	76
United	117	79	196
Duck River	93	0	93
Primitive	2,256	666	2,922
Two-Seed	50	5	55
Southern Convention	18,267	2,837	21,104
Negro Baptist Bodies, Totals	17,847	1,735	19,582
Colored Primitive	787	10	797
United American Freewill	250	1	251
National Convention	16,810	1,724	18,534
Grand Totals	39,610	15,255	54,865

[a] U.S. Bureau of the Census, *Religious Bodies: 1906*, Part II, pp. 45 ff.

[b] Includes the eleven ex-Confederate states and Kentucky.

[c] Includes all other states and continental territories.

Appendix C

BAPTIST BODIES IN THE UNITED STATES, 1906 [a]
MEMBERSHIP

	South	*Other*	*Total*
White Baptist Bodies, Totals	1,925,167	1,425,534	3,350,701
Northern Convention	0	1,052,105	1,052,105
General Six Principle	0	685	685
Seventh-Day	355	7,963	8,318
Free	11,559	69,800	81,359
Freewill	37,374	2,906	40,280
General	10,024	20,073	30,097
Separate	1,903	3,277	5,180
United	8,813	4,885	13,698
Duck River	6,416	0	6,416
Primitive	77,694	24,617	102,311
Two-Seed	726	55	781
Southern Convention	1,770,303	239,168	2,009,471
Negro Baptist Bodies, Totals	2,114,972	196,200	2,311,172
Colored Primitive	34,884	192	35,076
United American Freewill	14,439	50	14,489
National Convention	2,065,649	195,958	2,261,607
Grand Totals	4,040,139	1,621,734	5,661,873

[a] U.S. Bureau of the Census, *Religious Bodies: 1906*, Part II, pp. 45 ff.

Appendix D

COMPARISON OF SOUTHERN BAPTISTS AND METHODIST
EPISCOPAL CHURCH, SOUTH: NUMBER OF CHURCHES
AND SEATING CAPACITY, 1860 [a]

	Baptists		Methodists	
	Churches	Seating Capacity	Churches	Seating Capacity
Alabama	805	237,255	777	212,555
Arkansas	281	60,503	505	102,000
Florida	110	20,325	153	30,360
Georgia	1,141	376,686	1,035	309,079
Kentucky	788	267,860	666	228,100
Louisiana	161	47,785	199	58,181
Mississippi	529	172,703	606	168,705
North Carolina	741	271,086	966	328,497
South Carolina	443	169,530	506	149,812
Tennessee	668	210,381	992	288,460
Texas	280	77,435	410	103,799
Virginia	787	298,029	1,403	438,244
Totals	6,734	2,209,578	8,218	2,417,792

[a] U.S. Bureau of the Census, *Eight Census of the United States: 1860. Statistics*, IV, pp. 497, 499.

Appendix E

COMPARISON OF SOUTHERN BAPTISTS AND METHODIST
EPISCOPAL CHURCH, SOUTH: NUMBER OF
CHURCHES AND SEATING CAPACITY, 1870 [a]

	Baptists		*Methodists*	
	Churches	Seating Capacity	Churches	Seating Capacity
Alabama	786	189,650	991	218,945
Arkansas	463	103,250	583	91,890
Florida	127	21,100	235	42,600
Georgia	1,364	388,265	1,248	327,343
Kentucky	1,004	288,936	978	244,918
Louisiana	227	56,140	213	52,990
Mississippi	665	174,970	787	208,203
North Carolina	951	243,920	1,193	300,045
South Carolina	518	190,750	611	164,050
Tennessee	942	245,151	1,339	336,433
Texas	275	61,700	355	69,100
Virginia	795	240,075	1,011	270,617
Totals	8,117	2,203,907	9,544	2,328,264

[a] U.S. Bureau of the Census, *Ninth Census of the United States: 1870. Population,* I, pp. 507, 514.

233

Appendix F

COMPARISON OF SOUTHERN BAPTISTS AND METHODIST
EPISCOPAL CHURCH, SOUTH: NUMBER OF
CHURCHES AND MEMBERSHIP, 1906 [a]

	Baptists [b]		Methodists	
	Churches	Membership	Churches	Membership
Alabama	1,907	162,445	1,401	125,702
Arkansas	1,419	91,631	1,110	81,699
Florida	551	34,646	482	32,330
Georgia	2,159	232,688	1,546	178,307
Kentucky	1,703	211,552	1,047	99,355
Louisiana	610	49,620	381	31,639
Mississippi	1,350	123,357	1,113	94,845
North Carolina	1,837	202,798	1,532	151,808
South Carolina	979	118,360	801	84,266
Tennessee	1,617	159,838	1,480	140,308
Texas	3,107	247,306	2,354	225,431
Virginia	1,028	136,062	1,506	157,354
Totals	18,267	1,770,303	14,753	1,403,044

[a] Bureau of the Census, *Religious Bodies: 1906*, Part II, pp. 69, 471.
[b] Baptists did not count infants and small children as members.

Appendix G

SOUTHERN BAPTIST MEMBERSHIP, 1881, 1890, 1900

	1881 [a]	1890 [b]	1900 [c]
Alabama	76,200	97,918	131,280
Arkansas	37,111	55,497	71,419
Florida	9,958	19,067	25,369
Georgia	121,932	139,004	190,849
Kentucky	113,874	150,578	187,213
Louisiana	16,192	23,661	36,173
Mississippi	84,308	82,158	97,032
North Carolina	103,002	135,724	169,436
South Carolina	58,026	81,140	98,461
Tennessee	79,902	104,935	134,252
Texas	91,874	121,432	190,098
Virginia	69,702	90,600	121,547
Totals	862,081	1,101,714	1,453,129

[a] Southern Baptist Convention, *Proceedings, 1882*, Appendix E, "General Statistics," [p. LXXXIII]. Negro Baptists are not included.

[b] *Ibid., 1891*, Appendix D, "General Statistics," p. LXVII. Negro Baptists are not included.

[c] Southern Baptist Convention, *Annual, 1901*, Appendix E, "General Statistics," p. 206. Negro Baptists are not included.

Index